Jewish-American Writers and Intellectual Life in America

Series in American Literature

The Novels of Bernard Malamud
M. Rajagopalachari

The Novels of William Styron
S. Laxmana Murthy

Humanism and Jewish American Drama
D. Venkateswarlu

Jewish-American Writers and Intellectual Life in America

D. Venkateswarlu

PRESTIGE

Published by
Prestige Books
3/28, East Patel Nagar
New Delhi 110 008

ISBN 81-85218-67-6

Computerized Typesetting by
Laser Impressions
New Delhi 110 028
Ph. 537296, 537756

Printed at
Mehra Offset Press
New Delhi 110 002

Contents

Interviews

Essays

For my parents;
also for my teacher
Prof. Isaac Sequeira

Preface

In one of the debates on the post-Holocaust and the peculiar condition of "Chosenness," an avuncular rabbi once quipped to me, "Chosen for what? Chosen to suffer?" He did not expect an answer from me, but he symbolized in those questions an enduring dialogue between man and God which is so central to Judaism. It is even more instructive now, than at any time in the past, to systematize one's response to the protean character of the societal institutions and polity by looking into some specific problems as this work attempts in its fashion. What follows in these pages is an attempt at sifting through the contemporary issues for possible synthesis – even if it is not mentioned absolutely in clear terms; and even if it is not always round the corner.

The intellectual climate of Brandeis provided impetus and inspiration for these ideas which eventually took shape in a series of interviews with prominent intellectuals in America. It is difficult to put in words how much I value the affection and guidance of my teachers at Brandeis. Prof. Milton Hindus, Prof Leon A. Jick, Prof. Marshall Sklare, Prof. Marvin Fox, Prof. Eugene Goodheart and Rabbi Axelrod have been influential in many wavs. Prof. Hindus deserves a special mention here; and so do Eva, Myron and her friends. To me, Prof. Hidnus is an enduring example of a teacher, scholar and a humane individual – all combined in one. Being humble, he would not approve of this observation himself; but I would say it, any way.

I appreciate the time these interviewees have given me. They are all busy people – well respected and much sought after. Saul Bellow, Noam Chomsky, Norman Podhoretz, William Phillips, Robert Brustein, Wayne C. Booth, David Perkins, Richard Stern, Elie Wiesel and Marshall Sklare are extremely cooperative – to all of them I owe personal gratitude and affection. The Fulbright Foundation has given me encouragement in my intellectual pursuits: and I thank especially Mrs. Sharada Nayak and Dr. Jerry Prillman. Bob Hamburger has always been a good friend and I deeply cherish his enthusiasm for my work and the great moments I have had in New York in his company. Sam and Khalee have been the same old chums which is reassuring in this time and age of ever-vanishing values.

Mr. Kamran Latifi and Mr. Y.S.C. Bose deserve a special mention here. Mr. Latifi offered many useful suggestions and comments. He also entertained me with the memories of his Cambridge years. Mr. Y.S.C. Bose has always been very appreciative of my work and I greatly cherish his affection. I have benefited immensely from the intellectual discussions I have had with my dear friend Dr. B.D. Lahoti and Dr. K. Wilson.

The dedication of this book to my parents and to my teacher, Prof. Isaac Sequeria, is long overdue. It is too overwhelming to talk about such relationships and words are too inadequate to communicate them; without explaining much, I would leave it at that.

Department of English D. VENKATESWARLU
Osmania University
Hyderabad 500 007
India

Introduction

If I am not for myself, who will be for me? And if I am only for Myself, what am I? If not now, when?

Hillel

What is to say about these interviews? In actual fact, they speak for themselves. One finds in this collection, different thinkers viewing the same issue differently—sometimes disagreeing crucially with others. Often times, the discussions proliferate around the matters that concern the Middle East affairs, the status of the Jewish intellectual, anti-Semitism, professing in the context of the recent trends in theory and others. Most of the interviewees are Jews with an exception of David Perkins and Wayne C. Booth. To that extent, it would be interesting to recognize their observations with those of their Jewish counterparts. Among Jews too, Noam Chomsky not only disagrees with Saul Bellow on his perceptions of the Middle East scenario, but he even rejects his thinking as less than scholarly and, therefore, ideological. Inevitably, one finds in this strange collection, people of multiple intellectual persuasions. Neo-conservatives, liberals, liberatarian socialists, and many shades of these are reflected here in their deliberations, speculations and judgements. The reader (implied or actual) may feel some of their views repetitious. But when various intellectuals reflect on the contemporary scene, they are bound to come across certain seminal issues—which may also be significant for other thinkers. Even so, their perceptions are not necessarily similar. Again, coming back to Bellow's opinions on Israel, they may not be acceptable to certain others, say, Chomsky—for example.

What has happened to the profession of teaching especially to the teaching of English literature, is a pertinent theme for any one who cares to review and contextualize the philosophy and practice of liberal education. Post-war critical activities especially post-structuralism and the concomitant literary journalism have brought a new framework, thus bringing the profession and the discipline of English Studies into a ruthless critique—or, to reiterate from the position of theory-enthusiasts, enriched the practice of literary appreciation. Since most of them are teachers of repute, it should not be surprising that they have positions on these matters.

Is there a common ground for these people? In my view, the substantive humanism of one of the most revered Hebrew sages, Rabbi Hillel, can be re-situated in their convictions, be they socio-political, literary, cultural or any other. In the final analysis, this is probably the essential foundational structure that is acceptable to all of these eclectic minds who walk majestically through different disciplines of the American intellectual ambience. The much battered soul of humanity over the centuries, and certainly in this unwholesome century, occupies their acute sensibility and sensitivity. The implications and possibilities of redemption to such a context engage their most intense dialogue whether this is advanced in literature, theatre or foreign or domestic affairs. America suffered its own share of shocks in history, truncated by frequent blemishes such as slavery, the "plague years" of McCarthyism and, much recently, Vietnam War. The very emergence of the Civil Rights movement and New Left can be called, among other things, a direct backlash to the troubled fifties. Also, much to the embarrassment of everyone, the term "intellectual" became a tainted and even a painful expression. Easy conformism made several thinkers mere cowards. To be sure, the assortment of these thinkers, to my mind, has a strong belief that the tradition of a literate culture can still be established in American tradition; and such a tradition is the life force of any civil society. Although, the interviews collected here represent many facets of intellectual priorities, their collective voice belongs to the exigencies of the liberal tradition.

The essays in this book on the other hand are written over a long period of time and reflect my enduring interest in Judaic studies. Some of them are presented at seminars and workshops. Together, it is hoped, they provide constructive overview to the polyphony of Jewish culture and world view.

Saul Bellow

This interview took place at Saul Bellow's residence in South Chicago.

DV: Would you like to be called a Jewish writer? A simple question but, at least, some writers seem to be uncomfortable with such terms. In the forties, fifties, and sixties it was an interesting topic for intellectual discussion. I believe even today there are multiplicity of responses to such a subject matter. *Congress Weekly* in the fifties, *Commentary* in the sixties for the second time explored this theme.

SB: Well, you know, the people who call you a Jewish writer are not always friendly people. And from the Jewish side, I think Jewish community considers it good public relations that some of the best writers in America happen to be Jews. But I am not interested in public relations – theirs or anybody else's.

DV: What do you mean by public relations?

SB: Well, you know. That Jews can make a contribution to American life. Public relations in the sense that the Jewish stereotype has a different picture of Jews as corrupt money people and Shylocks and so on and so on. So, they are pleased when there are Jewish scientists and the people in the learned professions or writers or whatever because they feel it gives them a certain credit with gentile America. I am not terribly interested in that.

DV: Whether you are interested in it or not, you are a Jewish writer. Being a Jewish writer certainly makes a difference in terms of your creative writing and personal situation. Don't you think?

SB: Well, I *am* a Jewish writer. Well, you don't know. Public relations means advertisement in this country. I am not here to write advertisements for anybody. I am here to write novels and stories – not advertisements for any group even though I sympathize greatly with the Jews. Still, I don't think it's my role to improve their reputation. That's from one side. The other side: the Anglo-Saxon Protestants didn't always like it that the foreigners or ethnics of various kinds came to America and wrote in English. They were first generation Americans.

DV: They called you a foreigner . . .

SB: Of course, they did. I was born in America just as you were born in India. Born to speaking English. So, I don't like to have to apologise for myself. And I don't like to be put in a category which removes me from consideration.

DV: What consideration?

SB: They say you are a Jewish writer. You are not really an American writer.

DV: There could be an American-Jewish writer.

SB: No, I am just telling you what they say. I am not arguing anything. I am just explaining.

DV: But you are an American-Jewish Writer.

SB: That's right.

DV: Critics may have different attitudes towards you and your work. What you think of yourself is important.

SB: Oh, yes. I am not going to discuss my opinion of myself. Obviously, it is pretty good.

DV: Your fictional people seem to be thinking about their past all the time. They keep talking about their parents, cousins and uncles – the family structure, in other words, figures very prominently in your work. And also, they want to look back, possibly they crave for Old Country culture, values. Maybe they feel it provides security in gentile America.

SB: There are two kinds of Jews in the Western world. There are Jews who soon forget their history. The Jews who want to forget their history are the assimilationists, who want to rid themselves of their Jewish identity. But I think that would be a terrible mistake for Jews to turn away from their history. They mustn't. They have to be loyal to it even if they are not believing Jews; loyal to it, to the history of your people. That's another matter, you have to understand that. So, it does preoccupy me to a certain extent. I think in America it is rather exotic to have an attachment with family because the family is in the process of disappearing. For many Americans family does no longer matter very much. So, that's almost exotic, strange in a writer who doesn't do that. I explain to you my nephew is dead and I go to see my sister. Well, not all Americans do that kind of thing.

DV: I think I remember when Alfred Kazin was writing about you he mentions that only in Jewish-American writers one finds family. Where is family in Ernest Hemingway, he asks? He thinks family is an overriding concern for Jewish-American writers. I think that's pretty much what he says.

SB: Well, probably true. I think family figured very heavily in the life of Ernest Hemingway but negatively. He was doing his best to forget, but he couldn't truly forget. To turn his back on it. But he could not do it. His father was a suicide and so was he. That means something. Also, he hated his mother. The fact that you hated your mother doesn't mean that you lost your interest in the family.

DV: That's right. Since we are talking about the Old Country, when I read *Mr. Sammler's Planet*, I get the feeling that Elya Gruner needs Sammler because, he is a sort of personification of what is redemptive in the Old Country. Elya Gruner's life in America, his interaction with it, is not particularly sustaining. His daughter is a problem, so is his son. He himself has questionable connections. With this kind of situation, Sammler appears like an antidote or sustaining force for him.

SB: Americans are always looking for someone who can give them human nourishment.

DV: Elya Gruner is doing just that in *Mr. Sammler's Planet* ?

S B: He thinks his uncle can give him some human nourishment. And it is probably true because that's not what the American enterprise is about. American enterprise is power, money and technology and success and all these other things which are predicated upon the non-existence of the other human needs. You know you need these other things. They are just an obstacle to you. But actually many people hunger for them.

DV: But writers also make a lot of money in this country. You don't make a lot of money?

SB: I've lost most of the money I have made.

DV: But you *did* make a lot of money, didn't you?

SB: Let me put it to you this way. Until I was in the forties, I was living on the poverty level.

DV: Oh!

S B: It's true. It's true actually.

DV: You were teaching somewhere, weren't you?

SB: Now and then. I didn't teach as much as it appears. I used to have temporary connection. They would appoint me for a year at Princeton and not reappoint me. Or they would appoint me at NYU and not reappoint me. Or I was a Professor at Minnesota, I got a Guggenheim. . . .

DV: You were at Brandeis also, I believe . . .

SB: Only for a few months. Looks as if I had a permanent reliance on the universities. But that's misleading. Because I haven't. Here (U of Chicago), I came here because I was able to make my own terms. That's to say I would teach some courses when I was done writing every day. But I wouldn't really be an academic, that's to say, I wouldn't attend faculty meetings, sit on the committees and things like that. So, I had a special arrangement since 1963. That's twenty-five years that I had been here.

DV: What's the most difficult novel – difficult in the sense that you have trouble writing it.

SB: *Herzog.*

DV: Because it's too intellectual?

SB: No, it's not so intellectual. It is intellectual in a way but what it really does is to make fun. Highly educated people whose education does them no good in a crisis. And this is what Herzog discovers about his academic training. It's of no use to him. In an emotional crisis, he takes revenge on it by, as it were, destroying his education as he writes these letters.

DV: What's the problem with these people? Your characters seem to be likeable people in their own way. They somehow seem to make a mistake. They are intellectuals, nice and likable people and yet . . .

SB: You cannot lead a fully human life if you are nothing but an intellectual.

DV: They love their family, care about their children and parents. . . .

SB: But you see what it means to be an intellectual in the West in the twentieth century. It means, first of all, that the most powerful doctrines originating in the intellectual history in the eighteenth, the nineteenth and the twentieth centuries have a grip on the people. What do these theories tell you? If you are a Marxist, they tell you that your family doesn't exist any more, it's gone. Capitalism has destroyed it. If you have in mind Nietzsche, he tells you that God is dead, you are in a condition of nihilism. You know, these nice boys and girls up and down in American cities assimilate these doctrines. I have given you only two. I could have gone out to Freud as the third. This is what they are attempting to live with – uncritically. And it's a very hard going. It makes a career. But it doesn't make a human life. So, there's a difference between these two things, you see. That's the paradox. Because most of the most prestigious of the philosophers, the scientists of the last three centuries of the Enlightenment tell you these things, you know. They tell you what you are meant to be. Freedom for them is throwing off all the tradition of your fathers and starting a new page for your self. And you become successful by doing this. You become an intellectual and you are rewarded for demonstrating these characteristics. But in your private life, in your inner life, you feel disoriented by this. That's what I am trying to say to you.

DV: But can there be any solution to this?

SB: Well, the solution is in genuine personal independence so that you don't exist as an illustration of some theories. To which you are a capital. If you consider an intellectual in the same way as a capitalist, Marx talks about primitive accumulation needed in order to found an enterprise and so on. The Capital of these people consists of people like Adam Smith, John Locke, Karl Marx, Nietzsche, Sartre, Heidegger and so on – Lenin. They are the people who made a great impression on the modern man. Well, once you accumulated this capital by reading the difficult books and passing a lot of examinations, confirming your own life, you lock your career in this, you find it hard to be independent, you find it very hard to give up these facts. You follow me?

DV: Oh, yes. Yes. Yes.

SB: Which means you surrender your independence because you have an interest in protecting your intellectual accumulation of thirty, forty, fifty, sixty years that you have accumulated this intellectual capital. You are not going to throw it out of the window by changing your mind about all these things, by saying it's non-sense, you know. This is not in accord with my personal connection. So people have been trapped and falsified themselves through their education and are very reluctant to give up this illogical and dishonest way of living. That's what *Herzog* is about.

DV: You want to withstand these temptations, obviously.

SB: The book is really a satire-comedy. It makes fun of these people. The man makes fun of him in so far as he is taken to disagree with himself you know. So, he is writing letters to Nietzsche, Trotsky, Lenin – whoever it was. But in a way it is a joke. Because, in a way he is clearing himself from this baggage – mental baggage. You know a writer named Desani?

DV: G.V.Desani? *All About Herr Hatter*? Yes. What's your favourite novel, *Henderson the Rain King*?

SB: That's obviously your favourite novel. Alfred Kazin says how could I write a novel about a non-Jew? Henderson is not Jewish. You asked me before how I thought about being a Jewish writer. A man like Kazin takes it upon himself to decide that I am not in a position to write about American WASP millionnaire. How does he decide that? (laughs)

DV: Don't be so angry now. (He wasn't)

SB: He is a foolish person.

DV: Come on. You are not saying that.

SB: No, no. I don't agree with him.

DV: Apart from being a non-Jew, Henderson seems to have the same kind of life pattern as the Jewish novels. For instance, like Herzog, he also seems to be thinking about his family, his parents. He says he is trying to reach his father through his violen. (Bellow laughs heartily)

SB: After all, Freud says that you can never get rid of that. That's one of the things. You are born with an Oedipal complex. You know, it's an instinct you are born out of a struggle with your father or your mother. You can theorize as much as you like about the disappearance of the family, but if the family is disappearing why doesn't Oedipus complex disappear?

DV: Your fictional people seem to be thinking about the Old World all the time. But where do they find it in America? No *Yiddishkeit*, religion is no longer as effective as it used to be. Also, jumping into the melting pot or the mainstream. This situation inevitably creates an interaction or conflict. The only way of recovering, at least symbolically, is to visit the places of immigrant childhood. At least for a vicarious experience.

SB: What's wrong with that?

DV: Do you want to say something about it?

SB: Not really. It's very hard to keep up with America. It transforms itself every few years. So, what are you going to assimilate yourself to. It's not holding steady.

(The phone rings. It's his son Gregory from California. Bellow excuses himself and goes to answer the phone. May be his son wants to know how his father is taking his (father's) nephew's death. Bellow thanks him and says "I am on duty," meaning that he has a visitor.)

DV: You are all shook up, I can see that. Also, you are a very sensitive person.

SB: Well, you've got to be very sensitive. Do you have any more questions?

DV: Yes, yes. Generally, to my knowledge, you don't write about politics except that book on Israel (*To Jerusalem and Back: A Personal Account*). At the same time, there are implicit political views in your fiction?

SB: I think it's all over the place. Certainly predominant in *The Dean's December*.

DV: What kind of political position do you take at the moment? Do you appreciate the position of the Neo-Conservatives or liberals?

SB: I don't consider myself to be a Neo-Conservative.

DV: A liberal?

SB: I consider myself to be a classical liberal of the nineteenth century.

DV: J.S. Mill?

SB: Yes.

DV: About *Mr. Sammler's Planet* again. He is a survivor. Yet, he does not talk about or reflect persistently on the Holocaust or the War. It doesn't figure in the novel prominently somehow. Don't you think that's little bit problematic? For instance, he goes to Israel during the Six Day War but visits only the Christian sites. For a survivor Israel must mean more than that, a spiritual importance.

SB: He just wants to live an independent life.

DV: That's right. Being a Jewish survivor, Israel should have a special meaning in his life at that point of time (Six Day War).

SB: I want the survivor's view of America, not his view of the Holocaust. Of course, he went to Israel during the Six Day War because he felt so Jewish. So, that's that.

DV: But he visits the Christian sites.

SB: Well, he was not very Jewish too – he was an assimilating Jew.

D.V: What about the situation of the Jewish intellectual now? We have various Jewish intellectuals taking various positions. For instance, the editor of *Commentary*, Norman Podhoretz seems to believe in Neo-Conservatism. So does Irving Kristol. And there are *Partisan Review* and *Dissent* with a different position altogether. I believe there is a new one called *Tikkun*.

SB: I don't mix very much with these people. They don't have much use for me either. . . . Well, as a writer, I think, they are guilty of very poor taste in literary matters. That means a lot to me. Literature is something like my religion. So, if I say they have a poor taste, they somehow crippled themselves in a very important aspect of my life. They disqualified themselves in making intelligent judgements about a lot of things. I think people who have no poetry in them at all are dangerous politically. You can't trust them. They are strictly ideological. It means that to the extent they are strictly ideological, there is someone to humanize them. They make all their judgements on political basis. They have nothing to say about the soul of the people. They are not interested in that.

DV: Maybe they think that they are reacting to certain social and political situations.

SB: They think they are rescuing the West. They think they are rescuing the Western civilization. That's what they tell you if you pin them down. I am sure if you pin Podhoretz, he would say, "Oh, yes. I am rescuing the Western civilization from totalitarianism, from left wing influence, revolutionary influences or playboy revolutionary things." Because Americans on the far left are in a position of political privilege because they enjoy the protection of the society they criticize. And they would like to criticize and they would like to subvert. It's true they are dangerous people. They do bad things. On the other hand, somebody like Podhoretz who studied literature at Columbia University under Lionel Trilling now dismisses it as fraud – is not politically dependable in my view.

DV: He does not say bad things about Trilling. I had an occasion to meet him in New York city. He said that he maintained a cordial relationship with him. It's critics who created a misunderstanding between them.

SB: Did you read Podhoretz's. . . .

DV: *Making It*? I sure did.

SB: He mentions that Trilling advised him to attack the *Adventures of Augie March* to make his reputation that way.
(I laugh and Bellow joins me and says, "Podhoretz writes that, yeah.")

DV: What do you think about Irving Howe and his *Dissent*?

SB: Well, he is a sentimental socialist. He is one of these people who doesn't want to give up his intellectual capital. His case happens to be Marxism. He's faithful to it.

DV: You find it problematic?

SB: Yes.

DV: What's not problematic?

SB: Everything is problematic. I have a rather low opinion of Socialist movement altogether. I don't see that it makes much sense, for, Howe makes a claim to the old Socialist line.

DV: What do you think would be the ideal political situation? If you have to take a political stance, what kind of a political position would you take at the moment? Because liberal is such a dirty word to-day in America.

SB: It is not a dirty word to me. So I don't care what it is to America.

DV: But you live in America.

SB: Why do you ask me such a question . . .

DV: Do you think life of a writer doesn't matter when you appreciate his or her work? For instance, the writer's personal life, intellectual positions, to my mind, have some bearing on his literary output.

SB: Well, I can read certain Fascist Literature with great appreciation. I read Celine and I read Ezra Pound. I do not think in the end that their books are vitiated by their politics. And it is hard for me to read a poet like Pound with appreciation when I consider what he said about Jews during the War. No, I don't disconnect them. I take the ideas of the writers very seriously.

DV: Then, how do you define a masterpiece? What is a classic?

SB: Shakespeare, Homer.

DV: Shakespeare also wrote *Merchant of Venice*.

SB: Different in those years.

DV: Why was it different? It was so vicious.

SB: Well, there was no considerable Jewish population to persecute. And it was just traditional anti-Semitism in the tradition of Christianity which most people accepted without too much question because it was so exotic that they didn't know anything about it. But people coming from countries which have large Jewish populations who were anti-Semitic and no wish to do considerable harm to large number of people called Jews. That's very different from Shakespearean England where there were three or four Jews in the country.

DV: There could be many more.

SB: No, no. You missed my point. He wished no harm to any considerable number of Jews. He dealt with a Christian stereotype of the Jewish money-lender.

DV: How can you be so sure?

SB: Because Shylock has certain nobility in his character.

DV: That's Shakespeare's dramatic instinct. I think he wanted to make Shylock more human than a mere stereotype – and therefore, more villainous, as I see it.

SB: I think he wants to make Shylock anything. I think he felt moved to give Shylock certain more quibbles, certain words for Shylock to characterize Shylock. It wasn't just mechanical arrangement.

DV: What do you think about the Middle East?

SB: I don't know what to say. A person with a trained logical mind says to a problem, there's a solution. That may be true for physics. But that's not true for human affairs. There are no set solutions for any of these questions.

DV: But shouldn't there be? At least for the sake of peace?

SB: We suffered a great deal from people who thought they knew what the solutions were. For instance, Hitler thought the solution to the European political question was the extermination of the Jews. And Stalin thought that the answer to the Russian question was to destroy millions of people. Ukranians and Volga Germans so on and so on. May be he murdered a great many people. Those were the people who definitely knew the answer. They were very sure they knew an answer for every political question. I don't think it is like it's healthy to know, to be absolutely sure as the logician or mathematician would be.

DV: Are you writing your autobiography?

SB: No, I am not.

DV: Your characters like Henderson, though non-Jewish, appear to be intellectual versions of traditional schlemiel.

SB: That's misleading. Schlemiel is much more a character of satire than comedy. Schlemiel is just a fall guy.

DV: Do you go to shul?

SB: When I was a boy I went. I observe Yom Kippur (*The Day of Atonement*).

DV: High holidays. Rosh Hashana. Did you celebrate Rosh Hashana?

SB: No, my lady friend observes it.

DV: Don't you observe it.

SB: She does.

DV: What about you, sir?

SB: I observe her observe it.

DV: Did you read Edward Said's book on orientalism?

SB: No, I didn't. But I don't care much about Said. I think he is a terrorist. He is an official of P.L.O. It's hard for me to like him.

Richard Stern

DV: Maybe we begin with the Jewish writers . . .

RS: There are so many Jewish writers of different sorts. People who may not be Jewish, don't think of them as Jewish writers. But of course Saul Bellow is the world's leading writer of prose fiction and he happens to be Jewish. Philip Roth is also a very good writer and the late Bernard Malamud is a very good writer. Salinger is a fine writer but hasn't written for a long time. There are many others. Mark Harris is a fine writer who is little known. He is usually not thought of as a Jewish intellectual either. But he is a fine writer. Perhaps you know. His little book on Bellow *Drumlin Woodchuck*. It is a very amusing, interesting book – very odd. It's much more significant in a way that it appears.

DV: Bellow doesn't like to be called a Jewish-American writer.

RS: No, no. I don't think most writers who have a standing wish to be classified anyway.

DV: But they'll be classified anyway.

RS: They will be, certainly. It seems to limit their success. Bellow is particularly sensitive to ghettoization because it involves pejorative assessment. So, if one is an intellectual, he is an intellectual; if one is a poet, he is a poet. Yes, it may be one writes about a great deal about Dublin or about Chicago or about Jews or about people that happen to be Jews. If your subject matter is Jewish as Bellow's is in one way as Isaac Singer's is another, as Philip Roth's in a third way, then, I suppose, it is useful to examine your own Jewish roots or useful for a critic to examine those roots and see in what way certain experiences have led to the fictional transmutation, fictional creation. But there are certain writers like Norman Mailer who is Jewish but who is not Jewish in the same way. Their subject matter is seldom Jewish. The same thing is true in the case of Salinger and a person such as Mark Harris, though one novel of his is explicitly Jewish. And the same thing is true of myself. Only this year, in the forthcoming book of stories, collection of stories, which covers forty years – but in the three years did I write a story which came from heart as a Jew because I had an experience.

DV: What do you think of Bellow as a novelist.

RS: I have been a close friend of Bellow for many years. It's difficult for me to be objective in some ways. But to me, he is truly a magnificent writer. He is one of the two or three best writers that appeared in the United States of America. He has added something to American literature that is distinctly his – he, William Faulkner and Henry James. He is one of these Americans who has a long literary career. Indeed he may be said to, along with James, have been producing at a very high level for most of that career. Whereas Faulkner in the last years of his life was producing a very feeble work. Now, as to his novels, the people have said, his novels are the novels of education. There is a great deal of new exciting intellectual material which the leading character has to absorb in order to clarify his own personal situation. His intellectual situation and his personal situation is on the tracks on which the novel goes. They are sometimes in parallel and in other times there's distressing discontinuity between them. That makes for comedy. Indeed Bellow likes to think of himself as essentially a comic writer in that there is no great commitment to a tragic view of the world. Which means that though the world is taken seriously, it is so much of desperation, kind of race to understand this world that they have felt, accounts for the comedy. The people at times are pathetic and ridiculous and amusing. At the same time, they are touching. Now, in Bellow the danger is how to put these works together. That's why, I think he found a wonderful form, in this long or short novel form. The best example in the recent works is *Him With His Foot in His Mouth*. The early example is, of course, *Seize the Day*. It's a form in which Henry James also, interestingly enough, excelled. For Bellow the danger is that the character will write beautifully anything that crosses his mind. I think only Marcel Proust, among all the novelists of the world, has been able to write a novel in which that height of reflection has been absorbed in the narrative pattern sufficiently to say that it's not essay, a textual novel. I think Bellow at his best does this magnificently. And I am very fond of *Humbold's Gift* despite the fact that it is stuffed with reflection on all sorts of things. But he is a magnificent writer. The style is of course wonderful, mixing of demonic and intellectual. He is quite a good mimic – as Roth. But he is quite good. He is very skilful. Putting a novel together, when to stop and when to start, when a scene should be big and so on.

DV: Does he have the same kind of appeal that he had a decade ago?

RS: To youthful people?

DV: Both to youth and intellectuals.

RS: Well, no. You know there is always this literary stock-market. Bellow perhaps is not rated as much as he was. And it depends on the group. The New York group which sponsored him, loved him when he was their discovery. But I heard most of them say, "Well, after *Augie March* he went down." And it is ridiculous in my opinion. Some of them say that his best work is *Seize the Day*. Well, that's silly. It's a fine work. He has gotten much richer, much deeper, much more profound and beautiful. And then younger people were repelled by *Mr. Sammler's Planet* in which they felt the political slant repellent, that there was conservatism, the shrinking of sympathy which they disliked very much, the antipathy towards the young. They can point to certain events to Bellow's life, which they think augments this view of them. But that doesn't matter. In the long run, he would be read. And he is a great writer. He is still read today by young people as well as old people.

DV: What do you think about his last two books? *Him With His Foot in His Mouth* and *More Die of Heartbreak*?

RS: My preference is for earlier works. *Him With His Foot*, that particular story is as good as any thing Bellow had written. It is a masterpiece. He and I have an exchange about *The Dean's December*. It was not one of my favourite books and *More Die of Heartbreak*, it has some marvellous things in it. But there are always some ups and downs in a writer's career.

DV: He still has some magic, do you think?

RS: I hope so. I am looking forward to his new book. He has written a short novel which I haven't read yet. I used to see him more often than I do. And then I often read the works in progress. I haven't seen him lately.

DV: Bellow appears to be a very sensitive person. I met him couple of days ago. He gave all sorts of directions to make sure that I get to his place without much difficulty. Much later, he drove me back to my apartment. Maybe he thought, me being a foreigner and Chicago being what it is, I might find it difficult to get back. And of course it was rather late.

RS: Well, yes. He is a very fine man. He cares for people.

DV: Some say he is a smart person too.

RS: Yes, naturally. He is a man of genius.

DV: How do you view Neo-Conservatism?

RS: It's hard for me to say what my position is. But, on some ways, I am conservative, on some ways, I am a radical. Most people consider me much more radical than Mr. Bellow on my positions. On the whole, although I have published in *Commentary*, I don't sympathize with the positions of the Jewish intellectuals who have become somewhat overly defensive of American positions, almost automatically suspicious of the Soviet Union even though, of course, they were useful in seeing that there was duplicity, perfidy, treachery and viciousness in the Soviet Union at a time when the other people were expressively tender-hearted about the former ally. But now it's the reverse. Even though I published a story in *Encounter* which is the equivalent of *Commentary*, it seems to me that endless picking of Gorbachev and suspiciousness, watchfulness and varyness is excessively silly and wasteful and vulgar. I don't like the tone of the people who have themselves arrived and do not see young people are vivid and alive and have different positions on which to try things out. I am very antipathic to the people like Kristol and *Public Interest* group, Norman Podhoretz and so on even though in some ways these people have been worthwhile and the magazine they publish useful. And among the people here I like Allan Bloom personally. I think his book is interesting as a personal gripe but it should be a battle cry for the people, that it exemplifies a position is to me ludicrous. So many statements in this book are overly generalized and not precise. I like precision in my self although I am guilty of imprecision. I like case by case dealing with things more than overall assessments which run into a danger of racism or other overly simplistic forms. My own position – I don't know . . .

DV: Liberal or liberal-left . . .

RS: It's too easy to say that. But each term, as you know, is loaded with things. So, the liberal is practically a Kitsch word in America now because it is associated with the notion that government solves problems by spending money. I have close friends in the economics department here who have put me onto works which show that many governmental programmes have only, to use the old cliche, that Ronald Reagan got into office with exacerbated problems, to which there are solutions. To some degree, there is truth there. On the other hand, in a country like ours which is so rotten with poverty, unfairness, with ferocious, which at the same time sees its governing class drunk with a kind of not money-frenzy but athletic competitiveness in the realm of speculation money, in such a situation one must feel that hope that public leaders including those who in the government would call upon the high-minded qualities of the people and would realize that one of the aims of the life is an attempt to make others equal to oneself, to spread opportunities much more than it is spread. The meaning of the American Constitution and the Declaration of Independence seems to me to be rooted in that sort of charity. Charity is also a very desirable aim even if one's own heart is narrow, shrivelled and suspicious and worried about the young or the poor or those who are trying to take away from us what we have earned. At the same time, I admire them for some of the cautionary positions that they've had. I am, at the same time, also oversimplifying their positions because if we were in the same office and we were talking, I assume we come to an agreement of 80% or more of what we would discuss.

DV: "Liberal" is such a dirty word these days . . .

RS: Yes, it has become a dirty word. It is a political word. Any word that's used by politicians would become sold and polluted especially in our time. If you have seen the political campaign we have in this country recently, which is a kind of advertising man's dream, which is a substitution of reality. And it is a repellent demonstration of what's worse in our country and what's most dangerous in the world.

DV: ACLU liberalism and all those . . .

RS: And all those slogans and buzz words, as we call them. Yes, but of course one could do that with anything. And it's very distressing. It's the writer's job, above all else, to class up the political vocabulary, the intellectual vocabulary. That's his social job, social job of the writer. His individual job is the creation of the beautiful works which have nothing to do with ideology even though they sponsor one type of ideology or the other. The cleaning of the language, the refreshing of the language, the maintenance of clarity in the job of the intellectual and the writer. So, the political campaign of this kind is a comedy, comedy should rip the candidates and expose their treacheries of the language.

DV: They seem to be particularly against the New Left, the sixties generation.

RS: Both the candidates were the right of power. That's why Jesse Jackson with all his own defaults, rhetoric, defects and sins against the language, sins against the complexity, nonetheless appealed to many people because he had the freedom, at any rate, to talk about actual dangers and menaces, and also to establish a third position which is a traditional American position at least since the nineteenth century or even since the founding fathers.

DV: Do you have anything to say about Irving. Howe's *Dissent* and Phillips's *Partisan Review*?

RS: They were once prominent magazines. When I was growing up every issue of *Partisan Review* was bought by intellectuals, read and discussed. It was something that centred us and gave us place in all over the country. *Kenyon Review, Southern Review*, there are five or six magazines which were crucial to our lives. Now, there are hundreds of magazines, hundreds of publications and none has power. And the *Partisan Review* doesn't have any position now. Who knows? *Dissent* – how many people have read it? Now and then there is an interesting article but it is not central. *Public Interest* by one, *Commentary* by other and now the new journal *Tikkun* of less conservative Jews. There are so many. Look at the publications on my table. Last night I got *Encounter, Salmagundi, Harvard Magazine*, *The New York Review of Books*. I try and read them. This is just a position. *The New Republic, The Nation* and so on. *Spectator, The Economist, The Times*, *The New York Times*. One has to take in a great deal. At the end of it, can one have a position? There's a limit to one's time, one's patience. Where does it lead one at the end? I don't think it leads one necessarily left or right or center. One may change from one issue to another. So, one has seen a great deal of mixture. When I noticed it first happening, Daniel Moynihan and Milton Friedman agreeing on the issue of vouchers for schools – well, far right man and somebody who had at least been a liberal are agreeing now. Now, Moynihan is essentially considered a conservative. One sees all kinds of marriages these days; just as one does in sexual and erotic fields, one does in political field. It's a great mix.

DV: Do you have people like Philip Rahv and Lionel Trilling now?

RS: Yes, we do. I disagree. We have many Lionel Trillings. Nobody perhaps with that kind of position, with that kind of importance because Lionel Trilling spoke for the university position. You know, Jews were not allowed in the English Departments till the last fifty years or so. But Trilling made his way in Columbia. So, he had a university position. Secondly, he had written about Matthew Arnold and some standard literary figures. And that was rare in those days. And thirdly, he wrote about the liberal tradition which, he said, was lacking. Well, now you have a thousand Jewish intellectuals who have professional chairs of the same status. I say they don't have the same status because there was nobody else in those days. There was Trilling and the rest were tiny little people. And now everybody is a Trilling or more. Not everybody but many. They don't shine that much. You know Robert Martin Adams. Maybe you don't even know his name. he writes about all the time in the *New York Review of Books* and many other places. He writes about all sorts of things. He is every bit as good as Trilling, more knowledgeable than Trilling. But you don't know his name because he is one of the five hundred. Are there many? Let's say two hundred and fifty.

DV: Of Trilling's stature?

RS: Yes, of Trilling's stature. But again I have to say not of Trilling's stature because they cancel each other out because you don't notice them. Today, you don't even need a university chair. People even work in various places – perhaps librarians or newspaper people. I suppose you can say William Safire – I don't say he is a sensational journalist but he has a certain intellectual qualification. Podhoretz has certain stature.

DV: As you know Allan Bloom's book, along with E.D. Hirsch's created an on-going debate on many issues like American academic scene, liberal education and so on. Some critics also believe that Bloom romanticizes in certain ways. Do you participate in the debate? Do you share his views?

RS: Some of them. Again, as I said Allan Bloom is a very interesting human being, a kind of brilliant shlemiel and luckily because he has an individual character, he writes with a certain flair. He also knows two traditions: he knows Greek tradition and he knows the French. Well, these two strains and life-time spell of teaching, and because of his own personal energy and gripe, he was able to write a personal book which turned to attract more people of its sort than I have seen in my life-time. Now, when Bloom writes about music that young people listen to, even if I were a young person I might disagree, I find it quite brilliant and delightful. My own copy of Bloom's is marked with disagreements – overgeneralization, imprecise, overly argued. You see it doesn't matter if it is a personal gripe but if another person comes along to say, "well, that's my position," I say you don't understand, you haven't thought this out yourself, you've just vaguely seen in Bloom a bulwark of your own political position, or social position, or resentment of your own children, or hatred of rock-music or whatever. And your feeling that students don't read classics any more and they are too ignorant. I had two classes this quarter with students every bit as brilliant as the students thirty years ago. Yes, I would say on the whole they hadn't read as much. They know much more about the television programmes. They hadn't used that time to read George Eliot, Dickens and Eliot. But when they did read, they were very good and very intelligent and are eager to read and master the tradition now. And they are remarkable. Many of them came from broken families. Bloom is a philosopher. Many of the students who came from the broken families do not have the peace of mind required to be a philosopher. So, first of all, most of the great philosophers happen to have been unmarried and celibates and bachelors. It's rather an interesting thing Bloom himself is. But Hegel married and Socrates, poor fellow, married. That was overly generalization-notion I dislike. I disapprove the position, all those positions in his book in which he gets tired of thinking and becomes too automatically a voice of the conservative group and sounds like William Bennet who also occasionally says some intelligent things. When we get tired and stop thinking, we rant and then certain jokes or express sentiments. So, I am not sympathetic to that part of Bloom or his book. But I am sympathetic to the book as a personal statement and I think at times it is delightfully written and it challenges.

DV: Do you think anti-Semitism still exists in this country?

RS: Of course it does. Not as much as it did in my father's time. I am not as sensitive as Bellow or as Philip Roth. But there is doubt that just as there is anti-everything. Of course, there is a great deal of wildness in the country since there are so few people who have the genuine religious feeling, since there is no social order which is wonderfully defined. We have made gods of these celebrities—*The People's Magazine* and so on. And they are useful as lightning rods of resentment. Out of hatred, resentment and suspicion, lawlessness takes root. And so, anti-Semitism would be one of the outlets for it but compared to the past, it hardly exists. I have faced it very seldom in the whole life time. I am sixty years old. I have experienced three or four incidents in my whole life which I could characterize as anti-Semitic. And three years ago I experienced, I think I experienced, one on a train which was so shocking to me I wrote a story about it. But Saul Bellow doesn't feel that way and Phillip Roth particularly in England did not feel that way. It exists and it's a frightful thing. And the last night I was reading the case of Heidegger, Gadamer, Habermas and others who had written about Heidegger and how his philosophic position has led him into this tragic and horrifying mistake in which he identified Hitler as the existential force of being and was blind and repellently treacherous and blind to the violence of the movement. So, we can never slumber, we can never close our eyes to the dangers of any form of racism and anti-Semitism is one that is available here. Hitler did kill anti-Semitism than anybody else in the West.

DV: I listen to Talk Radio, for instance Larry King show, as often as I can. Sometimes the callers evince tremendous anti-Semitism. The questions they ask, the comments they make are disturbing to any one. The recent movies like *Mississipi Burning* and *Talk Radio* are powerful expositions of the underside of American society. The former is about the Civil rights movement and KKK in 1964 and the latter about a Jewish talk radio host who gets killed by pathological caller. Both of them underline racism that pervades the American scene. As I familiarize myself with the mass media, I am beginning to believe strongly that anti-Semitism is on the rise, perhaps in a subtle fashion.

RS: Of course it exists. Actually it exists more in intellectual world. The piece Gore Vidal comes from; whose life has been tormented by sexual irregularities, which he has, in the last twenty years, been allowed to more or less advertise. But his resentment of that and the fact that the Freudian-Jewish tradition is essentially a macho tradition and that love and works signal excellence in the Jews, identification of family in Jews and so on and such that he may tend to resent them. And the fact that Gore Vidal has not been taken seriously as a writer – only as an essayist. At a time when the Jewish writers have been exalted. And his resentment of Norman Podhoretz group, of the conservatism with whom I am partly sympathetic, led him to make those cheap, snobbish statements. But you are right, on many levels it exists. People around here now give voice to what used to keep silent. They feel, "Well, no body can be anti-Semitic. I resent you, period. And you happen to be a Jew. And that's probably the reason you are getting somewhere." But it does not exist to the extent it did in my father's day. The situation of the blacks has transformed in my lifetime.

DV: Do you think it would take dangerous proportions in future?

RS: It could always become dangerous in the hands of a demogogue. If there's a depression, you can be certain that anti-Semitism can increase, anti-black groups will flourish. They flourished already. They are not common part of my life. That doesn't mean that they shouldn't be. Bellow wrote a very good letter this summer about the ridiculous man here in Chicago, (Steve) Cokely who made the kind of speeches, among the most dispossessed of the people, that have broken the poorest parts of the ghetto. They have hungered for scholarship and wisdom and this man pandered to them by being blatantly and overtly anti-Semitic. And the mayor of Chicago took months before he fired this fellow from the staff. Of course, it was outrageous and the people were exploding about it – and rightly so. You should always be on the alert.

DV: I understand that, at least among certain intellectuals especially of liberal or liberal-left persuasion, neo-conservatism is viewed with disfavour – and obviously so. Norman Podhoretz would certainly have problems with this group. But some of the things he does, in my view, are commendable. For instance, how many Jewish intellectuals evinced timely response to Gore Vidal's near-venomous essay?

RS: Norman Podhoretz's article is absolutely commendable. He wrote a very powerful piece against Vidal's piece. I agree.

DV: What's your position on Israel?

RS: Well, it's full of problems. As a Jew, there is a natural and almost a magnetic pull towards Israel. And I am of the school that feels so specially constituted by a people which even though there's no reason to be superior, nonetheless have their survival in the world, by the troubles they have endured, by their special existence have, in a way, are in a way, chosen not by God but, in a sense, by history. When the State of Israel, in its public policy is not as generous as one likes it to be, there's a kind of shrivelling in one's heart. In the '82 war, I was terribly against the war. Timerman's wonderful book (*The Longest War*), I was totally sympathetic to that. I thought Israel was kind of gripped with madness in the person of Ariel Sharon and Menaham Begin. It was painful. Today with the Palestinians, it is a very difficult situation again. And I would hope that Israel will be able to converse with the PLO or anybody else which will see some broadening in the Middle Eastern situation – the establishment of the State of Israel and the granting of Arabs more rights in the Jewish State. And yet I know, that it is an enormously delicate and difficult thing, and that the essence of Israeli and Jewish position is survival as a recognizably Jewish unit. It is not just a State like another State that way either.

DV: Israel consistently relied on American support. Does it take away their freedom politically or otherwise to a certain extent?

RS: Well, I think just as Irishness in this country supported Ireland sometimes even in a bad way by sending money which has gotten into the hands of the Irish Republican Army and so on so there's a natural disposition on the part of Jewish-American to contribute. But if you mean the support of the United States, after all it's true that Israel is the only democratic state in the Middle East. And its interests and American interests are absolutely fused, almost fused – only now and then. So, naturally they make good allies, just as we are an ally of Canada. The United States is an ally of Great Britain, so we are an ally of Israel. It is perfectly natural. Since Israel is poor, certainly America must support it. It's because of the fact that it had the armies that would break the state, would bankrupt the state unless it had the support from the United States. Eventually in an ideal world "no."

DV: Do you even bother to reflect on Edward Said's position?

RS: Well, I am not sympathetic to Edward Said's position. Said is a Palestinian who is broad-minded, and he hopes for the establishment of the Palestinian State and feels that he and others had to help the PLO to bring to the position which Mr. Yarafat expounded two weeks ago. And I believe that Edward Said could sit down with those of us and, if he had power himself, we would arrive at some more equitable, apparently equitable, distribution of land and power in the Middle East. He had done a book on orientalism; though it is full of factual error and simplifications, nonetheless it remains the same sort of truths we have been talking about. That characterization and simplification of individuals as the basis of their easternism, their Arabism and their orientalism so that one immediately classified them in a different way. And, of course, it is ludicrous, terrible and harmful and some one like Edward Said is a perfect counter to this sort of thing. Edward Said, like any man who speaks a great deal, becomes popular. And often appears on the campuses. Whether it is Noam Chomsky or Edward Said the quality of their work must suffer. They do not bring the scholarly authority to every address that they did at their best. So, many of the positions they espouse are poorly argued. The evidence behind them is poor. And, of course, that's what happened to Heidegger in that terrible series of speeches beginning with his speech assuming as rector of University of Freiberg in 1933. That's true of all of us. I have been kept private all of my life – only four or five times I have spoken out publicly. That's I am a writer. I cannot bear the excitement and the spontaneity required of a man of action. I am not a man of action. I envy those few men of action who responded so wonderfully most of the time. But the greatest men of action have all made fools of themselves at one time or another. So, to blame Chomsky and Said for occasionally making repulsive or simple-minded speeches is disgusting. And people like myself should hold back from it. So, I am sympathetic to Edward Said and Chomsky.

DV: Now to the phenomenon of modernism and anti-Semitism. It is interesting to note that the canonized poets like Eliot and Pound have also expressed anti-Semitic positions.

RS: Pound I got to know in Venice and I wrote a book about him. And taught a course on him. It has always been an agony to me that he took the position that he did. Here is a brilliant book by Casillo (Robert Casillo, *The Geneology of Demons: Anti-Semitism, Fascism and the Myth of Ezra Pound,* 1988) published by Northwestern Press last year which made even my toleration for many of his positions shiver. I have been thinking about writing in the form of fiction – about the position of Pound and Paul de Man which you probably followed and the contortions that Jacques Derrida got into as he tried to extract him from these positions. Of course, he was a young man but a brilliant one. Heidegger, De Man and Pound – theirs are fascinating positions buy anybody who takes public positions, and the great many of them, is going to find that he has always simplified and made himself a mocking piece. That's why, some one who is able to see what he had done is so much more admirable than De Man who hid it and who constructed the whole literary theory in which historicity is smoke, in which a position one takes is smoke. And Heidegger who made only the feeblest sort of acknowledgement of the burning facts in front of him. Pound admitted that he was blind and simple-minded and had been gripped by stupidity. He admitted it. To that extent he is better than most of us. And many of us don't even admit it. And I will not mention.

DV: What do you say about the Jewish apologists for Paul de Man?

RS: Of course, there are. The people whose careers have been invested in exalting Paul de Man. Well, maybe you can find excuses for Paul de Man. The most interesting was the piece of Jacques Derrida in *Critical*

Enquiry in which he was able to deal every piece of De Man but one and then suddenly he broke down and said, "What am I going to do with this?" And here, he was a close friend of De Man, and he knew nothing of this. That was more interesting. The cover-up to use the Watergate term – that was the most interesting part. How many of us are brave enough to confess? How many of us don't have things that we are trying to hide? Practically all of us are concealing something from somebody and maybe from everybody. Our lives sometimes may be constructed about this concealment. De Man's, I am sure, was.

DV:–Let us come to the American mass media. It appears to me that there is a tendency on its part to focus on Israel, Israeli politics, PLO and so on. They are, it seems to me, pre-disposed to present Israel in a negative light.

RS: The only vested interest of the mass media as such, if you can personalize them which is always a mistake to some degree, is to become sensational, to become interesting, to maintain their publications – the constant exaltation and specific degradation of specific units Today it is 'X', tomorrow it is 'Y'; today 'X' is up, tomorrow 'X' is down; today 'Y' is up, tomorrow 'Y' is down. And yet it has always existed in the vocabulary of rationality and usually the clothing of rationality pretty well fits the situation but not very well. Now, today the general view of the many is that there is a unit called Palestinians and such a unit needs a nation. This is what they want and they should have it. Of course, they should not throw rocks and they should not blow up planes. And the general disposition, you can feel, is towards the acceptance of Palestinians as a State. And it seems to me that probably the times will have come in the next ten or fifteen years. But is it prejudice or something? Is it partly fuelled by the desire to make interesting headlines to agitate some people in Yiddish community? Certainly because it makes more interesting commentary.

DV: How powerful are intellectuals in this country?

RS: Well, it's difficult to say. It varies. For instance, in the last thirty years, the intellectuals who are economists have become very powerful. Social scientists, social doctrines, social scientific techniques have been a decisive element in national policy for many years. Then there is the tradition of the intellectual who is the State Department, who has essentially been a lawyer though George Kenan in his famous series of lectures talked about the danger of running foreign policy on juridical principles in as much as they involved contractual definition which are far too well defined for international fluidity. As far as literary intellectuals go, they are not powerful in this country. Literary intellectuals are not appealed in this country as they are used to be in the time of Vachel Lindsay, I don't know if you can call him an intellectual but he was a poet. But in his day when he wrote a poem on Panama Canal, President Woodrow Wilson called him into his cabinet and he read the pocm to his cabinet and he read the poem to the Congress. Can you expect this to happen today? No. Is Saul Bellow quoted on national policy? Seldom or never. Now and then Op-Ed page of the *New York Times* has opened up its pages to this sort of thing. Now and then we are questioned about our views. Now and then the President appears who knows the importance of the community in generating influence and makes a special appeal to them. John F. Kennedy is a special example of it who brought intellectuals to Washington D.C.; Alfred Kazin and others had lunch with him, talked about books. And then when they went home, wrote their opinions which were contrary to the opinions he willed them to espouse. He said such things as, "they were sons of bitches, wasted one and half hours having lunch with them." I have just come back from Australia, not just but this summer. In Australia, it's rather an interesting situation. They had a Premier in 1973 who was a true intellectual, who believed that the essence of the country is that expressed in its arts, who quite grappled the appropriation of the arts and who saw in his life-time the number of Australian novelists move from eighteen to a hundred and fifty. And the quality rise similar. And actually was actively involved in seeing that intellectuals were, writers and artists were, I should say, the proper expression of the society. Here is certain amount of lip-service, occasionally Jimmy Carter pins a medal on Saul Bellow. And for my money, that's good on the whole. I like the fact that the intellectuals, the literary intellectuals are not in power or allied to power because we should not exist as persons, we should exist as commentators. We understand, we do not participate. I have seen cases of writers occasionally, my old friend Ralph Ellison who was brought on to Washington by Lyndon Johnson and talked and feted – and what was the result? Where could his literary experience match that? He lost the idea of living alone with his resentment, his gripes, his feelings, his joys, his passion, his inspiration and putting them down in words. It's a danger even being a professor. It's a danger because one is so used to amusing the young. Any body can amuse the young, and to inspire them because here we have to say something you said five years ago which they haven't heard it. Their fathers may have heard it. So, it's a danger for a creative person, certainly it is a danger to be in politics; still now and then one wishes instead an actor being received as a God or listened to, would bring some one who is more interesting, a writer who has seen more, knows more, who would amuse America more, broaden it, rise it, elevate it intellectually and spiritually. I would like to see more of that. On the other hand, I do not want to see so much of that either.

DV: Who is a Jew?

RS: The Jew is somebody who is brought up to think that he is a Jew, considers himself a Jew and who is seen by others a Jew.

DV: Is it acceptable to the institutional religion?

RS: What institutions? You mean the Jew is somebody who is converted by the rabbi or born to a Jewish mother. That's the way they define it. Well, I have children by a woman who is not a Jew. And officially my children are not Jews? Each of them considers himself a Jew in part, knows that if he were in Germany in 1938 that definition would not matter. They would be sent to Auschwitz or Dachau and they would be exterminated. They are, to some degree, conscious of their Jewishness. My daughters married Jews who are more Jewish than my son who married a non-Jew. It's consciousness and other people's consciousness.

DV: Now, about the young writers – young in the sense that their literary career is still to be established firmly, like Chain Potok and Cynthia Ozick . . .

RS: I haven't read Chain Potok. I have never read anything of Ozick who seems to me powerfully interesting. She is an intelligent woman. I have never felt her as a remarkable writer. I have read couple of her stories but I think she is a much more refreshing writer. She does only a couple of small things, but she does those things beautifully.

DV: Harold Bloom mentions somewhere that there isn't really prominent Jewish-American poetry. Jewish-American novel has obviously attained significant status but . . .

RS: I don't think he knows. This is a great era in poetry and prose in America. We may not have a Shakespeare, we may not have a Milton, we may not have a Tolstoy.

DV: For Jewish poets too . . .

RS: Jewish poets as well. For instance, he probably has never read two books of Ellen O'Lerner. These are the works of genius. Now she stopped writing poetry but these are the works of genius. They are hidden away here and there. There is not Jewish poetry in the sense that there is a ghetto. The point is the community in which people write stories and poets do not think in terms of Jew or non-Jew any more. That situation has changed. Among my close friends, Jewish or non-Jewish, we almost never talked about it. There was much more talk about it today than there was twenty-five years ago. But they didn't talk about being Christian; they didn't talk about being Catholic. I guess I vaguely know whether one is a son of a Catholic or a Protestant. But to say that there is no Jewish poetry.

DV: He says actually that there are no significant Jewish poets.

RS: The situation is similar to Heine's time. Do you call Heine a Jewish poet? No. He is a great German poet who fled and lived in Paris.

DV: With the emergence of post-structuralism and deconstruction, don't you think teaching in traditional sense has become problematic?

RS: On the whole, yes. Extraordinarily little has come out of this enormous amount of activity. Now, I think, there you can make a case for Talmudic way of thinking. Since so many of the well-known critics are Jews in that sense. But for my money, I don't have the time and interest to read much. But I have read some. Now, Roman Jacobson as a founder of one of the sources of the school, he is a great commentator on the whole. And some of the distinctions he makes, say, his definition of poetic impulse, that's remarkable and useful. Jacques Lacan and the other Jewish thinker who atleast ten or twenty years ago is thought of great importance, I have been able to extract, maybe, one or two lines out of reading several thousand that have some wisdom in it. But the conscientious distortion of presentation in him is quite repellent to me. Paul de Man I heard give a lecture here. This is before I read anything about his past. I saw that this is an exercise in concealment from the way he used his accent, from the way he lowered his voice in crucial parts, the way he chose very obscure works to dismiss and only when he began to say something about Proust or the writer whom I know fairly well did I see that his views were deeply banal. He was not Jewish. I have never read anything of Paul de Man's that I found enlightening, *not one line*. I have never read much of Paul de Man but compared to Jacobson, he does not exist. As a linguist, brilliant. Eventhough, it is a critical age, I don't think that an enormous amount of work is done of significance. However, I have found that feminist critics have indeed shown me much, the better feminist critics have shown me much that I have missed in literature. I am interested in the political sources of criticism. There is no doubt that certain analyses have been enlightening and that one can learn. But I don't have time or interest to work through much of it myself. I have to reserve myself to what I do. It turns out that in teaching classes and in writing various essays that I have clumsily written along the lines of these people without knowing it and sometimes earlier than that. But I am not a good person to interrogate about this. I do feel that there is a powerful danger and I have seen that in the density and obfuscation of the criticism: one, in the displacement of clarity; two, in the nervousness about the authority, about creative authority; three, in the substitution of critical insight for, let's call it, artistic synthesis though it's not complete until, in some cases, it doesn't even exist until it has been given a reading. But such readings as Roland Barthes' Balzac's *Sarrasine* or some of the readings of Derrida are repellent readings. They do not attract. The number of insights compared to the number of repulsions is not great. Whereas William Empson wrote in six weeks the seven types of ambiguity. You could see his playfulness, you saw enormous amount of enlightenment; even when he tripped over himself and made mistakes, went on and on about something, you still felt the critical energy generating inside. Now, when Barthes introduced Michelet, there was a beautiful thing, there you saw insights, there you saw Michelet's brilliance set off properly by Roland Barthes. Towards the middle and the end of his life, I don't think he was doing significant work. Whereas Alain Robbe-Grillet, who seems to be one of the sources of Roland Barthes, has been fascinating in his discussion of the novel. Nobody reads him any more, nobody reads his criticism any more. That remains a challenge to students and helps rectify the works that otherwise will not be considered interesting. It is a great period of critical activity but how much of it is critical brilliance, I don't know.

DV: Do you think the theory has a vested interest? Which the magazines like *Critical Enquiry* legitimate?

RS: Most of the *Critical Enquiry* is unreadable. I myself have published two or three articles in it. Because they are readable, they are not even discussed. Now and then a wonderful piece is published. But generally speaking, there is a very small interest in the pieces. Now and then, there is a good issue – an issue, for instance, on race or psychoanalysis.

And the last week I was reading Heidegger there. And the editor himself was a friend of mine and that's why I published there. He says that it's such a struggle to get people to write clearly. It's a very difficult business. But it's an important publication. I don't want to denigrate it. Maybe out of heaviness and clumsiness will come a dancer who can dance on his toes, the intellectual dancer, but right now they are like rhinoceros, more or less trying to be ballerinas. They are clumsy and heavy and they overplay.

DV: Would you comment on the general political behaviour of the Jews – liberal, liberal-left, conservative?

RS: I have been on correspondence with some fanatic Jewish writers. It is considered the thing to be, to be right-wing especially if you have a lot of money, though I was glad to see my cousin in New York who is involved with Drexel and Burnham firm. His daughter, my cousin Millie, is married to the most conservative senator, the most backward senator, Gordon Humphrey of the New Hampshire. But I was delighted to see my cousin the liberal that he was in the thirties. He is still open-minded. He loves his daughter very much but he doesn't discuss politics with her. He says she is off the wall. Many people like my cousin who has money including this man who is a Chief Executive Officer of a very large cosmetic firm in Chicago, express views of a liberal kind. They pride themselves in being exclusive, the sort we discussed earlier. There is a variety of views. On the whole, seventy percent of Jews voted for Dukakis-versus-Bush and on the Hyde Park where I live now eighty percent of the Jews voted for Dukakis, and ninety percent – maybe. But still, I am a close friend of a wonderful economist, Gary Becker, who will receive the Nobel Prize even if he hasn't. And he with Milton Friedman and George Stiegler who is not a Jew and others here are very conservative in view. In Becker's case it is rational and well-thought out and he is open to all sorts of things. For instance, he wrote a piece on legalizing marijuana which, in general, is not considered a conservative position though Buckley, some one like Buckley, is for it. My own experience is that there is quite a great variety among my friends. I know leftists, I know rightists and I love centrists. And most of them can meet in a room and discuss things, arrive at a position which even if they wouldn't be identical atleast would recognize the rightness of each other's positions. We have at our university, two years ago, a debate on South Africa. I spoke, others spoke about it. It's a wonderful debate: should the university withdraw its involvement in the companies of South Africa?

DV: Did you have a radical past in the thirties?

RS: No, I grew up in the middle-class assimilated Jewish family, though I always considered myself to be more radical than a Communist at Chapel Hill. But I was ignorant and just ranted. I never joined any organization. I never was a Communist or socialist though my disposition would be more socialist than not. And yet I am unsure of that. I was of a generation which was literary than political.

DV: Coming back to Bellow, do you think there is a kind of misunderstanding between Mark Harris and Bellow? Harris thought that he was writing an official biography.

RS: Harris is a very odd fellow, and he says it. Bellow didn't mind that somebody is writing his biography; he did mind the idea. So 'yes' and 'no'. He didn't like some of the things he said and, in fact, he was angry with me for a brief moment for saying, – Harris must have asked me at one time, "Does Bellow have any games?" I said "philosophy and fucking." He was angry at me, once. I imagine if Harris comes to town, he calls on Bellow, but I don't know. Bellow is so much more famous, he had to protect himself from all kinds of intruders and also he is very very sensitive – exceptionally sensitive. But we all are. And he doesn't like to be thought of as a person of certain sort. I myself had been quite embarrassed with Harris's book. I thought I looked ridiculous some of the time in the book. He described the fact that I was wearing an overcoat that my father found in a restaurant. I was a little embarrassed. He makes me look like a fool, I don't mind. And still it is a brilliant and interesting book.

DV: Bellow somehow thinks that there is always somebody out there to take advantage of him.

RS: He does feel that. It's true.

DV: Well, Harris did write a book which embarrassed him.

RS: It has both good points and bad points. They were never really close friends – I don't think. Listen, Bellow and myself had this misunderstanding this summer because I wrote this piece in *Critical Enquiry* about P.E.N. conference in New York, actually in two parts. I quoted something Bellow had said to me. He felt that I made him out a racist, saved by his talent. Well, I said, "Saul, I don't think you are that way." But we got over it any way.

DV: These things happen.

RS: These things happen, yes.

Norman Podhoretz

DV: I would like to know your opinion on Lionel Trilling and his critical enterprise. I believe you made some remarks which later became quite embarrassing for both of you. It created a kind of controversy.

NP: Yea, it was in my book, *The Breaking Ranks*. Well, he was my teacher and was also a friend. And I knew him for a long time, quite intimately in that long part of the time. And I think he was certainly one of the most important American literary critics of our time, one of the two or three most important, I would say. And he was special in that he would talk about literature within the social, political context without ever violating the principles of autonomy of literature. He was able to do both of those things, keeping in view the independence, sovereignity and autonomy of literature and, at the same time, to see the significance of literary works in terms of surrounding world. Most of the critics, of Marxist and semi-Marxist persuasion, who can talk about of social and political context but who do not appreciate aesthetic dimension and there are many who can focus on aesthetic dimension without paying attention to contextual factors – Trilling was not entirely unique but he was one of those who was able to do the both simultaneously. He was also, in his own right, a very interesting writer. As a critic, his essays are very interesting and vital and his own role in the history of American intellectual life is extremely important and influential. He became, of course, best known as a critic of liberalism from within. He always considered himself a liberal. But I sometimes thought that with such friends liberalism did not need any enemies. He was an incisive critic practically of all the liberal attitudes of his own day specifically the kind of liberalism that was vaguely sympathetic to Communism in the thirties, upto the forties and the fifties. He was a strong anti-Communist. My own relationship is very good till his death. The controversy you alluded to earlier was created after he died by the critics. When I talked about him in my book, *The Breaking Ranks*, I also said some of the things I just said to you and I also spoke about the disappointment, not my self alone, but several of us felt at his refusal to play a leading role in fighting the New Left and the wars of the late nineteen sixties and into the early seventies. I made his wife and several other people very angry in saying that he held back out of fatigue and an unwillingness to engage in the kind of ideological framework that he once engaged in when he was younger. But I think that my treatment of him was respectful and I never accepted the criticism of my book. I don't think that I treated him disrespectfully or misrepresented anything that he said. I don't think it is justified criticism of my book. There was also some anger about the story I told of his reaction to my earlier book *Making It* which he had advised me not to publish. When he read the manuscript, he did not like the book and he advised me not to publish it. I am very bitter about that as any writer would be. But his wife Diana Trilling, whether she forgot or not, denied that he had said it to me. But he said it to me, you know. No question about it. On Jewish issues it is quite interesting. I had many talks with Trilling about Jewish issues on several occasions. He never denied that he was Jewish or in any way pretended to be not that sort but it was not a big issue with him or a salient issue with him, I would say. He once wrote an essay called "Wordsworth and the Rabbis." So, he also had some connection with the magazine called the *Menorah Journal* which was edited by my predecessor Elliot Cohen, the founding editor of *Commentary*. He also had a close relationship with Elliot Cohen in the early years of *Commentary*. But he did not have a high regard for Jewish culture, did not know a lot about it. I think he certainly had a low opinion of the American-Jewish community which he considered bourgeois, philistine, self-satisfying. He never identified closely with Jewish affairs and Jewish interests and he actually once wrote a piece in which he said that he saw nothing creative, nothing valuable in Jewish culture. I used to argue with him about all of these issues eventhough I was his student. He was very intrigued by the fact that I was interested in Jewish affairs. When I was an undergraduate at Columbia, I used to also attend classes at the Seminary College of the Jewish Studies after the few blocks up where I did eventually a valid degree, Bachelor of Literature. I also got a B.A. at Columbia at the same time. I was his favourite student. He once gave me the honour saying that I was the best student he ever had. He liked me personally and he had a high opinion of me as a kid. And he was simply, I think, he was slightly puzzled by the fact that I am studying at the Seminary. There was rabbinical school in Seminary. The branch I studied in had an academic branch. It was sort of Jewish liberal arts college. He would often ask about this. I'd say that he was quite intrigued. In later years, we often discussed this whole issue. I guess that he was a man who was very much interested in Freud and psychoanalysis. He himself had been psychoanalysed. He had a lot of psychoanalytic view of life. So naturally any one with that sort of view of life who is Jewish would be interested in his own Jewishness, its importance in his own identity. But, as I said, beyond that he had no real concern or involvement. He is much more interested in Freud or even German literature than anything Jewish. And I think that it is a limitation on his part although everybody has limitations and strength. That's roughly what I would say about Trilling.

DV: When Trilling made those unfortunate comments on American Jewish community or, for that matter, anything Jewish, he must have been very young. He himself had written two or three articles from a Jewish viewpoint much later in his life.

NP: The article appeared in *Contemporary Jewish Record* which is the predecessor magazine of *Commentary*. He was not that young. He wrote that article in 1944, I think. There was a symposium. He would have been forty years old by then, I guess. He was not that young. This was during World War II. While the Holocaust was going on, people were not conscious then. On the writers that interest you like Malamud, Saul Bellow, and others, he had a mixed attitude towards them – justifiably so. He did not think that great stuff is coming from the Jewish fiction. He thought highly of Bellow, but not that highly. And I think he had similarly benign attitude towards Malamud, but I don't think he was very much impressed with him. Or with Philip Roth or with any of the others. Some of them are half-forgotten now. He was much more interested in Norman Mailer although Mailer is the least Jewish of the American-Jewish writers. I may have introduced him to Norman Mailer. No, no – Lillian Hellman introduced both of us to Norman Mailer, come to think of it. I became a close friend of Mailer for some time. There was a time when he and I were very close, he also came to know the Trillings quite well. But Diana and Trilling were impressed by him personally and also as a writer.

DV: What do you think of the present Jewish writing. Has it come of age? Who are the prominent Jewish writers, according to you?

NP: Saul Bellow, maybe. Well, he is certainly the most gifted of them. As a novelist, as I conceive the novel, he is not a great novelist. I think he is something else. He mainly writes monologues disguised as novels.

I don't think there are any characters in his novels. Occasionally, maybe, but fundamentally he is always talking about himself and his feelings, very brilliant expositor of his feelings and ideas. He is an involved intellectual. But I don't think he has the true gift of a novelist which is to bring the world to life, at least not for me. Many people disagree with that. He has got a high reputation, as you know. He is a man of immense intelligence, learning and skill. He doesn't have the novelistic gift. Malamud, of course, is dead now. I still think that he wrote some wonderful stories which would probably endure. Again I don't think any of his novels stands up as a perfectly realized work. I have come to think better of Philip Roth as he and I have gotten older. I quite liked some of his recent works, Zuckerman trilogy, not all of that. I mean the character in the book, not treated very gently. But some of these come to life. One or two of his recent books I found even touching. Although he is a limited writer, he is always his own subject. Many of the others, you may find here and there lasting pieces. Cynthia Ozick – she wrote " Envy" which we have published in *Commentary* originally. I think it's a great work – a small masterpiece. I don't think her other novels very satisfying. As I say, there are many of them, who have a story here and a book there. It's hard to say. Maybe because I am so close to them. How much of it really amounts to real literature? I know that it has become fashionable among certain circles that the whole movement has been overrated. And from a strictly aesthetic point of view, that maybe true. Some people say, it's all finished now, it's all over. In a certain sense that too is true. In a sense that every school and literary tendency has a life span and sometimes it reaches the end of its vitality. But, I would say, that even if it is overrated, in one sense, nevertheless, it is very interesting and is an influential explosion of the creative energy on the American scene. I think it broadened several new qualities in the American novel. First of all, there is a strong emphasis on ideas that is generally common, a raciness of idiom and language, a nervous urban style with some influence of Yiddish particularly in Bellow and Malamud, a new boldness not in style but in subject matter particularly in Roth – so there's something there, they tried to know exactly what's tender in the subject of eternity, how important it really is. The people you have talked about, the Jewish dramatists, I have a low opinion on all of them both as writers and Lillian Hellman was once a friend of mine, I know Arthur Miller.

DV: Miller again is a peculiar example. He seems to be forever avoiding Jewishness in every possible way. His plays are ethnically anonymous although one could clearly perceive Yiddish flavour and typical Jewish ethical structure in his plays. His treatment of Jewishness is certainly surprising . . .

NP: Well, it's not so surprising. That's the style among the Stalinists of his generation. They thought the way to achieve universality is to eradicate every trace of particularity. In *Commentary*, long before my time, there was a wonderful article on Arthur Miller. I remember even the name of the person who wrote it. Not so much the article that was wonderful but the title. The title was wonderful. It was a review of the translation into Yiddish of the *Death of a Salesman*. I said Stalinists earlier. I didn't mean the members of the Communist party. But the liberal fellow traveller which Arthur Miller certainly was in his younger days. The culture of the period. It was true in the case of Lillian Hellman as well. *The Little Foxes* was about a Jewish family, her own family. There is no indication that these people are Jewish at all. Similarly with Miller, *All My Sons* and *Death of a Salesman*. These people had liberal internationalism. They thought of Jewishness or any other ethnic or even national identity as limiting and also reactionary. It was like bourgeois reactionary. You were not supposed to pay any respect to this kind of interest or preoccupation. The way to achieve a great universal art is to be general. Of course, a lot of it is a rationalization in disguise of their own feelings of discomfort at being Jewish, their feeling that somehow if they come forthrightly Jewish, no one will be interested in what they had to say, what they were writing. But whatever the psychology behind it, the work that was produced was highly superficial. In the case of Lillian Hellman very melodramatic and politically tendentious and it was wrong tendency. You mentioned Clifford Odets. He was highly talented. He has a talent. Well, *Waiting for Lefty*, was agit-prop, Communist Party stuff. The famous ones are *Awake and Sing* and one or two others. But he never fulfilled himself. As for Elmer Rice, I think he is forgotten now, I don't think people would remember if you mention his name. There are some American Jewish poets. Now, the most famous is Allen Ginsberg. I am not a great admirer of Allen Ginsberg. But many people are. You know, there have been very good American-Jewish poets.

DV: How difficult it is to bring Jewish sensibility to poetry? Does it involve structural problems? Do you think that the American Jewish poets are successful in blending Jewish sensibility with the tradition of poetry? Because I remember that Harold Bloom is saddened at the fact that Jewish poetry has not been effective nor does it really create a peculiar style that can truly accommodate Jewish sensibility. Charles Reznikoff, in this connection, is a very good example.

NP: Well, I know him. I don't think it creates any structural problems. I don't remember the essay you have been talking about, so I cannot address his particular argument. But what many people have said was that the problem of writing poetry was that it's impossible to achieve greatness as a poet without being deeply rooted in your culture. It's the theory of culture of anti-Semites in Europe including (Richard) Wagner who said that Jews could never be creators, they can only be critics because they are so rootless, they are rootless Cosmopolitans. Unless you are in tune with a folk or soil, you couldn't produce great art. And this is the theory Wagner developed in the famous pamphlet, "Jewishness and Music." It became a theme for cultural anti-Semites in the 1920s in Vienna and Berlin. In a very attentuated and modified form, such an idea has also circulated in the United States just about the poets and also about novelists. There is a small element of truth in this idea, but that is a very small element of the truth. I don't think it applies hardly at all to the modern period, certainly not in the United States where every one is relatively rootless – most of us are. So, I don't see any structural problem. You know the great poets are very rare. Even Harold Bloom exaggerates the number of great poets. He thinks Wallace Stevens is a very great poet and I doubt it. There have been a couple – I mean there haven't been more than two great poets in English in the entire twentieth century, T.S. Eliot and Yeats. There have been some good poets. So, the fact there haven't been any great poets of Jewish origin in English isn't particularly surprising, if it is true.

DV: When critics talk about great poets, I wonder sometimes how they define their greatness. To take a specific example, you have poets like Ezra Pound and Eliot. Their poetry has been elevated to the status of literary canon. I can't think of any literature programme anywhere in the world which doesn't include them. And yet, if one has to evaluate their positions on Jewish question or consider what I would call anti-Semitic slurs in their works, it would create problems in dealing with them. Do we have to forget about ethical or moral aspect when we are talking about greatness of any particular artist? If that is the case, what could be the function of art in a society, indeed in the context of human civilization? I don't know how to separate these two, art and ethical structure.

NP: Well, nobody does. It's an extremely difficult question. I never thought of this before. You are trying to study the Talmud. There is an interesting law in the Talmud. That has to do with the dietary regulations where something is Kosher. You can't mix meat and milk. But there's a formula – I don't quite know how to translate. It can be cancelled in the sixtieth part. If only it is one sixtieth part of drop in the meat, it is okay. If it's not more than one sixtieth, then it's okay. And that's one way of looking at it. How much of it is there in a particular work. In the case of Pound, it's lot more and in the case of Eliot, he wasn't certainly an anti-Semite. But in his poetry, there's only a faint trace of it. In the case of Pound there's a lot more. On the issue of relation of morality to art, there's also the question of distance. In other words, things in the works of Shakespeare and Chaucer are very shocking by contemporary standards. But it was a long time ago and somehow one doesn't, at least I don't, respond in the same way.

DV: Some people do. For instance, Arnold Wesker does.

NP: Yes, some people do. But I don't. Again, I am not talking about the anti-Semitism. For example, some one wrote a very powerful novel or book celebrating Hitler or Stalin, I would find it impossible to admire no matter how wonderfully it is written. But if you read about, I don't know, Genghis Khan or somebody, tyrant of past centuries being celebrated even by Shakespeare, the distance seems to cancel out the moral offense. It's a very difficult problem, it is an extremely difficult problem. It has never been satisfactorily resolved. There is a big controversy here about Picasso. Because there's a biography of Picasso showing what a monster he was and arguing lot of this was reflected in his work. People have been fighting about Picasso's moral monstrosities and his painting. So, I was talking about Trilling earlier and the autonomy of art. One has to respect the autonomy of art in the sense that it has its own laws and according to these laws a piece of art, painting or poetry achieves even the right to be considered as art, quite apart from any other considerations. In other words, noblest moral sentiments do not make a piece of writing into a work of art if it takes the aesthetic power. It's very difficult to define that and it is abstract but the critic knows it when he sees it and he would respond to it. Otherwise, he can't be a critic. So, I think one has to respect that autonomy, those laws, those aesthetic laws. But one shouldn't stop them. Again, that's what Trilling did. He was able to do both: understand aesthetic laws and moral, social and political dimensions in the work. When I did criticism, even when I do occasionally, I try to do both. But some cases are very very difficult and almost impossible to deal with but as there's a maxim the lawyers use, that hard cases make a bad law. And I think the same is true of criticism. If you take the writer like Celine who was an apologist for Nazism, fascism but he was a great stylist of certain kind – even Genet. There are the worst cases. Pound – it's almost impossible to settle his issue. But in the case of Eliot, I don't have that much of difficulty because, as I say, in the most of his work that I admire, there's no trace of anti-Semitism. "Four Quartets" . . .

DV: As I look at the Jewish intellectual scene, I see a tremendous interest in their tradition. There was a time in the thirties, forties and fifties and maybe up till recent times, Jewish writers and intellectuals are somehow embarrassed by their Jewish identity. Now, the students at prestigious universities like Harvard, Yale, MIT, Brandeis and the others are proud of their ethnic background – if you look at the Hillel programmes. Jewish intellectuals at the moment are trying to see connections and establish a useful context between their Jewish heritage and whatever other intellectual priorities they have. In literary theory and criticism, it is particularly evident. Harold Bloom establishes a parallel between Kabbala and literary theory. Geoffrey Hartman edited a book called *Midrash and Literature*. There are surely many more examples. The situation happily has changed for the better. How do you view this changing scenario?

NP: Well, there's a paradox here. You know Heinrich Heine who was Jewish and converted to what he called a passport into European civilization. He never took his conversion, I think, seriously. He was a very brilliant man. He once said – my German is not very good but I translate it – "How are Christians, so are Jews." In other words, Jews are always trying to imitate what the Christians are doing. The fact is that it has become fashionable in recent years, not just among Jews but in this country, to be ethnic or to identify one self. When I was a kid, the early period – I am not as old as I look – that was the time when it was unfashionable. For Lillian Hellman and Arthur Miller to come out strongly as Jews would have taken certain courage. I mean the fact that they didn't do it. There are many reasons. But still, it was not regarded as such a wonderful thing. And in certain circles it was regarded as bad taste. You are supposed to assimilate. The opposite is true today. Now, every one is something. So, Theodore Roosevelt once said that there are no hyphenated Americans meaning that we are all immigrants. Now, we have only hyphenated immigrants. Every body is Italian- or Jewish-American. Everybody is mixed. Partly this is the consequence of the loss of nerve, loss of confidence in central WASP culture which used to dominate and no longer does. We were supporting the country where immigrants were not required to learn English or there is whole fight over whether English should be declared as official language of the country. There is a bilingual context with Hispanics. This would have been once inconceivable. It has been taken for granted that you have to learn English. That's all there is to it. If you want to be something else, learn some other language, it's your business. But you have to learn English. Out there in the world, you lived in English. There's a time when that confidence, those unifying centres totally had broken down, they lost their authority. You see a kind of break-up of what you called the Balkanization of culture. You also see it in politics where every member is a part of a group, ethnic group, religious group, now even sexual group. So, this phenomenon of Jewish intellectuals being proud of their roots and culture is a part of the general pattern and fashion of the general culture at large. So, I do not see it as necessarily expressing a greater pride or deeper interest in Jewishness although it probably does in many cases, very likely in most cases – I don't really. I am just observing that this is a new fashion and if fashions were to change I am not so sure that if these people would still go to synagogues, writing books about Kabbala. Still, what's happening now, atleast to Jews, is healthier than the older fashions, feeling obligated to assimilate and shed your Jewishness as did so many intellectuals once felt. I think this is healthier and better.

DV: I am trying to think about what you have been saying all along. I remember a book written by Susan Handelman called *Slayers of Moses* where she attempts to view the recent critical theories especially deconstruction from the viewpoint of Rabbinic Judaism. There are some other studies of this type as I mentioned earlier. Do you think such attempts are superficial?

NP: Well, I think it is superficiality. I think obviously there is some need there to make it Kosher. I don't think deconstructionism is rabbinic or anything like that. Or I don't see anything Jewish there either.

DV: What do you think about Paul de Man controversy these days? As you know, he has his own admirers or apostles trying to justify him or whatever?

NP: Well, Geoffrey Hartman wrote an article more or less justifying him. I think that it's disgraceful. I think that Paul de Man was a Nazi obviously – no question about that. He was whatever he was. He was an anti-Semite and a Nazi. There's no denying that. The question that was raised whether it had any connection with deconstructionism, here is a furious debate whether it does. Some people say 'yes', some people say 'no'. My own position is that deconstructionism is a form of nihilism. To the extent that Nazism is also a form of nihilism, there is some deep affinity there. But I wouldn't press the point too hard. I think that De Man should not be justified. I was appalled to see Geoffrey Hartman's essay. Hartman is a good Jew. Unlike some of the people I have been talking about, Geoffrey Hartman genuinely is interested in Jewishness. He is a loyal Jew, no question about that. He is not being merely fashionable. His Jewishness was not stronger than his commitment to deconstructionism. His friendship with De Man overcame his Jewish instincts in this case.

DV: What do you think about *Partisan Review*, its past and present?

NP: *Partisan Review* is not what it was. It was a great magazine once upon a time. It's a shadow of the former self. Really it's sad to me . . .

DV: They never even discussed issues of Jewish interest or Jewish culture in the old days, although you certainly find a change of heart now?

NP: Well, when I first met Elliot Cohen, when I was the editor of *Commentary*, and I was a young writer and I had already written for *Partisan Review*, he said that the only difference between *Commentary* and *Partisan Review* is that we admit it and they don't – meaning of course Jewishness. Most of them are Jewish, major contributors. But they were in a period when the magazine was most influential and powerful. It was the time when Jewishness was not particularly acceptable among intellectuals when most of them were stiff if not Marxists, atleast heavily influenced by Marxism. Mostly, they thought they were indifferent to Jewishness or hostile. That changed to some extent in the fifties when even in the *Partisan Review* you find open traces of

Jewishness, now some of Malamud's stories published there, Bellow's stuff and also Isaac Bashevis Singer was published there. I should also mention Delmore Schwartz who also wrote some Jewish stories, published in *Partisan Review*. For most part, that was the intellectual generation, like Lionel Trilling, who were not particularly involved in Jewishness or Jewish affairs.

DV: Well, coming to the American political scene, there are many advocates of Neo-Conservatism at the moment. You are an influential theorist and supporter of this particular school of thought. How do you define Neo-Conservatism? Where is the point of departure, if at all, from the old-style conservatism?

NP: The term Neo-Conservatism was, of course, invented or used as a derogatory epithet. Many of us have surrendered to it. It's not a term we ourselves have used. 'Neo' means new, of course. We conservatives were new because we all have started on the left and moved, as we thought, to the centre and other centre of the right, the right of the centre. But, in any case, we were newly arrived at this position from a point somewhere on the left. Many say that Neo-Conservatism is Jewish but that also is very much exaggerated. Many of the leading Neo-Conservatives are not Jewish, are not, were not. People like Jean Kirkpatrick, Daniel P. Moynihan who since changed his position and moved back to the left. But he was one of the founding fathers of the Neo-Conservatism. James Q. Wilson, I can mention many others who are not Jewish. And we were all reacting against some of the radical tendencies of the 1960s. That's how this movement—this is a movement because it does not have any other organized existence or party line. It's a tendency. Those of us who showed this tendency all had one thing in common which is that we were repelled by what was happening on the left, in the middle of the late sixties both politically and culturally. Neo-Conservatives have all come together usually spontaneously and independently in opposition.

DV: You are supposed to be one of the champions.

NP: Well, I am one of them. There is Irving Krystol. In my case, I am very much a member of the radical movement.

DV: You are the moving spirit of Neo-Conservatism.

NP: One of them. Generally, Irving Kristol is considered the grandfather of Neo-Conservatism, as he is called. He is ten years older than I am. He preceded me in this position. So, in my case, I have written about this, I was unable to stomach the anti-Americanism that developed in the radical movement. This eventually came to include Israel and also to Jewish interests and concerns. Although some say that I became a Neo-Conservative, because of Jewish concerns, it's not true. It just happens not to be true. It was the other way round. The hostility to Israel developed on the left because of their hostility to America and the West. Israel was considered an appendage of the American imperialism, the fifty-first state, the representative of evil culture in that part of the world. So it was derivative. Anti-Americanism came first, anti-Zionism came second, subordinate, corollary. And it was anti-Americanism that I responded to, rebelled against, that has led me to the whole reconsideration. My political views about this country and about the Western civilization generally and ultimately, also the role of my own Jewishness in relation to these larger issues. So, when you asked me the relationship with the old conservatism, that cannot be answered in terms of propositions because what was true in 1968 and 1972 – the answer to that question then would have been different than the answer to the question today. Because the traditional conservatives have also changed. You have a dynamic situation. For example, originally the difference between tradition or paleo-conservatives and Neo-Conservatives is the attitude toward the welfare state. Neo-Conservatives have accepted the welfare state, they didn't want to turn it into a socialist state. We accepted the welfare, they were against it. But they are not against it any more. They, especially since Reagan, didn't undo the welfare state. There is no longer counter-revolutionary move against the welfare state among traditional conservatives. That's finished, over. So, that difference has disappeared because they have changed. On the other hand, we too have changed, moved closer to them on some other issues, so-called social issues. They are not of a large part of the new thinking twenty years ago than it is the case today. So, these have been convergences. People on the right have moved to the left-ward, I don't mean the left, shifting and becoming more moderate. We were on the left, moved to the right. We would, sort of, admit vaguely in general area to the right of centre. There are still differences. If you want to be crude about it, if you want to ignore complicating, you can define in ethnic terms. I said before that the Neo-Conservatism is not entirely Jewish, lot of Neo-Conservatives are Jews, but most Jews are liberals still. But if you want to say that most of Neo-Conservatives are Jewish, you can say that. The older conservatives represented by *National Review* are more or less Catholic and the New Right is more or less Protestant and the fundamentalist Protestant. We have difference of ethnic and religious causation.

DV: Why is 'liberal' such a dirty word today?

NP: 'Liberal' became a dirty word because the liberal tradition was captured, kidnapped really, by the New Left in the late sixties. Many liberals have allowed this to happen. They did not fight against the usurpation of the term by the New Left. They allowed those people to be called liberals. So, liberalism got identified with ideas, attitudes, positions that are very foreign to the liberalism that had existed in this country before the late sixties. There was a time when it was not only an honourable word but people fought over it—"I am a liberal," and so on. The term 'liberal' got identified with the attitudes that were associated with the counter-culture and the New Left. When older liberal acquiesced to this, allowed the word to be like that, it gradually reached the point where we are today. The word became dirty. Liberalism in the sixties was associated with the idea of strong foreign policy. That's what Kennedy meant. John F. Kennedy said, pay any price, bear any burden to ensure the survival of the success of liberty. He was in favour of strong defense, strong foreign policy to contain the expansionism of Soviet Russia, to fight Communism. Kennedy was also in favour of economic growth and tax-cut which he had initiated. They were strong defenders of traditional, liberal, bourgeois liberal values. That's what liberalism stood for in those days. The New Liberalism stood for something else, it was neo-isolationist, hostile to economic growth and it was fundamentally hostile to traditional values, so-called bourgeois, middle-class values. The term liberal came to mean what it did not mean before. And the New Liberalism has proved itself to be very unpopular, in my view, quite justifiably so. But, the fold is not just Ronald Reagan, that's ridiculous. It wasn't Ronald Reagan who made liberalism a dirty word, it was the liberals who made liberalism a dirty word.

DV: As I was discussing some of your positions with my fellow scholars at Brandeis and also with some of them here and elsewhere (mostly Jewish), most of them didn't seem to accept your positions. In fact, they expressed a tremendous surprise at my being interested in meeting with you at all. Why is it so? Is it mostly because of your association with Neo-Conservatism or is it because most Jews are still liberal and, therefore, they can't go along with your political agenda?

NP: They consider me a traitor, I think.

DV: Did you try to answer those accusations, if any?

NP: Not any more. I wrote million words clarifying but nobody pays any attention. Certainly I wouldn't have any interest in explaining to these people who don't have any interest in understanding. If they have any interest, it's easy for them to know. Most of them don't read *Commentary*, for example.

DV: I think I completely agree with you there. For instance, for most Jews or Jewish intellectuals, Gore Vidal's article in *Nation* called "Empire Lovers Strike Back" does not mean very much, or maybe, as I gathered, some of them aren't even aware of it. Similarly, when I mentioned "Whose Palestine?" an article published in *Commentary* responding obviously to Joan Peters's book *From Time Immemorial*, most Jewish intellectuals I happened to meet were either incredulous or expressed, again, astonishment. Much of this happens, I think, because of their pre-conceived notions about *Commentary* and its editor, yourself. Why don't they analyse instead Gore Vidal's anti-Semitic rhetoric? Why is it so?

NP: These people are sunk in a reflexive, mindless ideological position they are not even aware that it is ideological. They take it so completely for granted, they are dogmatic, they are close-minded, they are bigoted. It's almost like a religion in that any one who doesn't share is the heretic, an apostate, or an enemy. And yet, it is ironic that these people use the term 'liberal'. You asked why 'liberal' is a dirty word. Once 'liberal' used to mean open mind, tolerance, believing in freedom and free discussion. Most of the people you are talking about, Jewish and non-Jewish, are close-minded, intolerant, not interested and not even capable of listening to other points of view. And that's another reason why they acquired a bad name.

Noam Chomsky: I

I met Noam Chomsky in January, 1989. Chomsky took me to his room at MIT and told me that he was in India to receive an honorary doctorate from Delhi University. What surprised him was that he was heavily guarded. When he visited Asia Fair along with the then Prime Minister Indira Gandhi, he felt he had heavy surveillance, even more than the Prime Minister herself.

NC: There was a soldier outside my room. He would nod every time I go out, he would nod every time I come in. There was a soldier down the hall with a rifle. There was awful lot of security. And I asked at one point: what's it all about? And I never had any security. Then they told me. In fact, I walked through the Asia Fair. There was an Asia Fair going on. I walked through with Mrs. Indira Gandhi. My impression was that I had more security than she did. I never had plain clothes people following around. It looked, at least, it looked as if I was under more of surveillance and control than she would. Then I asked at one point. What depressed me was, I never had any body following around any where. They said, "Well, we looked up your biography and we discovered that you were Jewish. We thought, you might be a target for PLO terrorists." I thought I might be a more likely target for Mossad. But that didn't convince anybody.

DV: I remember a comment made by a responsible college professor in my country. He said that the only person worth paying attention to in America is Noam Chomsky.

NC: Yes, I had a good time there. I talked at Jawaharlal Nehru University and to various other groups. It's quite interesting, I always wanted to get back to but I was never able to.

DV: You have been around for so long. You have taken controversial positions which is so uncommon among American academics. In retrospect, do you think that some of the positions you have taken in the past cause any embarrassment now?

NC: Embarrassment to who?

DV: Embarrassment to you. I mean, have you revised some of your opinions?

NC: Well, of course. If I haven't revised my opinion, they assume I am dead. Nobody fails to revise their opinions if they are alive. The world is much too complicated a place but, for example, in linguistics which is linguistics and philosophy in my professional field, I have revised my opinions quite substantially. In fact, the question is an old one. In the natural sciences, for example, if you still believe the things you believed in thirty years ago, you might as well retire and go sailing. I mean the field is dead. So, of course, every time a paper comes out, you think about it and revise your opinions. With regard to international affairs, I think there is much less reason to revise one's opinions because the points are no theories, no intellectual depths to the analysis. I think what happens in the world is relatively obvious. Of course, I revised my opinions, I learned a lot more because there's lot of documentation which has come about that was not available as that time. If I were right today, twenty five years ago, I would have different kind of evidence, different kind of understanding, and would give a different slant to it undoubtedly. That's why I keep reading the classified documents, for example. You learn more about the background of things. Things I would only speculate about twenty-five years ago, you could now present a lot more evidence for. And some of the things have to be revised because new things have come out.

DV: Does it bother you some times because you have many critics here certainly? People disagree with you a great deal . . .

NC: I don't have many critics here. People disagree but they are not critics. To be a critic, you have to come to terms with something. For instance, some one with an article saying this man deserved to be shot. I don't regard him as a critic. If some one says that here's something wrong, that it doesn't have reasons – I agree that's being a critic. But virtually there's no such material. I don't know which tries to engage intellectually. It is mostly just denunciation, which is not considered criticism.

DV: There is a general tendency these days either to reject or disown the ideas of the sixties?

NC: There's this tendency where?

DV: For instance, I remember an article by Melvyn Lasky in *Encounter* . .

NC: Does he accept the ideas of the sixties? I mean, CIA never accepted the ideas of the sixties. They didn't like them in the sixties, they don't like them now. Why should they?

DV: I like to know your opinion on Neo-Conservatism. It is almost a permanent item on their agenda to denounce the New Left?

NC: I think you have to check up what happened. In the 1960s, a lot of things happened in the sixties, there were lot of popular organizations, lot of development among general population, began very much among the young people and spread to various sections of the people. New questions were asked, there was lot of dissidence, there was skepticism, activism, refugee political organization and so on. All that terrified elites, elites want the population to be passive, pathetic and weaning. They are expressive about it. In fact, there is a remarkable book on this topic. This is the only book that came in 1975 which is called *The Crisis of Democracy*. (Michael Crozier et al.)

They are liberal elites, international elites, Japan, Europe and the U.S. Their general opinion was there was a crisis in democracy. The general population which was generally apathetic, obedient and silent had become mobilized, and was beginning to enter political area and to put forth political programmes and, of course, that's totally intolerable because democracy means elite world, what we call democracy in the West means business-run societies of which general population is silent. They will have to ratify occasionally what it wants but nothing beyond that. This was all being questioned in the sixties. In the universities, they were terrified because the students were asking questions instead of copying down what they were told. Terrifying, you know. The interpretation was, the universities were all burning, all kinds of fantasies developed about what happened. What happened basically was the breakdown of the pattern of authorities. When the pattern of authorities breaks down, strange kind of things happen too – lot of freaking thing. The focus is on how they are trying to undermine dissidence. But the main thing that happened was just intellectual arousal, cultural improvement. The country has become a much more civilized place, not among elites, not at all. But the general population in many ways. Out of this fervent came, especially a group developed in the 1970s, even more the 1980s. By now, it's all over the country. It's just not the students. But things like, say, the anti-nuclear movement, the Feminist movement, the environmental movement, the extension of the Civil Rights movement and so on. These are all at large scale of the populist organizations with no elitist participation.

Just as the Peace Movement in the sixties had virtually no elitist participation. I mean, the intellectuals were strongly in favour of the war in Vietnam. They deny it to-day but one can prove it if you look back. They were very divorced from the general popular movement. The media, for example, even liberal media, never departed from the very narrow, gender blind – they had different tactics, maybe. By 1968, the Wall Street was bent against the War, just not worth pursuing at that point. It should be liquidated. After that, liberal elites began to raise questions about tactics and so on. But, by and large, they were mainly populist and spontaneous movements with very little elitist participation. By about the 1970s, during by-polls, somewhere between two-thirds and three quarters running right up until today regards the Vietnam War fundamentally wrong and immoral, not a mistake. Among opinion-leaders the number were far lower. Among the intellectuals virtually nobody unless it is a statistical error. Those are big changes in the country and what they have led to is a very sharp-split. There's a general population which remains disobedient, questioning, enquiring, more so than force, and there are the narrow elites who, in fact, did undergo a right-turn. They became not conservative, just reactionaries – statists. This split is quite noticeable. So, for example, I can measure it in my personal life. I can see it by noticing the audiences. I am booked up solidly years in advance for talks, big audiences, sophisticated audiences. I can talk on a level which I would not talk to in the sixties. We just understood a lot more. The country has become more civilized, more informed and so on, outside of the elites. They have become more narrow, more rigid, more ignorant, more difficult to talk to when you talk about the country, you can't just talk about and you can't just go by what is there in the journals. You read journals, you read elite opinion and elite opinion happens to be quite divorced from whatever is happening in the country.

DV: How do people view the Vietnam War now? Because I remember there was a movie called *The Apocalypse Now* which, I thought, depicted the troubled American psyche. and now more and more Hollywood movies like *The Killing Fields*, for instance, would seem to underline the savagery of the post-American intervention?

NC: The *Apocalypse Now* is not a vigorous critique of American intervention. It accepts the legitimacy of the American intervention. *The Killing Fields*, first of all, does not say much about the American intervention. This was the sort of time one would expect from Russia or any totalitarian country. It is an extremely dishonest film. Notice how it began. It begins in 1975. It has one scene which refers to something that occurred before the bombing of Nah Trang. Why did they pick up this case? Because that was one case in which the bombing was by error, because that was the case in which the bombing was of the government outpost. That was tolerable for the propaganda system. They were tolerable if you admit they were errors. What they don't discuss is that there were lot of issues which were not errors. For several years prior to that, Cambodia had been subjected to the most heavy bombing in history and it was not by error. They were targeting the most densely populated peasant areas, not by error. There is nothing about that in *The Killing Fields*. They probably killed hundreds of thousands of people. That was a huge massacre helped organize communal sense (kind of a ruse?), probably counted for their substantiality of their brutality. But *The Killing Fields* starts afterwards all over – and pretends nothing ever happened before. And just of no where, except this one error, came these mad men coming out of Cambodia and started killing everybody. That is propaganda. That is simply vulgar propaganda which exonerates the United States. It starts where the U.S. atrocities ended because the U.S. was forced to withdraw. It talks about the only atrocities that followed. For example, a couple of years from now if the Russians are put on the film in Afghanistan which would start in 1989 and start about the Mujahuddeen, it would probably be very ugly. Well, maybe what the movie talked about is accurate but it is ugly because there's something which happened prior to that. If you skip that you are lying and you are lying in a vulgar and ugly way. So, of course, the propaganda system which includes cinema would try and exculpate the United States. Naturally, that's the job. It has been doing it right through the war. I mean there's no change. Take a look back. I studied this since my childhood. I have co-authored a book called *The Manufacture of Consent*. It's about media and intellectual opinion. Almost half of the book is devoted to the media coverage of the Vietnam War from 1950 up un-till 1988. And there is no change. Throughout the entire period, the media were very much within the propaganda framework. We paid attention mostly to the liberal media.

DV: Are you saying that mass media is subversive in this country?

NC: Subversive? Subservient, yes. Press, media – ideology of a corporate consensus, state corporate consensus. And then it's particularly true of the liberal media. So, when you talk about a shift in this matter, that's not correct. There's a major, major effort after the war on their part to reconstruct, to reimpose—I mean. What happened in the sixties and the seventies is that the usual controls broke down. Usually, the population goes along with state propaganda which is presented through the media, the intellectuals and journals and so on. But in the sixties the whole set up began to break down, which is why everybody is upset about the sixties. Normal disciplined authority broke down and stayed broke down. Among the general population, seventy per-cent of the population, you still get the saying that the war was fundamentally wrong, immoral and not a mistake.

DV: But some intellectuals still justify the American intervention in the Vietnam.

NC: They all do. They always did. They did this all through the war. That's the point you are missing. You go right through the war, you find rarely exceptions, people accepted this. Take, for example, the journal like *Dissent*, that is as far left as you can go and still be visible in the United States. They were criticised by Bertrand Russell in 1964 because they advocated American intervention. At the end of the war in 1975, they said they thought their position was correct, apart from the nuances. From 1964 to 1975, they maintained the position that the United States has a right to send troops to Vietnam. If another country does that we call it defense of freedom or something like that. But they took that position; they never changed it all through the war. That's just as far left as you can go. Of course, by the time the corporate elite turned against the war and came out in the favour of withdrawal, today that's not very interesting, that's tactical judgement. And if you take a look at the mass media, I have been doing it for quite a few years, I have never seen criticism against the war that even reaches the Soviet criticism on the war of Afghanistan. Soviet Union recognises it as an invasion. We don't recognise that we invaded South Vietnam. Of course, we invaded South Vietnam. When John F. Kennedy sent out air force, not disguised, but actual air force, to bomb the South Vietnam villages in 1962 that's aggression. We do not regard it that way. You do not find any comment on it in America. Nobody describes it as the U.S. aggression. That's the degree of subservience to the state propaganda which is pretty remarkable, which comes down to hundred percent.

DV: If this is the case, don't you think it is extremely difficult for a common man to maintain objectivity? Since he is exposed to the biased, state-subservient mass media?

NC: Of course, it is difficult. What is interesting is that so many have done it. Take, say Nicaragua. There has been tremendous effort to demonize Sandinistas, as they put it, and gain support to the U.S. terrorist states in the Central America, El Salvador and Gautemala. Which like to slaughter their citizens. The extent of this effort is pretty remarkable, which has been revealed partially recently, in fact in Congressional studies and other studies, the government carrying out illegal activities to target their own population. But there is lawless administration, so nobody is surprised to-day. It's the biggest propaganda effort on the part of the state that has ever existed in the U.S. history, probably one of the biggest in the history of Western democracy, maybe—*the* biggest maybe. Well, and the media went along with it. I have studied this in a great detail. There is virtually no departure from this on the part of media. But the population did not. Take for example, the recent hurricane in Nicaragua. The hurricane was devastating. It cost probably a billion dollars in damages and it is a very poor country, virtually destroyed first by Samoja and then by the war. The United States exulted. The U.S. government, of course, wants people to starve and of disease and so on. And that's the whole point. Naturally, they are happy about the destitution from the hurricane. They did not give a penny for a relief. They were able to intimidate their allies. Of course, they didn't give any relief, either. On the other hand, there are tiny little groups in the United States. There's a Jesuit Centre in North Carolina with virtually no resources. They were able to raise millions of dollars for aid, from the ordinary Americans who were not brainwashed by the media or the intellectuals and who managed to hold on to elementary moral values. That reflects the country. On the one hand, you have the sadistic elite who exult in suffering and starving and disease. It's terrific. On the other hand, you have general population, a large part of it at least has remained separate from this elitist culture. You don't see any reflection of that in newspapers and journals, of course. But it's true.

DV: I have been watching Presidential debate. The Republican candidate George Bush has consistently attacked ACLU liberalism. I got the feeling that 'liberal' has become a term of abuse in his eyes.

NC: Well, it's a part of the right-turn among the elites. Meanwhile, the population has become more liberal. If you can look at the election of the 1980s, the U.S. is the most heavily polled country. The reason is the business wants to keep its pulse on the public, they want to know what the people are thinking. They want to control the people, so they better know what they are thinking. So, there is a tremendous amount of public opinion study in the U.S. Mostly for business purposes. You look at it. But studies show quite clearly that through the 1980s, there is a drift towards the New Deal style liberalism. For example, when people asked, "Do you prefer military spending or medical spending?", they said they preferred medical spending over military spending by huge factors, by 41% or 71% depending upon the question they were asking. "Would you prefer higher taxes if they are for education, welfare and environment?" Majority of the people agreed. There is a continuous drift towards New Deal style liberalism. At the same time, liberalism has become a dirty word among the elites. Because they are opposed to it. What they want is a shift of power towards wealthy and privileged which they happen to want to represent and be part of it. I am not terribly surprised. I will be surprised if anything different is happening. So, yes, of course. So, among the extremely powerful elite culture, liberalism has become a dirty word. But among the general public – may be they aren't using the word – they are becoming more liberal. Even the mainstream *Commentary* conceded at the end of the Reagan period. A large increase in governmental intervention in creating a welfare state. That's the effect of the Reagan period.

DV: Let's shift to a different subject. Is peace ever possible in the Middle East?

NC: Well, it depends. If the U.S. change its policy. By Middle East, you mean the Arab-Israeli conflict, because there are lot of other things in Middle East. Well, since about 1971, the U.S. has been buying the peace process. There has grown an international consensus in the form of a political settlement there. The consensus went through two phases. You can't date it but roughly from 1970 to 1975. The consensus was rejectionist. It called for basically the United Nations 242 as it is understood throughout most of the world outside the United States and Israel, meaning return to the pre-1967 borders with some slight modifications. Various guarantees for the territorial integrity and security laws in the region. Now, that's rejectionist proposal that offered nothing to the Palestinians. That was the proposal pursued by most of the world. So, non-aligned countries, Soviet Union, major Arab states, most of Europe, virtually everybody outside Israel and the United States and some marginal groups in the Middle East. In fact, the President Sadat of Egypt offered such a proposal in February 1971, virtually in those words to Israel – secretly. Israel rejected it and sent back its rejection – and so it confirmed it. But about 1975, the terms of international consensus shifted to include a Palestinian state in the West Bank and Gaza Strip, again with the same territorial guarantees. In fact, that came to the U.N. Security Council in January 1976. There was a proposal by Syria, Jordan and Egypt, backed by most of Europe, by Soviet Union overtly, P.L.O. quite openly. In fact, P.L.O. preferred the proposal, vetoed by the United States – a bid called for political settlement with Palestinians being offered the right to establish the Palestinian State on the West Bank and Gaza Strip. Then it just repeated the words of the U.N. 242 with the territorial guarantees and right to live in peace of all states in the region, I am using the words of 242. That was the first time when P.L.O. was on record as endorsing explicitly in those words. Since that time, there have been repeated proposals of that sort. Brezhnev made an explicit proposal in February 1981 at the Presidium of the Soviet Communist Party in which he explicitly mentioned Israel, with rights and security and territorial integrity and that was unanimously endorsed by the Palestinian National Council couple of months later. All of this was suppressed in the United States. Nobody ever talks about it. It is just not there. It's down the memory hole. Because, again, the war of the intellectuals is to serve power, not truth. The truth did not help the power to bring out these facts. You cannot find them, not on front page or back page, not in scholarship and so on. But it's true. There are plenty of such initiatives now. The State Department in 1971 was in favour of Sadat's proposal. In fact, Sadat's policy more or less reiterated the official U.S. Policy. That was the plan of Rogers in 1969. But there is an internal struggle in the U.S. that is symbolized by the conflict between Rogers and Kissinger. In fact, the State Department, lot of corporations and lot of diplomatic services are in favour of political settlement. Kissinger was in favour of a stalemate, meaning Israel should keep its control over the territories.

DV: But there are studies, for instance Matti Golan's book, which states that Kissinger also betrayed Israel, in a way?

NC: Only a fanatic would believe that. Well, I think Kissinger betrayed Israel, too, but by blocking peace. Kissinger, first of all, knew nothing about the Middle East. His writings are so embarrassing by their ignorance. But he does understand violence. That is one thing he seems to have a grasp of. And in 1971, he believed at the time, including intelligence services, that the Israeli power was so enormous, that no combination of Arab States could ever threaten it. So, naturally since the only thing he understood was power, he supported Israeli power. In 1973—the war was mostly because of Kissinger. Kissinger continually rejected Sadat's peace proposal. He was continually flooded with information from American corporation, ambassadors and so on that if the U.S. blocked Sadat's peace initiatives, Egypt would have to go to war. There's no other choice. He could not understand it. Nothing ever penetrated that dense mind except violence, that he *does* understand. So, he rejected all of this, backed Israel. Israel also rejected it. They were in a mood of extreme triumph in that period. They didn't take Arabs seriously. When October 1973 came along, they were all very much surprised, as you may recall. Everybody was astonished and shocked at the early success of Egyptians and Syrians and that penetrated Kissinger's mind. He could see that. And, therefore, he moved to the next logical position. If Egypt cannot be dismissed, as he assumed, it has to be excluded from the conflict. He was to exclude the major Arab deterrent so that Israel can integrate the occupied territories and attack its northern neighbour with the main deterrent removed, that's Kissinger's step-by-step diplomacy which was accommodated in Camp David. It's obvious at the time, by now it's even conceded, by most strategic analysts. But the effect of Camp David, it was obvious that this was going to be the effect, was to exclude the major Arab deterrent so that Israel can proceed with the U.S. aid. It was sharp fifty percent in the U.S. budget. At that point went fifty percent of the whole of the U.S. budget to Israel. Israel proceeded to occupy the territories, exactly what you expect when you remove the main deterrent—if you have any brain in your head. And of course that is what exactly happened. Now, the people who say that Kissinger betrayed Israel mean that if they kept Sinai, there would be never any trouble because they will be facing Egypt as well as the rest of the Arab world. I don't think it is harmful to Israel or helpful to Israel. But if you want Israel to be a smarter, a kind of military outpost, a strategic asset, if that's what you want, this is helpful for that purpose. It removes the major Arab deterrent and gives Israel more flexibility and freedom. And that's exactly what Kissinger wanted. The U.S. position is that Israel should be a strategic asset, meaning basically a mercenary state, a militarized mercenary state. There may be adjustments here and there. But basically from 1971, that pretty much defines the U.S. position.

DV: What would be the solution to the crisis, if there is one at all?

NC: I suppose there's one. But there can't be any unless the U.S. stops its rejectionist policy. The U.S. has been adamantly opposed to a political settlement and remains so. Until December 1988, it has been so vehement in its rejectionism, then it would allow Palestinians to select its own representative or eventual negotiations. That's really extreme. That's as if in 1947 saying that Jews do not have any self-determination, they cannot even be represented by the Zionists. If somebody had to say that in 1947, he would be called a Nazi. That's the U.S. in the 1980s.

DV: So, much depends on the U.S. . . .

NC: The U.S. is the dominant outsider, much depends on Israel too and something depends on the rest of the world. But nature and power in the region is such that the U.S. is the decisive influence. As long as the U.S. is opposed to the political settlement, there is not going to be one.

DV: In the meantime, there is so much of terrorism.

NC: There's so much of terrorism going on. So much of it is the U.S., Israeli terrorism. There's also, some of its Palestinian terrorism. Now, the propaganda system tells you that you are supposed to look at terrorism conducted by the other gangs. I do not take orders. Terrorism is terrorism, no matter who carries it out. When Israelis bomb refugee camps in Lebanon, that's terrorism. Last year, according to Lebanese police, they killed one hundred and thirty people. There were about twenty-six bombings. That's terrorism. The U.S. supports. The last terrorist act was in December (1988) 14 or 15 approximately. The U.N. condemned it and the U.S. vetoed it to Security Council because the U.S. supports terrorism. I do not support the wholesale terrorism of the U.S. and Israel or the retail terrorism of the various Palestinian groups. Why should I? But there is no one in America who condemns terrorism. They condemn the terrorism of the enemy. That's not opposition to terrorism. Supposing some in Soviet Union condemn the terrorism of the Afghans without talking about their invasion of Afghanistan, we just laugh. It is not terrorism, it is commissars. Virtually, one hundred percent discussion in the West is about the commissars. They are the commissars. They talk about the terrorism of the Palestinians but they don't talk about the terrorism of the U.S. and Israel which is far greater in scale and has always been.

DV: It seems to me that Israel-bashing has become increasingly a marketable commodity especially for the press. Also, one sees subtle variations of anti-Semitism.

NC: Where do you see anti-Semitism?

DV: Especially among the blacks. I believe Saul Bellow published an article in a Chicago-based newspaper responding to this something ago.

NC: Saul Bellow went to Israel and wrote a book of a kind of the most absurd Stalinists when they travelled to the Soviet Union in the thirties. It's also about the magnificence of culture, how well the Arabs are and so on. It's so disgraceful. What Saul Bellow tells you about the blacks is as interesting as a Communist hack tells you about the Capitalist oppressors. If you want to know about the blacks, you have to look back and not what Saul Bellow says. Where is anti-Semitism among the blacks?

DV: Louis Farrakhan, Steve Cokely and Jesse Jackson made some unpalatable comments and still do. Edward Said, a Columbia professor, some people believe, is an anti-Semite.

NC: You have to look at what they mean by anti-Semitism. There's so much of anti-Semitism in America.

DV: Certainly among intellectuals and in the press both right, left and centre.

NC: Not right and left, overwhelmingly on the right. In fact, you find it right in the midst of major supporters of Israel. For instance, one of the major supporters of Israel is Christian fundamentalism which has a strong streak of anti-Semitism. But it happens to support Israeli power. This is not in support of Israel but Israeli power which is quite a different thing. I think it's very harmful to Israel. The call for support for Israel here in this country means support for Israeli power. This is very strong in Christian fundamentalism which has a strong streak of anti-Semitism. In fact, you find it at the top of the Bush campaign. We know that this is kind of kept quiet by the press. The Republican election committee has an ethnic outrage group, the organization of ethnic groups. It was discovered that they were run by a bunch of Nazis. Ukrainian Nazis the people who deny that there was no Holocaust supported by Nazis, the whole bunch of Eastern European Nazis who were brought over here after the Second World War. They were at the top level of the ethnic outrage campaign. Well, some of them were dismissed although most of them reappeared in the Bush campaign. Of course, they did not make a point about it, the Jewish organizations did not make a fuss about it. *The New Republic*, which is an Israeli propaganda journal which has an interesting editorial in which they said that the fact they were Nazis at the high level of the Bush campaign is not important because that's what they called anaemic and antique anti-Semitism, Nazis's is the anaemic and antique anti-Semitism. And then they said that the real anti-Semitism is the Democratic Party. And why is that a real anti-Semitism? Because they debated a resolution for the Palestinian statehood at their convention. That's the real anti-Semitism, not the antique and anaemic anti-Semitism of Hitler and Goebbels. They didn't care about this.

DV: This was when?

NC: Must have been in October or something (1988).

DV: In the *New Republic*? But Martin Peretz, the editor, is Jewish.

NC: Yes. The point is Martin Peretz does not really care about anti-Semitism. He is perfectly happy with the Nazis as long as they support Israeli power. In fact, if you notice, the Democrats did not pick this up. I'll give you another. Very little of this is in the newspapers, I should say. Because they understand from the major Jewish organization like the Anti-Defamation League (ADL), so they are not going to press this news. These groups are sufficiently pro-Israeli. So, they are not going to care if they are Nazis. It's fine. At the same, right here in Brooklyne (Boston). They are trying to put together an educational programme for schools on the Holocaust. For years, they have been submitting proposals to the National – whatever it is called. The Israel supports educational programmes of this sort. And they were always turned down. The way they were turned down. They always get a positive approval rating from the people who recommend but they have turned down. Well, lot of information came out as to why they were turned down. They were turned down because lot of right-wing Republicans condemned the programme because it did not give the required time, enough time to the Nazis and Ku Klux Klan, Nazis and KKK to express their point of view. So it is biased, other arguments of this sort. Now, all of this came out in public. In fact, the only way to have turned it down in 1988 is to cancel the entire category to which this belongs. So, there are no categories to allow this in. This is anti-Semitism. But nothing about it in the campaign. William Bennett, who is in charge of it, has now moved to become a Cabinet member. *The New Republic* did not comment upon it, the Anti-Defamation League did not raise a finger and the Democrats never talked about it. The reason is the right-wing Republicans support Israeli power. They don't care about anti-Semitism. Nothing would prove more easily, it's a traumatic proof. In fact they say so. Take a look sometime at a book by Nathan Kramer called the *Real Anti-Semitism in America*.

He was a national director of the Anti-Defamation League. He is dead now. He is supposed to be concerned with anti-Semitism. And the book is called the *Real Anti-Semitism in America*, which came up three or four years ago, five or six years. He says approximately this. By all conventional indices, the anti-Semitism is down: there is less discrimination. Jews can get into professions more easily. He says that this is an illusion and there is a serious kind of anti-Semitism developing which is more dangerous than the old kind – what the *New Republic* called anaemic and antique anti-Semitism of Nazis. What's the New Anti-Semitism? The New Anti-Semitism is, he says, that the people question the U.S. defence budget, or the people who criticize the American foreign policy. He says, peacemakers of Vietnam vintage, I am quoting now, people who give war a bad name and peace a face of progress. That's real anti-Semitism. And then he identifies them. The National Council of Churches, for example, sniping away the American defense and military budget. That's real anti-Semitism. And the liberals who say that America should not invade Central America. That's real anti-Semitism. What does he mean by that? He means something. For the Anti-Defamation League, there is a particular party line, Israeli power should be maintained. The party line says that you have to maintain an Israeli power. You got to maintain Israeli power. That's where you find the interests of Jews. If the people oppose the interests of Jews, they are anti-Semites. So, if there are some who think that there should be a political settlement in the Middle East, they are anti-Semites – by that party line. Now, the way to keep Israeli power is by keeping the United States strong and keeping it violent. So, therefore, any one who opposes it gives war a bad name, peace a favourable Press, and is obviously an anti-Semite. That's exactly what they say. Given those assumptions, you can understand why the *New Republic* would describe Nazism as antique and anaemic anti-Semitism whereas the real anti-Semitism is the willingness to debate a political settlement of the Middle East crisis. Now, when you quote these people, remember what they are saying. Look at the facts. It's not that there is no black anti-Semitism. Of course, there is black anti-Semitism. If you take a look at the ethnic conflict and study the urban ghettoes in the United States, you would discover that every ethnic group hates every other ethnic group. The Italians hate the Irish and they both hate the blacks and the blacks hate the Jews. That's the nature of urban slums. There's plenty of it. In fact, it has increased in this case by the fact that the Jewish immigrants are a generation earlier; they moved up. They are now the bureaucrats and the teachers and civil servants and the lawyers and the real estate agents and the store owners and so on. Whereas the blacks are the new immigrants. There's plenty of opportunity of conflict there, which will turn into ethnic conflict and then race conflict, but to talk about anti-Semitism as Saul Bellow talks, about the oppressed and deeply oppressed black community, that's cynicism – pure cynicism. If he is worried about anti-Semitism, why doesn't he condemn the New Republic? He doesn't. He writes for them. Because he doesn't care about anti-Semitism; he cares about privilege and power.

DV: Are you suggesting that Bellow doesn't reflect Jewish values?

NC: What are Jewish values? Jewish values, like the values of any other culture, is a very complex affair. If you go back to the Bible, you find a conflict. On the other hand, you have the Prophets and remember the Prophets were the people who were driven out of the society because they were so much hated, they were driven into the desert and condemned and they were the people who were hated at that time because they were telling the truth. On the one hand, you have the dissidents who were expelled from the society and on the other hand, you have the mainstream which was just genocidal. The Old Testament of the Bible has the genocidal chapters in the whole literary canon. Which are the Jewish values? There is no answer to that question. Like any other rich culture, they are all over the place. When Rabbi Kahane says that he is expressing Jewish values, he is exactly right. There is a mainthread of Jewish values which would lead to Rabbi Kahane. When the members of the orthodox Rabbinate appealed to the Biblical charge to destroy Amalakites down to the last man, woman and child and say, "Well, that applies to the Arabs," they are appealing to something in the Jewish tradition. You can't deny that. On the other hand, if there is someone else who says that Jewish tradition says that you should care about widow and orphan, that's also right. You can't say which are the Jewish values. They both have their sources in the tradition. Should Jewish intellectuals pick their values, they can pick any of the values. Which Jewish values, which human values? Which human values to be picked? Well, you make your choices. If you happen to be committed to human rights, freedom, human dignity and so on, you make certain choices. And from those, then come hard questions. How do you apply those choices to real political and social world? That's not so simple.

DV: Assuming that there was a relationship between blacks and Jews, why do you think it was broken at all?

NC: Why is it broken? There was a relationship. Well, for a long time Jews were supporting the oppressed people. Let's remember what the truth is about that because it was all suppressed in the propaganda system. Some of the main support for blacks among Jews is from the Communist party. Now, nobody is allowed to say that in the United States because you are not supposed to say nice things about the Communist Party. But the fact of the matter is, when you go back to the people who were doing the hard civil rights work in the days it was really tough, you could get killed for it, it was very much the Communist part and lot of them were Jews. That was a big component, probably the major component. And then more peripherally, there was liberal support for the blacks, much more peripherally. And that means signing a statement, and occasionally going down to a big march. And the real hard work on the scene was from Jewish radicalism or whatever you may call it – very much Communist Party based for a long time especially in the thirties and the forties when these were unpopular causes. These alliances up to a certain extent had broken down because of the changes in both the communities. Jews were an oppressed group. I grew up in a very anti-Semitic neighbourhood. We were the only Jews of the neighbourhood of German and Irish Catholics. My brother and I know couple of paths if you walk on them, you could get killed. First of all, they are pro-Nazis, openly pro-Nazis. I remember a beer party celebrating the fall of Paris in my neighbourhood. It wasn't so unusual either, it was in the late thirties or early forties. During the Second World War, I was living in Philadelphia. During the Second World War, the race conflicts and ethnic conflicts became so extreme, that we (blacks and Jews and Italians and everyone else) were under curfew, the teenagers were under curfew for some time. We were not allowed out in the streets after eight o'clock because of race and ethnic conflicts. There's nothing new about that. What happened was that Jews, more or less, pulled out of that. My family, at that time most of my relatives, my uncles and aunts were working class and lot of them were in Communist Party, left-wing Trotskyist circles – that's all gone. Jews are now moving to upper middle class. They are no longer the oppressed minority in the United States. They are relatively wealthy and privileged minority. When I got to Harvard in 1950, that was late, but there was virtually no Jewish faculty – two or three Jewish faculty may be, there's plenty of anti-Semitism around, very overt anti-Semitism. Within a few years that is pretty well disappeared and now the Jewish faculty at Harvard is well beyond the proportion of the Jewish population in the nation. As the Jews moved into more privileged circles, not surprisingly their positions have changed and their relations to other oppressed minorities who have not advanced have also changed – not entirely. Jewish attitudes still tend to be somewhat more liberal than the mainstream, probably more supportive of the civil rights than the mainstream. But there have been changes in the black man. The black communities are much more oppressed and depressed than they ever were in that past; there is real demoralization inside the ghetto societies and it takes violent forms and even self-destructive forms, an awful lot of drugs and crimes, these poor people are preying on one another. You have to look more broadly to know what's happening in the United States. Up un-till the thirties, there were waves of the immigrants, like my father, for example, coming from basically the peasant society in the Eastern Europe. These waves of immigrants could be absorbed. They worked at starvation wages. It's a rich country and it was an expanding economy and it could slowly absorb them. My father used to work in a sweat shop. But then he was able to go to college and I could become a college professor. That's the kind of thing that happened for a long period. But in the nineteen thirties something very substantial changed. The United States economy stopped growing. Since the nineteen thirties, of course, there was a lot of growth that could absorb the poor people, poor immigrants. It's mostly high technology and services and so on. It's the kind of thing that basically absorbs the privileged and the wealthy and the trained and the educated, not the masses of population who could attend school. They are not absorbed. So, we didn't come out of the Depression from that point of view. What got us out of the Depression was military spending and high technology and so on but that doesn't absorb the new immigrants. At the same time, there was a new wave of immigration, two new waves of immigration. One was blacks, now that was internal immigration but still immigration. They were driven off the farms in the south with the mechanization of agriculture and they moved north. They filled up there in the ghettoes. There was nothing for them to do. They could not become the sweat shop workers the way my father could and move up through the expanding economy because there was no expanding economy for them. And the other immigration was Hispanic. They are somewhat similar. Basically there are the two huge immigration pools but without the technique of absorbing that we had in the earlier days of expanding economy. So, the result was they were basically put in a concentration called urban slums where they arė supposed to prey on one another, where they are terribly demoralized. You go through Harlem to-day, there was nothing like it even in the worst days of the Depression. I remember when my family was unemployed living in what was then called extreme poverty, there was nothing like black slums today. You didn't have to have your grandmother sitting with a baseball bat to kill the rats. That has to be taken into account too. There were beginnings of attempts to get away in the sixties with the black nationalist movements and black panthers and so on and they, like any thing that came off the urban slums, have lot of very complex properties, ranging from violent, criminal to reconstructive – the constructive parts were destroyed in the large part, by the state violence. It was striking that the government was involved in the murder of Fred Hampton. They didn't try to murder Huey Newton. The reason was Huey Newton was just a criminal, was exploiting the panthers and Fred Hampton was a constructive organizer and so he was killed by an FBI initiated police assassination. Nobody talks about it. This happened in Chicago where Saul Bellow lives but you don't hear. Saul Bellow is not talking about him because he doesn't care. He knows about it but he doesn't care. If you check his writings and find out about Hampton assassination, and the black panther organizer, I predict you will find that he said nothing about it. Maybe I am wrong in which case I'll retract the criticism. But take a look. The effect of that kind of thing, the effect of repressing, killing off the main constructive organizers is that you are left with the criminal gang which is what they wanted all along. When you are left with the criminal gangs, of course you are getting demoralized. And you have all sorts of anti-social elements in it then like drugs, anti-Semitism and everything else. But to discuss anti-Semitism and not to talk about those topics is just obscene.

DV: Would there be any possibility of ever patching up the relationship between the Jews and blacks?

NC: I have never seen relation difficult. I have always worked with black groups and I am a Jew. For instance, I was at Fred Hampton funeral. I was one of the few white faces at Fred Hampton's funeral. I never had any problem with them. I still do. What's the problem? If you want to work with the blacks, you work with the blacks.

DV: I read an article some time ago in *Commentary* on racial perversity in Chicago, written by Joseph Epstein. He is pained to see the strenuous relationship between the Jews and blacks. The article is mostly autobiographical. For instance, he writes about how his father was especially nice towards blacks. Obviously, that sort of relationship does not exist any more, what with black leadership like Steve Cokely, Louis Farrakhan and even Jesse Jackson.

NC: Did he talk about the assassination of Fred Hampton?

DV: I don't think he did.

NC: No, he doesn't. Because he doesn't talk about anything that needs the situation changed. What he wants to do is to look at all the faults of the blacks. I haven't read the article, so I am only guessing.

DV: I think he principally talks about the painful awareness that there is no good relationship between these ethnic groups.

NC: But why is the relationship bad. It is not just that the blacks have wrong genes. Things happened, things he did nothing about. For example, I was at Fred Hampton's funeral. I flew in from Boston for it. I bet he didn't walk across the street for it. There are reasons for that. I pick this one example because it's a very dramatic one but dramatic enough that Saul Bellow certainly knows about it. Because the whole story is very widely exposed in Chicago press and it was very important. It was that kind of thing that cut off the constructive elements in the black nationalist movement and left with the criminal elements which these people can now deplore. But they contributed to their ascendence. It's very easy to sit in rich apartment and condemn the poor people struggling in streets.

DV: Are you saying in other words, that most intellectuals in this country are irresponsible?

NC: I would say that it's virtually a tautology. The people who are not irresponsible, we don't call them intellectuals. In order to make it to become intellectual you have to pass through several gateways. Powerful institutions do not reward people, who want to undermine them. You gain the rewards and privileges. You can be five times as smart and five times as informed and be a critic, but you are not an intellectual, you are on a street somewhere. We have to be careful about how to describe these things. This is not true only about the U.S., this is true of any society. The groups that will be respected are privileged intellectuals. That begins in schools. If you are obedient in schools, you get good grades. If you have independent mind, you would probably be thrown out as a behaviour problem. Does it mean you are less of an intellectual? No. It just means that you are not a conformist and obedient.

DV: Marxism is such a hated concept in this country? Is it because that most people make up their mind on the basis of mass media? Or is it because they are not properly exposed to the complexity of Marx's philosophy?

NC: Nobody here is exposed to Marxism. So, what they refer to is a devil-version of a pervert. I don't think there would be such a notion as Marxism. The whole idea of Marxism, in my view, belongs to the idea of history of organized religion, intellectual history. Is there anything like Einsteinianism in physics? In serious fields, you don't deal for individuals and study their works as holy-writ. Marx is a human being. He had interesting things to say, he had wrong things to say. Some of those things may be applicable to a period or a century after he wrote, some not. So, if you are in a serious field, you treat Marx as a person who made contribution you can accept and reject. But the idea of Marxism or Freudianism or anything like that is just an indication of intellectual bankruptcy. That's not the reason why Marxism is rejected in the U.S. That would be, in my view, the right reason for rejecting Marxism. Here it is rejected because it is a term of abuse. Nobody knows what Marxism means, or what communism means – it is merely a term of abuse, some bad thing you are supposed to hate. But nobody knows what it is.

DV: Does Communist Party exist in the country? Are there any lessons to be drawn from the nineteen thirties?

NC: Well, there are lessons. The Communist Party did some very positive things. As I mentioned, they were in the forefront of the civil rights. It was not so simple in those days. It was so tough. They played a role in labour organizing. They were also completely subordinate to the most grotesque Russian propaganda. They supported Stalin's crimes. I remember this very well. I was anti-Communist then, I was anti-Bolshevik leftist. I remember huge battles when I was twelve years old among my relatives who were supporting Stalin-Hitler pact. Large part of the destruction of the Communist Party was self-destruction. So, it's like a lot of things, it's a mixed story. Life is not so simple. For those people who were working in the Communist party, what it meant for their lives, it's not Stalin's pact, they did not believe in that because it's the bourgeois press; what it meant for them, was defending the rights of blacks, labour organizing, going to a picnic with your friends—that was the way of life. It's a working class culture. It's important from that point of view. It's an important working class culture which happened to destroy itself, in part because of its subordination to the propaganda of a foreign state. In this respect, the persons like Saul Bellow remind me very much of the old Communist Party. The way he writes about Israel is about the parody of the way Communist Party members used to write about Russia. I pointed this out in the review of his books. In fact, the nearest thing to the Communist Party in the US these days is the American liberal Zionists. Their attitude to Israel is very reminiscent to that of the Communist Party in the thirties. That's been pointed out by Israeli doves in Knesset who repeatedly condemned what they called the Stalinist features of American Jewist life.

Noam Chomsky: II

DV: In fact when I showed your picture to a friend of mine in Washington D.C., they told me that you look quite young and so on. I mean, you have been so popular and you know they thought of you as some kind of an elderly gentleman with long white hair and all that. . . . Sir, tell me about your formative years and religious and other backgrounds and how you hit upon the kind of ideas you have. Did you face some problems in the process?

NC: Well, I grew up in the later part of Depression. I was born in 1928. Then the Great Depression came, I was a child and those were my formative years in fact. My parents had jobs, they were teachers – Hebrew teachers. I guess, you'd say a lower middle class existence. I mean, perfectly comfortable but not unusual at the time because plenty of the people didn't have jobs. Yeah, my immediate family – my uncles, aunts and so on were mostly unemployed or occasionally employed working class – Jewish working class in New York. At that time they were still very timely – rather radical working class culture either around the Communist Party or the anti-Bolshevik left or something and I grew up in that year. I didn't live in New York but whenever we went there that's – where we gravitated towards and by the late nineteen thirties, by around nineteen forty when I got about old enough to take the train by myself and go to New York and spend a couple of days there, then eleven or twelve years old and spending all my time hanging around anarchist book stores and anarchist offices and picking up literature and even the . . .

DV: Sir, did you read a recent book written by Carl Bernstein's called *The Loyalties*?

NC: I didn't read the book, I read the reviews. His background is different. He comes from what's called the 'red diaper baby'. He came from a Communist Party background. And this is my own background. I mean they were bad uncles and aunties in the Communist Party but my aunt's associations were quickly anti-Bolshevik left, either left-wing Marxist or anarchist. And these were very live issues at the time. It was very lively culture, not just political, it was an intellectual culture so this was more part of – you know – string quartets and arguments on literature and Freud. And it was just a very lively and, in fact, the most exciting intellectual environment I have ever seen way beyond Harvard, say. Although many of the people had no formal education at all – they were self-educated or they may be going to High School or something like that.

DV: As you were growing up, there were so many things happening to Jewish people elsewhere – you have Holocaust and. . .

NC: Yeah, that was a couple of years later and after that came the war. I was very much involved in what then was called the Zionist movement. Now it would be called anti-Zionist for the same ideas – I was part, I was involved in that part of the Zionist movement that was opposed to a Jewish state, I was interested in Arab-Jewish cooperation, and I meant socialist by nationalism. When I finally got to college around 1945, I was primarily – I was studying Arabic and I had all sorts – I intended in fact to go live there and . . .

DV: Now your position wouldn't be too popular I suppose because some time ago Abba Eban was at Brandeis University and he obviously has the same kind of attitude you have I believe and . . .

NC: Well, Abba Eban is – you see it's a very difficult thing. You see for example, Abba Eban back in the early 1970s bitterly attacked people like me in particular but also people like me because we were . . .

DV: Now he is once again attacking . . . ?

NC: Well, now he's shifted, he's shifted, he's shifted quite a bit and he's joined a position not unlike the one he was attacking at that time. Although, you know until about a year or two ago Abba Eban has never come out in favour of Palestinian independence. He said that maybe that we shouldn't oppose it but he has never come out in favour of let's say a two state settlement or anything of that kind. And as of about two years ago he was opposing it. Up until the last clear article of his that I saw was in 1986 in which he was basically supporting the Labour Party position of, you know, what they call territorial compromise, meaning they keep what they want. I think, that was before the *Intifada* and now it's probably changed.

In the early forties I was part of the Zionist movement and thought that the whole idea of the Jewish state was wrong. And I still think it's wrong, just like I would be against a Christian state.

I think that the Enlightenment ideals are basically correct. You are a citizen of a country or something. I mean what happens to a Jew in a Christian state. Well, he's not, he's obviously not an equal citizen and the same is true of a non-Jew in a Jewish state and for the very reason, I mean, the very same people who became outraged at a statement by the Supreme Court saying that the U.S. is a Christian nation and rightly so; those very same people are in favour of a Jewish State in Israel and you can't have both positions.

DV: I still see in newspapers some anti-Semitic incidents occurring over and over again. . . .

NC: Anti-Semitic incidents? Oh yeah, but there's look, there's, I mean, there's anti-Semitic incidents, anti-Stalin incidents, anti-Irish incidents, anti-Semitism has a somewhat special quality because of the history . . .

DV: But I also listen to talk radio programmes, and I hear sometimes alarming voices of some people so pathetically, I mean, it's almost pathological, I thought . . .

NC: Anti-Semitism?

DV: Oh, yeah.

NC: Did you ever walk through Dorchester (Boston)? Do that before you leave but be careful because make sure somebody is with you because you could easily be attacked. There is a very, there is a very rabid anti-Asian racism.

DV: This side of America is hardly well-known outside . . .

NC: Well, the fact is . . .

DV: When I first came to this country I thought it's a glorious country, American Dream and so on. Everything beautiful, affluence and all that . . .

NC: No, you should see the city slums before you leave . . .

DV: I am literally scared, watching I mean the University of Chicago I was awfully scared . . .

NC: Yeah that's true. Ah, see, Chicago is, well, I don't know how much you know American Literature at all and have you ever read things like, have you read like, say, James Farrell and people like that? Well, you know, he is writing about ethnic hatreds in the cities and in fact I remember that very well, that's exactly the way it was. We were the only Jewish family in Irish Catholic and German Catholic neighbourhood and they were rabid anti-Semites and in fact in those days they were openly pro-Nazi. I mean it wasn't secret. I remember there were Beer parties in my neighbourhood when Paris fell into the Nazis. It was only when the United States was attacked, you know, we got into the war, that was no longer a possible position. But, it was violently anti-Semitic and there were, you know, if there were, Farrell describes areas of Chicago. There were Irish and Italians; they were killing each other. I was a teenager in the early 1940s. They had to declare a 7 o'clock curfew for all teenagers. We were not allowed on the streets after 7 o'clock and it was just because of race riots. Every group was trying to kill every other group and a lot of that still goes on. I mean now, by now, the anti-Semitism's dropped a lot. When I got to Harvard in 1950, Harvard was very anti-Semitic. There was virtually no Jewish faculty. I remember very well when the first Jewish mathematician was appointed at Harvard, it was the early 1950 . . . there were, maybe handful, maybe three or four Jewish faculty. And it was an upper class WASPish place, you could feel the anti-Semitism. I mean, you know, I mean these guys didn't think Jews ought to be around. That was only thirty years ago and by now that has dropped. By now anti-Semitism has virtually disappeared in more or less middle class or elite circles. It still exists at the community level like every other ethnic rivalry, and hatred exists and, of course, it exists in other respects in the U.S. For example, the fundamentalists, the fundamentalists are very strong in the U.S. There is no other individual country that has anything like the American Fundamentalist movement. The U.S. is like Iran in this respect, there's a deeply fundamentalist element which you don't find in other countries, and that is mixed, a lot of that is very anti-Semitic and the same people can be both anti-Semitic and very pro-Israel, as you know, and so it is not any kind of a contradiction.

DV: Is this a common theme with ethnic minorities?

NC: Well, I mean, the fundamentalist's story is complex because, the same people who are, say, pouring money into Israel to build a third temple, tear down Al Agsa and build a third temple, those same people can be very anti-Semitic. They are doing it because in the book of Revelations it says the Gog and Magog are gonna fight to the death in Armageddon and after that all the good people, mainly them, would be saved and, of course, all the Jews will go to hell, you know.

DV: Now when you look back, what are the significant moments?

NC: . . . in my life?

DV: . . . significant moments?

NC: No, no, no, there were plenty of significant moments, I would not say that any time in which my political views underwent any kind of radical change, I mean there were times when things happened in the world that you had to react to, like the Second World War, the discovery of the holocaust, the atom bomb, the beginning of the Cold War, Vietnam War, I mean obviously one had to react to all those things and obviously one's views change over time but mine are radically different from what they were forty years ago.

DV: Do you have any or did you face any problems for the positions you were holding. Did you face any sort of problems like some kind of criticism against you for the kind of ideas you have?

NC: Well, I was always very isolated. I never could join anything, even, as I said, when I was a kid the things I was most involved in, in fact very much involved in was the Zionist movement so I was all involved in Zionist youth movement. I went there in summer, Zionist summer camps, I was a leader, youth leader for Zionist groups but I never joined any of the organisations because I disagreed with all. Even the bi-nationalist ones which I agree with, there were some that I more or less agree with on Palestine. The Zionist left which was socialist bi-nationalist, I thought and still think that was correct. But I couldn't join those groups because they were either Stalinist or Trotskyite and I was anti-Stalinist and anti-Trotskyite so I couldn't and as I say these were very live issues at that time. I had associations with them and I was always isolated. In fact, I was very skeptical about the Second World War. . . . While it was going on, I would spend time in the Philadelphia Public Library reading, you know, odd, marginal publications with tiny left-wing sects which were critical of the Second World War and described it as a capitalist plot to wipe out the proletariat of Europe and all kinds of weird ideas and there was enough sense in it. I didn't really agree with it but then I didn't dismiss it either. And later I found that there are a real elements of truth in it; in fact, particularly the war in the pacific was very mixed affair. I mean it's not good versus evil, the pacific war by any means. It was a very complex interaction and at the time the U.S., I mean, the anti-Japanese racism in U.S., it was indescribable. It was like the Nazis and the Jews. If you want to get a picture of it, read John Dover. He's a very good aged scholar. It's forgotten, it came out a couple of years ago, it's a well known book, you'll find it all over. And he describes the Japanese image in the U.S. and the U.S. image of the Japanese in the early 1940s, very accurately, I remember it very well. I mean people were anti-German but with regard to the Japanese they were vermin. They had to be crushed and destroyed, you know. I mean, it was just vicious racism and I was appalled by that at that time and . . .

DV: What is your political position now?

NC: My political position?

DV: What do you consider yourself as? There are neo-conservatives, Irving Krystol and Co and liberal left which doesn't seem to be popular at the moment.

NC: Well, I mean I'm not basically what I was then and kind of a socialist anarchist, a libertarian socialist anarchist. I think that's right, I mean radical democrat. You know there are lot of names for it but it's all the same thing.

DV: What do you think about Irving Krystol, neo-conservatism and he has some big allies you know, Jean Kirkpatrick and Melvyn Lasky and all those people especially those magazines *Commentary*, *Encounter*. *Encounter* is virtually a refuge for ex-communists who have things to say about Communism and everything.

NC: Well, they are basically Communist, I mean they kept the same views they had when they were Communists, some views except . . .

DV: They want to glamourise America.

NC: But they just changed the idol of their veneration, now they serve the American state whereas, as a Stalinist, you'd serve the Soviet state. But the same ideas. They are not conservatives. They are radical statists. They want a very powerful state, powerful and violent state is what they are in favour of and there is nothing conservative about that – it's the opposite of conservatism. I mean the term neo-conservatism is ridiculous. All of these people want a very powerful, violent state, in fact they want a welfare state. They just want it to be a welfare state for the rich whereas the liberals talk about a welfare state for the poor. But, and you can see it in the Reagan administration then, in the Reagan administration, government expenditure relative to GNP went up faster than in any peace time administration in history. The Reagan administration was more protectionist than any post-war, post-Second World War government. They want a powerful state. They introduced state censorship to an extent unique in recent American history. Well, they want a powerful, violent state which is lawless, is not subject to any controls, is separated from the public.

They want the public to be marginalised not to do anything to do with it. They created the largest state propaganda agency in American history, the office of public diplomacy. There are precursors but this is really unique. In fact, it's a kind of craze. . . . It's the opposite, any conservative would turn over in his grave to see what's called conservation today and as far as Irving Krystol is concerned, well, his view is, as he put it, that insignificant nations like insignificant people may get exaggerated views about their own importance but we have to teach them their place and we should do it with force. He said, you need police to keep order in the city and you need American gunboats to keep order in the world – in case any of these insignificant nations get out of place, that's his view. Why? You know Hitler would have been happy with that.

DV: That's Irving Krystol you say?

NC: That's right, that's Irving Krystol, I'm quoting, that was, he was talking then about Arabs at the time. This was the time when the Oil prices went up higher than he thought they should and his idea was why use violence because there are insignificant people who were getting exaggerated ideas of their own significance and therefore we returned the gunboat diplomacy. That's exactly what he thinks and that's his position and that's the position of Jean Kirkpatrick – let's take her. Her position is that poor in the world, miserable peasants, don't mind it. She said that. They she says . . . India. She says the untouchables really don't mind it because in these traditional societies, she said, people are used to their own misery, they take it for granted, the miseries of ordinary life are tolerable to these people, say, to the untouchables or to the starving farmers. They just don't mind when their children are starving to death and when they are working twenty hours a day and dying at age forty. They think that's perfectly okay because they are used to it, and she knows that from her wealthy apartment in Washington. She knows that the miseries of ordinary life are tolerable. That's her famous article that made her famous on dictatorships and double standards. You can't believe that a human being can write those words and the neo-conservatives are always fine because they agree. They agree that the miseries of ordinary life are tolerable to ordinary people and it's a very convenient view for the privileged. So if people are sleeping in the streets, well, you know, Calcutta or something, it's fine. They are used to it, they don't mind it and at the time when Government of El Salvadore was moving up to real genocide, I mean they were killing thousands you know, thousands, tens of thousands of people and you know not just murder but mutilation and torture and rape, I mean it's real pop style killing. Right at the point, she praised the moral quality of the government and said it's unfair to blame the Government for the atrocities which they are carrying because we don't know that they are carrying them out. Sure, we, first like we didn't know that Hitler was carrying out the Holocaust. I mean these people are unbelievable.

DV: But they seem to be having a field day at the moment?

NC: Well . . .

DV: . . . more confident than liberal left intellectuals?

NC: Well. What kind of field day are they having? I mean, they've got plenty of wealth behind them. As long as you have plenty of wealth behind you, you always have field day. How can you fail to. That's I presume why they join that group because that's where the wealth is. Whether that's the reason or not, it is perfectly obvious that they take any position however horrendous if it's supported by private wealth, it's no problem.

DV: Do you find yourself in sympathy with magazines like *Dissent* and *Partisan Review* at the moment?

NC: *Partisan Review*, actually, the editor. The Anti-Defamation League in Boston has a very leaky office and the Anti-Defamation League is actually largely devoted to defamation as anyone would expect in the age of Orwell; so, it collects defamational material about people who they think are not loyal enough to their version of Israeli politics and it distributes them or invents them or invents lies which it distributes and so on. Somebody, for example, from the office leaked me a copy of my life about 150 pages of, like an FBI file, I mean half truths, lies, correspondence. People took notes of talks that I made and sent them in to the Anti-Defamation League office and so on and so forth. This, they distribute when I give a talk somewhere or I'm in a debate somewhere. They send that out so that people can pull defamatory material from the file and use it to try to prevent the talk or something like that, that's their function. One of the leaks I got from the office had to do with *Partisan Review*. A person working in office was appalled, informed me about correspondence that was going up in which the editor of the *Partisan Review* offered – this was late in 1982 – after the Lebanon war. The editor of the *Partisan Review* wrote them and said he was upset about the negative publicity that Israel was getting and he wanted to offer the *Partisan Review* to the Anti-Defamation League as a platform for discrediting critics of Israel – one in particular. That's straight Stalinist.

DV: Why?

NC: Why? Because these people are basically Stalinist. It's not Russia now, it happens with Israel now. But the attitude of these people towards Israel is just a mirror image almost of the attitude of American Communists towards Russia in the 1930s. In fact, sometimes it's a paradox. Did you read Saul Bellow's book *To Jerusalem and Back*? I'm amazed at his naivette. It's exactly the kind of ridiculous childish nonsense that every loyal communist who was writing about the happy peasants in Russia in the 1930s. Same cliches, same stupidities, you know same racism, it's a whole book about Jerusalem. I think there's one Arab to whom he refers you know, a taxi driver, who tells him something he wants to hear. I actually wrote a review of it but it was just comical and William Phillips, who is the editor of *Partisan Review*, he comes out of the background, he was a Trotskyite. But Trotskyites and the Stalinists weren't all that different. The Trotskyites were just the Stalinists who lost. I mean their basic attitudes weren't all that different and he carries them over now to his service to Israel, so it appears. As far as *Dissent* is concerned, I know the people but they are some mixed story. There are some things in it, they are interesting. I think their actual record is pretty awful, Irving Howe and Michael Waltzer. Well, it takes Israel again; their attitude of apologetics for Israel is just grotesque. I mean Howe devoted much of his career to defaming, to inventing lies about critics of Israel, some of it is just unbelievable stuff. In the early 1970s he was exploiting the general popular support for Israel as a way of undermining activist elements in the peace movement to which he was very much opposed. If you want to get a picture of Howe, take a look at what he thinks as important. He wrote a book called – he edited the book of democratic socialist essays on the Middle East about early 1970s and the final item you know which he reprinted in an op. ed. of the *New York Times* in which he writes approximately as follows: He says that why is it that the whole left is so anti-Israel, why do they all want to see Israel, driven into the sea and the Jews killed and so on and so forth. He says, well, what could Israel do, there is nothing Israel could do to get their left back on its side. He says the only thing, and he has a suggestion, what Israel ought to do is, have a bloody fascist revolution and as soon as the whole left including Jean-Paul Sartre and I think he's the only person he names and others will all flock to Israel to take part in the wonderful events because now there's a bloody fascist dictatorship and they'll celebrate the planning and law of the blood flowing in the streets. He describes it as the whole left from Palanetta to Scarsdale, the terms are selected with meaning. I don't know if you know what they mean, but Palanetta as far as Scarsdale are two upper class subrules and the implication is that the New Left which he hated in just a bunch of rich kids running crazy as compared to the sort of working class types who sit in the *Dissent* editorial office and who really are part of the kind of ordinary working class. So there's this, those serious people, the serious working class socialists and then there is this New Left who're flaky rich kids who like blood and violence and they'll all flock to Israel to celebrate the bloody dictatorship and, he says, Jean-Paul Sartre and Simon de Beauvoir will write a thousand-page-volume extolling the new dictatorship and getting all the facts wrong and so on. That's what he wrote. Now the fact of the matter is, at that time Jean-Paul Sartre was getting an honorary degree from the Hebrew University because of his services to Israel but facts don't matter. The point is that he didn't know the story about the New Left from Palanetta to Scarsdale, that's just a way of undermining the peace movement. In fact, the whole thing was a way of trying to undermine activist elements of the peace movement and was basically pro-war. And that's the method that he used to do it. Now that's again in style, there's no content to it, it's just mud throwing, no content whatsoever. But the style is very staunch, that's the style of the connoisseur and he learned it, he learned it in the '30s – that's his training. When Daniel Berrigan, around the same time, had the impudence to say that everything wasn't as beautiful in the occupied territories that everyone was claiming that it was – Howe wrote a vicious attack on them, full of all sorts of ridiculous falsehoods and so on. If you want I have a, I've written about this, I have a response to his attack on Berrigan and the last chapter in the Middle East . . .

DV: Is this part of your . . . ?

NC: No, I don't think so. It's in – you'll find it in peace – the last chapter of my book *Peace in Middle East* has some material on that. But in *Fateful Triangle* with a little bit of reference to it. You look up Howe in the index you'll find it. These people are just unspeakable. I take Waltzer; Waltzer didn't go this far but you know Waltzer was basically in favour of transfer. I mean his position in the early 1970s was that in Israel the people who are original to the nation ought to be helped to leave. That's rabid Kahane you know. The people who are marginal to the nation are the Arabs. Why are they marginal . . . ? First of all, why are they marginal to the nation? Now, if you are an Arab citizen of Israel and what do you expect? Then, you are marginal to the nation. Am I marginal to the United States because I'm a Jew? Suppose somebody said, suppose some American Nazi got up and said this is a Christian State, people who are marginal ought to be helped to leave, like me, how would we react? That's Waltzer on Israel. People who are marginal to the nation, that is, Arabs ought to be helped to leave. Well, you know Kahane would agree, he doesn't think they'll kill them, he thinks they'll pay them to leave. That's Michael Waltzer and, for example, Irving Howe as late as 1982; now, they all have a story about themselves as advocates of a political settlement and so on. That's all very recent. Throughout this whole time Howe was describing Israel as highly democratic, socialistic country advancing towards socialism and so on. This is the time of the first repression when he finally, in 1982, for the first time he wrote something in which he conceded that maybe the occupation wasn't as beautiful as he thought it was. But after years of repression and torture and humiliation and so on, finally in 1982, in the *New York Times*, he wrote a review in which he said, "well, I am appalled to discover that it isn't all the sweetness and light and," he says, "besides it's wrong." Instead of putting money in the territories what Israel ought to do is use the money for the Galilee settlement in Galilee. Because he said it's, which he referred to it as, the underpopulated – Galilee. Now that's like somebody saying that New York is underpopulated because it has too many Jews and not enough WASPs. I mean, Galilee isn't underpopulated, it's just that there're too few Jews, plenty of Arabs. What makes it underpopulated is that there aren't enough Jews. They're Arabs, they're all stuck into their villages because they're not given any land on which to build since the land is owned in the name of the Jewish people in this democratic, socialist state that Howe is so excited about. But to call that the underpopulated, Galilee, is like calling New York underpopulated because there are too many Jews and too few Christians. These people are unbelievable. On the other hand there's good stuff in the sense that . . .

DV: I believe Bellow ran into a controversy recently . . .

NC: Who?

DV: Saul Bellow. He published a novel, a tiny little novel, where he almost gives the impression that minority is dangerous to American Society or something like that and I also believe that he supported Richard Daley and when I think about all these things and remember my reading of his novels, I get the feeling that black people always appear as gangsters, pickpockets in his novels. I think there is always an ideology in literature that keeps bothering me but the point is when some one like Saul Bellow writes the reader is always under the spell of narrative magic and he almost forgets this side of it. This is one of the reasons why I get the feeling that literature always has some kind of ideology any way.

NC: Yeah, and that's something that Irving Howe rather wrote well about. Incidentally in the 1950s, he wrote a book called *Politics and the Novel* which is quite a good book in which he has many good things to say. The person has some talent you know.

DV: What do you think about the New Left movement now? Does it have any significant place?

NC: Much more significant . . .

DV: Everybody seems to say bad things about the New Left now.

NC: New Left of the '60s? Everybody hated the New Left because it was too successful. It changed the country in a very healthy way, I mean, one of the reasons why Howe did hate the New Left from Scarsdale to Palanetta. Well, you know students were asking embarrassing questions. They were not just obedient, they were thinking for them selves. They became politically organised. They acted, they just didn't sit around. They acted in favour of Civil Rights and the peace in Middle East, they were challenging authority. That was frightening, was frightening that lots of people were becoming politically involved – were entering the political arena or becoming organised with thinking, were setting up . . . journals, were questioning orthodox views and so on. Now in any popular movement you do find a lot of crazy things specially when the popular movement is young people. I mean there are young people coming out of nowhere, no cultural tradition of dissidence at all, inventing everything from themselves. I know a lot of it was very crazy, freaky, you know, violent and so on. That was the fringes and all that remains is that that's the only thing you're not allowed to know about the constructive work that was going on, which was the overwhelming majority of it and the reason is, that was much too threatening and that had a very positive impact on the society. This is a much more civilised country than it was 25 years ago. I mean, in all sorts of respects; take, say, the feminist movement and that came out of the New Left. You know the ecological movements came out of the New Left, the solidarity movements with the third world that didn't exist before and internally these movements now are not students; they are not young students. It's all over the society, it's just mainstream America where rather substantial or, take something as simple as the attitude towards native Americans. We went through 200 years of history pretending that there weren't any native Americans – just a few hunters running around who had to defend themselves against, you know 'what can you do' cowboys and Indians, cowboys and Indians, you know savage Indians like monkeys or something.

DV: Stereotypes, etc.?

NC: Yeah, well, until the 1970s that it became impossible even to face the facts and even anthropology couldn't face it – the scholarly disciplines couldn't look at the facts until the 1970s since they looked at the facts after 200 years they discovered that it wasn't a million naked savages running around. It was maybe 8 or 10 million people living in advanced civilisations, more advanced than their colonists in many respects, you know, stone houses, complicated social organization . . . agriculture; they were wiped out like genocide. Well, that whole history has been suppressed for hundreds of years and it's just begun to come out in the '70s. It's not accidental that it came out in the '70s, that's part of the opening up and challenging of the authority and the questioning and the willingness to enquire and so on, the freedom that was part of the New Left. It's all very important, you know it's a long way to go but it's changed the country in a very substantial way. When you talk, when I give talks now as I do all the time, everybody is much more sophisticated and knowledgeable and thoughtful and so on than they were 20 years ago. And that's part of the effect of the New Left. There's been a counter-reaction, reaction against it. One of the reactions, the sort of right turn what's called neo-conservation or it's absurd term, that's a reaction to this and, of course, it is among the privileged. Among the privileged there undoubtedly is a right turn, among the general population there isn't. General population continued to move towards more and so called liberal positions in fact democratic socialist positions. You look at opinion studies and you discover that through the whole 1980s all this right turn was supposedly going on. The public was becoming more committed to sort of New Deal style liberalism right through the whole of 1980s and in fact there was overwhelming opposition, public opposition to virtually all of Reagan's policies.

DV: What do you think about the political situation in Soviet Russia at the moment? They have Glasnost, Perestroika and all those things. Does it have any impact on American foreign policy?

NC: Yeah, it'll have a big effect on American foreign policy because, well, . . .

DV: What happened to Soviet Communism?

NC: Well, you know Samuel Huntington, the Government Professor at Harvard. He's a professor of Government at Harvard and a long time government advisor. Back around 1981 he pointed out quite accurately that when we undertake intervention in the third world there are other forms of an alternative action; it's necessary, I'm quoting him, it's necessary to create the misimpression that it was the Soviet Union that we're fighting. That's what we've done ever since the Truman doctrine. And that's quite true. If you carry out intervention, say in Central America, South East Asia or something, you always have to pretend to the population here that you're fighting the Soviet Union. Because, otherwise they don't see any reason to do it, you know, why send troops to kill Vietnamese. Because we must be defending ourselves from the Soviet Union which is after all a big dangerous enemy. And the same is true domestically like when the Reagan administration decided to expand the power of the State and to use it as a welfare state for the rich by forcing the public to subsidies of high technology industry which is basic Reagan policy; when they did that, they had to claim that we were doing it not in order to make rich people wealthy, – you can't tell people that – we were doing it because we had to defend ourselves from the evil empire. That system of funding high technology is called the Pentagon, that's the way you force the public to like Star Wars, a ridiculous idea. Nobody with his head screwed on thought a bit about the weapon system, it's a great way to fund fifth generation computers and lasers and in fact the whole range of new technology; it's funded through that system and the public pays for it because you have to defend yourself against the Russians. Well, if the Russians become less threatening it's harder to mobilise the population to defend itself by paying off the wealthy and supporting torture and murder in the third world and so on. So that's gonna be a problem. On the other hand, and this is discussed in elite circles, they also see a sort of silver lining in the clouds. So, for example, take a look at the talk I gave in England which was published there, but at the end of the year, *New York Times* had an op. ed. by Dimitri Simms, who is the senior fellow of the Carnegie Endowment for International Peace and he gave a sort of wrap up for the year on Glasnost and what this all means; he is a Soviet expert. And he said that there are some good things about all these developments, he said, it does make the World system more complex and, you know, we lose the simplicities and the certainties but there's some good thing about it. One good thing is that we won't any longer be exploited, the third world won't be allowed to exploit us any longer. So, for example, in the third world debt problem, he said, they can sort of play the Russians off against the Americans but if they can't, if they are not, if they've got the Russians to turn to them we can be much harsher. And we won't be mistreated by the undeserving poor, that's one good thing about it. The other good thing about it, the best thing about it, he said, is, it's gonna free us up from military intervention in the third world. We've always been cautious about military intervention in the third world. We've always been cautious about military intervention. He gives two examples, because we're afraid of the Russians; the official story is that we deter the Russians and we contain the Russians but the real truth is they deter us and they contain us. You have to say that but if you look at history it's quite true. And now the Russians are looking less menacing, it's possible to say what has always been true. In the case of Arabs, when the old prices went up too high, we should have invaded because they have no right to do what they want to do with their own oil – it's ours, not theirs. But we couldn't because there was too much fear that the Russians might get involved and there could be a global war. But if the Russians back off with their new thinking, then we can invade the Middle East. We won't have to worry about and the other example he gives is Nicaragua. He says we had to be somewhat cautious about Nicaragua because you never could be sure that the Russians were gonna react. Now that the Russians back off, we can just use military intervention outright, send them reins. We don't have to worry about what's gonna happen and that's good because we're not deterred anymore so that's the good part of that 'Glasnost'. Well, that's the Carnegie Endowment for International Peace and the *New York*

Times and in fact that's happening, I mean, take a look at this morning's paper, you'll find a little thing in the *New York Times* in which James Baker says we have to test Gorbachev's seriousness, we have to see if he's serious about 'detente'; if he is, he's gonna back off from supporting Nicaragua and Cuba and then you know the only countries in Central America and the Caribbean that are under military threat have to be disarmed and the reason is we're the military threat. Now you know Gorbachev did offer to stop sending military aid to Nicaragua if we would stop sending military aid to El Salvadore and Guatemala. But that was ridiculous. 'Detente' means he allows us free rein to do anything we want – that's the meaning of 'Detente' and unless he goes along with that that shows he's not serious about 'Detente'. Now that position is accepted across the border. That's the position of American liberals too. For Gorbachev to show he's serious about 'Detente' he has to let us do anything we want to do in Central America and Caribbean. I mean, if Gorbachev were to get up and say: if the Americans are serious about 'Detente' they have to stop supporting solidarity in Poland you know people just laugh.

DV: Is it good for the Russians? over there?

NC: Is it good for the Russians? Yeah, constantly good for them at the moment but it's very chancey, it's very complex, I mean the Soviet Union is not like the U.S. I mean, it's more like India. It's an internal empire; it is a sort of homogeneous society more or less. It's got ethnic problems and so on, but there isn't any separatism like the Italians are hung up on forming their own state in the U.S. But in the Soviet Union, you know the Azer-baijanis and the Georgians and the Estonians and sooner or later the Ukranians who are 50 million people. They don't want to even be in that state; they regard themselves with some justice as a part of an internal empire, Russian run empire. That means the whole thing can fall apart and that's a difficult one to deal with . . .

DV: What's going to happen to Communism as a political philosophy?

NC: There is no such thing as Communism and there hasn't been since 1917. In October 1917, in my view at least, in October 1917 when the Bolshevik coup took place, they destroyed socialism in Russia. I mean, the first moves of Trotsky and Lenin were to eliminate the socialist institutions. First thing they did was, to get rid of the factory councils, reduce the power of the soviets, really eliminate them, develop a central or state authority, turn it into what Trotsky called a Labour army. Now, that's the opposite of Socialism, like they moved at once to eliminate the socialist institutions. Now if the world calls that Socialism, there's a good reason for it. These two major propaganda systems in the world, the main one is the American one, but the next includes England and France, the next bigger one, biggest one is the Soviet system and both of those propaganda systems claim that this is Socialism and do it for opposite reasons. The Soviet Union claims that it is Socialism because they want to take for themselves the moral prestige of authentic Socialism. So they claim that what they're doing is Socialism. The American system calls it Socialism because they want to defame Socialism by associating it with the totalitarian Russian State. So the world's two major propaganda systems are united in calling this monstrosity Socialism and, I think, it's the worst blow the socialist movement has suffered in the twentieth century viz. the October Revolution. They should basically, I mean, quickly destroy possibility of Socialism in the Soviet Union. Actually Lenin, who is a pretty good Orthodox Marxist, he agreed with this. Lenin to the end of his days never thought that there could be socialism in the Soviet union. As a good Marxist, kind of an Orthodox Marxist, he assumed that a Socialist Revolution could only take place in the most advanced capitalist country, at this time he meant Germany. So his conception was that the Bolsheviks were trying to maintain things until the revolution would take place in Germany and then they would be on the margin of it because they were not ready for socialism, but Germany is, because Germany is advanced capitalist. Well, that's orthodox Marxism. He believes that he is in Orthodox Marxist, and when the Revolution was crushed in Germany they had to adjust and then it's all taken over by State politics and international politics. But Lenin was basically right. I think, there was a possibility for Socialism there, but he destroyed it with Trotsky's help. That's why I'm not at all impressed by people like, say, Irving Howe, whom you mentioned, or Irving Krystol who you mentioned or William Phillips of *Partisan Review* who are so proud that they were Trotskyists in the 1930s. To say that they're Trotskyists in the 1930s is to say that they approved of the destruction of Socialism and the imposition of totalitarianism because that's what Trotsky did.

DV: At the same time we have, for instance, Frankfurt school of thinkers—especially Adorno and they have their own version of response to Marxism. What kind of importance do they have today?

NC: What kind of importance? I guess they're important. Personally, quite honestly, I'm personally not interested in, I don't really, I shall look at it. I don't think it tells me a lot.

DV: Is it one of those academic things that are happening?

NC: I don't know, all I can say is I don't find it interesting or informative. If other people do, fine. I mean, my own feeling, honest truth is that what is understood more or less about the world is rather simple. If there are more complicated things they are not understood. Now we can either describe them in simple terms, relatively simple terms, you know, simple words and so on. Well, if we want, we can develop very complicated theories about them which don't say anything more than the simple words do and if you're an intellectual you better do the second thing. Otherwise you don't have a craft and you don't look important and you can't write a thousand page book and get professorships. So intellectuals tend to create these complicated theories and discuss them and be interested in them. When I read them I don't see anything.

DV: Like Deconstruction?

NC: I mean Deconstruction is the extreme example of this. I think, that's just pure irrationality as far as I can see. When I read, I try to read this material, I mean, I must say, I literally, I look at a page of Derrida and I can't understand one sentence. Now you know there are two possibilities. One possibility is that it's just beyond me. I'm not smart enough, that's possible. But I don't really believe it because there are plenty of hard things that I can understand, like I can understand advanced mathematics and if I read a page of quantum theory I also can understand it. Well, I know what I'd have to do to be able to understand it. If I want to understand quantum electric dynamism I know I could do it. I have to work and I know what I have to do and so on. But I can never understand the page of Derrida and there's nothing I can do to understand it. Well, so one possibility is that all of a sudden the literary critics have developed a field that is vastly more advanced and complex than theoretical physics and advanced mathematics – that's one possibility. The other possibility is, it's all fraud – Take your choice and it's obvious what the answer is; but I'm not telling other people what to say. I've tried to read the parts of the stuff that are close to my own discipline. It's just childish nonsense. The arguments don't work, the facts are all wrong, it's gibberish. In fact some of the people involved in my view are just pure charlatans. Jacques

Lacan, for example whom I knew a little bit. My frank impression is that Lacan was just trying to figure out how crazy he could get and still have people in Paris take him seriously. So he would do one, here we say OK, "I'm gonna have five minutes psychoanalytic interviews" and everybody would say "oh! boy, fantastic innovation." They take that seriously. And some other mad idea, and they will take that seriously and finally couldn't think of anything else. There comes a point when you've done everything and can't think of anything more. The last thing you could think of is to close down your psycho-analytical institute. Everybody took that seriously, front-page story in Le Monde. I mean, at what point you begin to laugh you know . . .

DV: In fact, I remember Professor Goodheart who says that these people are . . .

NC: Who?

DV: Prof. Goodheart. He says that these people are taking a power trip at the expense of literature.

NC: I tend to agree with that. I mean, look, undoubtedly there's serious stuff there, I mean, they are intelligent people. I'm sure if you read it all, I'm sure you'll find something that'll make some sense. But as a movement, I can't figure out what's it about. What's deconstruction, what's deconstruction supposed to be. I mean, you know, anybody for ever has tried to read texts and is figuring it out, telling of truths – if the arguments work and if the facts are right, you know, if the arguments are coherent. If they are biased in their selection of sources, if they're framing the issue in ways which reflect ideology and that's the way we read everything. That's the way we read the morning newspaper.

DV: What do you think about the recent controversy about Salman Rushdie's book? Do you see any major political . . .

NC: Well, you know the idea of a death threat for a novelist is so outlandish, you can't even discuss it. It's a major atrocity, doubtlessly. On the other hand, I should say, the people standing out for Rushdie are mostly total hypocrites. I mean they never take a position on . . .

DV: Like Norman Mailer?

NC: Well, I mean, I never saw him you know.

DV: Anyway it's a belated response in America.

NC: Let me give you an example. When Canada blocked the import of Salman Rushdie's book for several weeks, they did that because they wanted to see if it conflicted with certain Canadian laws. Canadian laws got an anti-hate law. It's a law which makes it a crime to publish any—to publish false news. That's something right out of the middle period. That law goes back to 1275 when it became part of British common law that publishing false news is illegal—meaning, the state shall determine the truth. And if the state says this is true and you publish something else, that's false news and therefore you get arrested. That's what the Canadian law says and it also says it is illegal to publish anything which is considered by the state to be against the public interest. Well, that law was meant to stop people from denying the Holocaust and in fact there's a guy who's facing, I think, about a year's jail sentence because he published privately a thirty page or something, a small pamphlet in which he probably denied the existence of the Holocaust or maybe he's a neo-Nazi or something like this, I don't know. He was brought to trial, convicted, he went to appeal, he was reconvicted on appeal and so on. It's the same law, same law that stopped the import of Rushdie's book. Well, that was known there. I found three articles in the *New York Times* about it. When the trial was going on there was an editorial in the *Boston Globe* local journal applauding the decision, applauding the decision of the court saying, finally, the jury had enough courage to shut these guys up, make them stop writing what they're writing and so on and so forth. You know it's the same law that stopped the import of Rushdie's book. When they stopped the import of Rushdie's book everybody was screaming about this violation of freedom of speech. They believe in freedom of speech for the views they like. Hitler believed in that too. Now if you believe in freedom of speech, you think that it's appalling for somebody to be sent to jail for publishing a pamphlet in which he denies the Holocaust. I mean, freedom of speech means freedom to tell lies—doesn't mean freedom to tell what you think is true. I mean, from the point of view of the Ayatollah Khomeini, Rushdie's telling lies. Telling lies not just about anybody but about Muhammad. So, therefore, it's the same principle. The fact of the matter is that everybody is in favour of freedom of speech. When you are sure that you've got half a billion Westerners up there in front of you, then you're very courageous. But how about taking this same position in a serious case when you don't have half a billion people up in front of you. Then everybody's quiet and there is case after case like this. I mean, take this morning's *New York Times*. This morning's *New York Times*, there're two stories, kind of interesting. One is a little news item saying that a certain Palestinian journalist was arrested on the grounds that he is one of the leaders of Intifada. Another is a column by Anthony Lewis who is referring to the fact that the same guy, several months ago, was arrested and put under administrative detention. I think, it's the third or fourth time that it had happened. Well, you know, Lewis didn't know that same guy was going to be arrested in the news column today, but has there ever been a protest about this? Is there going to be a protest this time? In fact, you know, if you're a Palestinian editor you can. Early this month, the March 9th, one month ago, this guy's from Jerusalem, on March 9th, an Arab from Nazareth, that's inside Israel, nothing about occupied territories or anything like that. An editor from Nazareth had a press conference at the place which is more like the National Press Club; that means every journalist was there and if you wanted to be, well, you only have to know when. But everybody knew about it in which he called the press conference to protest the fact that the Israeli Government had closed his newspaper, forcefully closed his newspaper. In Israel, you have to have a license to publish. Not that you are permitted to have a license, it'll be taken away for any reason whatsoever. They took away his license to publish his newspaper on the grounds that—they couldn't criticise anything that was in the newspaper because it all passes through military censorship. But they claimed he had some connection with hostile elements or something. See a thing like that in *New York Times* or any American newspaper? No, because nobody cares about freedom of speech. Had it happened in Nicaragua there'd be a three inch headline. What they care about is freedom of speech they like. For example, Anthony Lewis was best of them; you take a look at his column and he says there's terrible situation in Israel. It has freedom of speech for Israelis but not for Palestinians. They don't have a free speech for Israelis either, they've got some of the most draconian censorship laws in the industrial world and Hebrew newspapers can appear with a blank editorial because the censor took it out. Last Fall, during the election campaign, one of the little peace groups tried to run an ad on Television—showing a film of Yasser Arafat offering to negotiate. Television wouldn't run it. When this went to the Supreme Court, the decision was: that's correct, the state had determined that the PLO is a terrorist organisation. And therefore television is not allowed to show anything that's inconsistent with that. That's freedom of speech? Now Anthony Lewis who is that most outspoken critic of this says: Well, there is freedom of speech in Israel. But not for the Palestinian. The fact is that concern for freedom of speech here is very low and, yes, it's easy to get excited about the Rushdie case because it's enemies who're doing it. Everybody hates Iran, everybody hates Islam, so therefore you can attack them and because you're very safe. Hundreds and millions of people agree with you. So you can look like a hero. I signed with Rushdie league that's true but there's plenty. I do care about the other ones also and that infuriates everyone, of course.

Elie Wiesel

DV: Who is a Jew? This seems to be coming up for discussion over and over again. And you are the better person to reflect on this.

EW: I don't really think of myself as a better person. A Jew knows who is a Jew and we should not raise questions that are not timely. Well, this question, as you know, has done much damage.

DV: Yes, indeed.

EW: For two thousand years, they didn't ask this question. A Jew knows who he or she is. A Jew is someone whose destiny is linked to the destiny of the Jewish people. As simple as that.

DV: It has been more than four decades now after the World War II. How does he fare today?

EW: How he fares? Today? You mean, is he better or not? I think he is better after all because of Israel. It's his life, it has been a dream. It's been under threat but it is there; it makes not only a tremendous difference, it makes an essential difference in Jewish life everywhere and its centrality to his own Jewish life cannot be disguised. And here and there, there are problems of course. But when you compare it to the Jewish situation in '33, '45 and today, their situation is better now. On the other hand, because the Jewish people are wounded and the wounds appear and the scars appear. In '33, they did not have those wounds and the echoes of those Jews are still alive. So, it is not a simple situation. But then being Jewish is not so simple.

DV: Soon after the war once again there have been disasters; Vietnam and you have problems in Afghanistan and Korea and so on. When does humanity ever learn? Do you think we have learned anything at all from history?

EW: Individuals learn here and there, students may be; but the group of people, human family, the society unfortunately, they do not learn – although I never compare. No tragedy should be compared to any other – surely not what happened to the Jewish people. But in the area of lessons we may say that the world has not learnt anything. Except if he doesn't learn, (humanity) it is doomed to die.

DV: Not many writers in this country seem to deal with the Holocaust in their works although there are some who do.

EW: Some do.

DV: Probably Edward Lewis Wallant's *The Pawnbroker* is a rare novel which does attempt to grapple with the dense moral and historical context of the Holocaust. Bellow touches this here and there but in a marginal fashion.

EW: There are some less good writers. We have of course Styron.

DV: But don't you think he generalizes the context?

EW: I don't like it. It's not a good book.

DV: Obviously, you are talking about *Sophie's Choice*.

EW: But then he is not so dull. He is tactful. Minor writers have written about this but not the serious writers.

DV: Now, the situation of the Jew in America. Uptill the fifties and the sixties, the Jew has essentially been a liberal, supporting black people and things of that sort. Now it has changed in some ways atleast thanks to the Jewish enthusiasts of Neo-conservatism. I don't think they support welfare state concept vigorously nor do they support affirmative action any more.

EW: I would not generalize. It's a pluralistic society. Some people are still liberals and fight for racial equality but others are not. But you can't say the Jewish community is doing that.

DV: The Holocaust puts such ideas as progress of humanity, Enlightenment, man's estate, and man as a moral being into a serious critique. It was the time when each man was for himself fragile and helpless. Does it mean that man in extreme situation would clearly slip into the animal kingdom instead of hanging on to his enviable place just below angels?

EW: Humanity is fragile and humanity of man is even more fragile. What is needed is a kind of ethical strength to be built up in every person. If not , culture is not enough, science is not enough, military strength is not enough. One is not alone, what everybody does, one does on behalf of so many others. In good and in bad.

DV: After the Holocaust, Jewish theology has seen many vigorous viewpoints. Richard Rubenstein, Emile Fackenheim and others. How do you view their viewpoints?

EW: I am not a theologian. Therefore, it is not easy for me to comment. Everything had to be revised after the tragedy. Philosophy, history and literature. Language, strength, ideas were altered. In the course of it history underwent tremendous revolutionary need for change. So, I imagine, for theologians it is a problem, of course, it is a serious problem, meaning God, God in history, God in man, God in humanity. Where are the limits? Where are the boundaries?

DV: In the recent years, one finds fictionalized versions of the Holocaust, William Styron's *Sophie's Choice*, John Hersey's *The Wall*. Indeed when Styron's novel was published, *Commentary* carried a very negative article – if I recall correctly. Now, how far this trend in literature – that the Holocaust could be fictionally recreated and imaginary characters could be placed in such situations – is acceptable? Would it be that in such gestures there is a disservice to the suffering of people in the camps, and to history?

EW: I couldn't do it. If they feel they can do it, they do it. John Hersey's *The Wall* is a very good novel. But the others I am afraid . . . I don't think the Holocaust can be treated as fiction.

DV: Again the definition of a Jew. This topic certainly rattles the mind of many people. It has always been, maybe. Elie Kedourie wrote an article about it in *Commentary*.

EW: It is a non-sensical debate – ill-deviced, ill-conceived, ill-timed debate. A Jew is some one who links his or her destiny with Jewish people – period.

DV: I believe when Indian Jews went to Israel, they had some problems. Especially Bene Israel community of India faced certain embarrassing moments with the Chief Rabbi.

EW: I know there were some problems. But they were solved. I don't think these problems lasted. I mean these problems did not last.

DV: What do you think about the Middle East situation now. Is peace ever possible there? Whatever happened to classical Zionism?

EW: There must be a solution. There will be a solution. I don't know what it is. I think it is a tragedy, tragedy for everybody. And tragedies cannot last, should not last.

DV: How does the present generation of Jewish youth, for which the Holocaust is probably history or even one of those dark chapters of Jewish past, can come to terms with the Holocaust?

EW: I don't think any one can come to terms with the Holocaust. It will remain as a wound, it must remain as a wound, an open wound.

DV: What approaches should they have towards it?

EW: They have to study, learn, study and study more.

DV: I think there is a growing interest in Judaism and the roots among the young people. Having participated in Hillel groups at Brandeis, I feel that this generation is consciously making an attempt to study and analyse Jewish history and tradition. Do you want to comment on the various denominations of American Judaism – Reform, Conservative, Orthodox?

EW: I don't know, I am not a sociologist, I am not a rabbi. But whether it is Hinduism, Islam or Judaism I believe in study. They must study and learn – study more. Study with tolerance. Whatever you think is true, is true. Whatever other people think is true, is true for them. Probably the source is the same but the paths leading to the source may be many. One is as good as any. Knowledge is good for all. The absence of knowledge is bad for all.

DV: When I think about Hitler, I cannot help wondering that Germany which is supposed to respresent the best of Western culture and a civilization in terms of art, literature and music has also produced monsters like Hitler.

EW: I don't know. That's a big question. One doesn't understand. Germany has the best universities in the world. And killers came from those universities. Why? The question you ask is a very serious question.

DV: Hitler did not come on to the scene just like that. In fact, I remember an article written by George Steiner probably in *Encounter* where he tries to reason out Hitler phenomenon. He says that if one looks at the German cultural past, among the Greek epics, Homer is exceedingly popular. And Virgil is not all that appreciated. Homer celebrates war, heroism, massacre whereas Virgil's *Aeneid* is a search for home, planting roots again, building up of a community all over again. It is interesting that Hermann Brock who was forced into the Nazi camp, wrote *The Death of Virgil*. Also, German intellectuals like Richard Wagner, Heidegger and others have their own part in the emergence of Hitler.

EW: No, no. He did not come from a vacuum. History of Anti-Semitism. There is a kind of dehumanization in their concept of humanity, in their concept of history, in their concept of art. Once you humiliate humanity in one group, all groups are affected, are marked.

DV: How do you view the present Germany? Neo-Nazis, chemical factories . . .

EW: Oh, I am disturbed. Oh, I think it is terribly disturbing, disturbing to me. Nazis on one hand. That's right, chemical factories. Normalization, what they call normalization of history. Policies. I am disturbed.

DV: What is the status of the Jew in Soviet Russia. You once wrote *Jews of Silence* about the Jews in Russia. You have just come back from Russia. How are the Jews now in Gorbachev's Russia. With his much-talked about Glasnost and Perestroica . . .

EW: Much better, much better now. I think Gorbachev is trying to open many doors, inside and outside of Russia. And I think we should help him. He is probably our best chance. If some thing happens and he is asked to give up his position, there will be a return not to Brezhnev but to Stalin. At the moment, he is doing many good things. He opened many possibilities.

DV: How much of Yiddish culture survives there in Russia now?

EW: Of course, the great many of the Yiddishists were killed by Stalin and his men. But there is today, there are enough people in every city, Jews who want to remember, who want to study. That's why they want to open a Centre there. That's why I went there. I just came back last night; I am optimistic. If Jewish culture survives even if in muted form, it always comes back. And it is a good sign.

DV: I.B. Singer comes to mind immediately. He tries to bring back the Jewish culture of pre-war Europe, although his dybbuk-strained theme is repetitive. But Yiddishkeit is recreated in his highly readable works . . .

EW: He picked up Yiddish culture, of course. But there are many other writers too. I like him. I like his brother, I.J. Singer. He is a great writer. Sholom Aleichem, Der Nister, David Bergelson. It is a great, great culture. I hope it will remain.

DV: Among American writers, I think Cynthia Ozick is showing lot of interest in Yiddish culture. Philip Roth too. Philip Roth may be one of the under-estimated of the Jewish writers.

EW: I like them . . .

Marshall Sklare

DV: I have been reading Jewish writers for quite some time. Now, you have done extensive study on Jewish communal life, Jewish sociology. Do you think the Jewish writing reflects Jewish tradition in any way? Or does Judaism mean anything to the Jewish writers?

MS: First of all, I don't think you can generalize. Cynthia Ozick, obviously, is so much more Jewish than probably anybody else. She has a strong background of Jewish culture and she writes very much about the Jewish things. The others may write about people who are Jewish or situations which are Jewish, creating a difficulty of what is a Jewish situation. I don't think you can make a generalization about all of them. My impression is that the Jewish novel is not as popular as it was before. It would seem to me that the height of it – maybe ten years ago, fifteen years ago, twenty years ago – seems to have diminished at the present time. That may not be such a serious thing because all of these go in cycles. So, one cannot expect everything to be either on a level or always going up. And, if I am correct, the down part of the cycle will later go up again. The novelists like Bellow, Malamud, Roth are second generation individuals and came from first generation homes, that is, their parents were immigrants. And that has given them a strong background in, what you may call, the folk-Jewish culture – Yiddishkeit. None of them had any background in high Jewish culture, Jewish humanities. Their background was in mother's kitchen, family apartment and in the neighbourhood. And that's what their writings reflect. That's very important because most people in that milieu and most people are subjected to their milieu. Most people are not learned in the Jewish humanities. In a certain sense, they reflect the Jewish street – you might say. But they reflected it so frequently on intellectual level, reflected on a level of anecdote. They raise it to artistic production. But the limitation of their work is their lack of learning in the high Jewish culture. They reflect the Jewish street and they may raise it to artistic level but I would consider it a limitation. We do, through their novels, get a reflection of the Jewish street. That's still valuable. It's valuable to my work because I have to know the culture of street as well as high Jewish culture. Some one who is not as limited as that is Alfred Kazin. *A Walker in the City* is the best, at least to me is the most interesting.

DV: And *Starting Out in the Thirties*, the *New York Jew* and so on.

WS: *A Walker in the City* is interesting because he has no high Jewish culture; he has no knowledge of the Jewish humanities. But he is an acutely sensitive individual, he is fundamentally a critic. He is extremely important to me because he indeed takes to the Jewish street as he did in *A Walker in the City* and tries to analyse what is Jewish about it; what is his reaction to it?; how did he come to it? What are parents' feelings about it? What are his feelings about it? Can he live there? Can he move to Manhattan which to him is the great frontier?

DV: The city beyond, as he says.

MS: Yes. So, I find Kazin very sharp. Sometimes I find better analysis in his work than I do in the novelists.

DV: You seem to suggest that the interest in Jewish literature is diminishing, at least temporarily. Which is rather interesting because when we, back in India, think about the twentieth century American literature, we invariably talk about the Jewish writers, at least we recognize the significance of their contribution to the novel, drama and poetry. Thus, we have Bellow, Arthur Miller, Allen Ginsberg and so on.

MS: What I meant was that Malamud is not replaced. There was this efflorescence – Bellow, Roth and Malamud. They are either dead – as Malamud was – or . . .

DV: Not getting that much of attention these days.

MS: Well, they are getting attention. But their successors do not seem to be around in the number and with the thrust and perhaps potentiality for fame that they did. So, that's what I mean by this somewhat a decline. But I say these things work in cycles any way. Maybe that ten years of fifteen years from now, a new generation will raise. But that generation was built up on son and daughter of an immigrant. But writing generally reflects their second generation stance to America, feeling about their parents and feeling about their being in culture, and that, of course, cannot be duplicated because people are now third generation or fourth generation who are writing. I don't see third and fourth generation writers to the extent I see the second generation writers.

DV: Do you think inevitable assimilationist tendency is responsible for its decline – if it is a decline at all?

MS: I think they don't have the experience of the Jewish street as the second generation had. Well, they can't because the Jewish street is no longer what it was. The Jewish street is now suburban and even though it might be eighty percent Jewish or seventy percent Jewish, it has a general ambience and is not specifically Jewish and it doesn't lend itself to the kind of writing they were doing. I am not a specialist on literature. I read literature like anybody, and I read it to get a sense of Jewish life.

DV: How do you view Bellow in Jewish context? To my mind, he seems to use Jewish background in a subtle fashion, although he generally writes about Jewish characters who do not greatly reflect on specifically Jewish issues. But the Jewish concern for family is there in his novels also. Uncles, cousins, wives and, inevitably, ex-wives hover his fictional landscape. The protagonists always look back and indeed very much yearn for the past as if the present American situation – both familial and societal – is very sterile and, therefore, shrivels the soul of man. Isn't this quiet essentially Jewish?

MS: Well, perhaps the Bellow book that I find appealing and gives a good knowledge of Bellow is *To Jerusalem and Back*.

DV: That's non-fiction, of course.

MS: Yes, that's non-fiction. What I find in that book, first of all, is his acute sensitivity to Jewish patterns of life. You remember the way the book starts. When Bellow sees Hasidim, he quickly orders a Kosher meal. You may say it's human but it's much more than that. He knows exactly what to do. Isn't there something about arranging the seats so that his wife is not between them? and then there is a funny conversation between the Hasid and Bellow. Well, he notices that Bellow does not eat Kosher meal. He thinks maybe because it's too expensive. Kosher meal is generally very expensive. The Hasid says that he would subsidize. It's very funny because Bellow made a lot of money. He spent a lot of money with his various wives; it has been a big expense to him. But, any way, he can enter into such a thing because he knows what the man is and what he is thinking. And there is this funny thing. His wife is a non-Jew. The Hasid talks to him in Yiddish. Well, Bellow knows Yiddish. Bellow was born in Montreal and he was brought up in Chicago in the neighbourhood where Yiddish was commonly spoken. When the Hasid notices that his wife does not participate, he asks Bellow about it. And Bellow says that she was brought up in a non-Jewish neighbourhood. He doesn't want to hurt the man's feelings. He always has this acute sensitivity and sensibility. Of the writers, he knows more about the Jewish culture than the others.

DV: He makes a very subtle use of it in his works.

MS: Well, yes. He is not throwing it at you. He is not trying to instruct you. He is telling a story that presumably happened and telling you in an artistic way. I think a lot about him, at his ability to handle Jewish culture whereas some of the others are less facile, less knowledgeable, more crude than he is.

DV: In my view, Chaim Potok is someone who consistently weaves his narrative in a Jewish context.

MS: Chaim Potok is in a different league altogether. First of all, his knowledge of Jewish culture. He has a knowledge of high Jewish culture, knowledge of rabbinism and he was a student at Yeshiva University and frequently his novels deal with people who are part of high Jewish culture – some of them modelled on famous rabbis.

DV: He also succeeds in telling the story without giving the impression that he is more interested in proving the Jewish ambience.

MS: Well, he is a very good dramatist, sort of.

DV: He does not make Jewish context prescriptive. He is not overly instructive. The context fits in with the discourse of the novel. So anybody can read his novel as a novel and still experience Jewish culture. In a novel called *My Name is Ashev Lev* he projects the theme of a Jewish painter in modern times. What it means to be a Jewish painter? What are the problems that come up? And how the tradition of Jewish orthodoxy responds to it? Whether this response is conducive to the growth of a painter? If not, what is the price one has to pay for choosing to become a painter in this context? How does one come to terms with it? These are interesting questions explored meaningfully by Potok.

MS: Well, you see the problem for him is how do you remain true to Jewish identity and Jewish tradition and, at the same time, participate in the modern world. I don't think that's true of the other writers you have mentioned. Because they have moved over to the general world and, therefore, it's not a problem for them. But he comes from a very intense Jewish background. And for him the question "how to live in two worlds?" is very significant and it is there in his fiction. Whether it is the Jewish painter, Jewish mysticism, relation with a father who is rabbi and who wants his son to be rabbi – these are constant themes. How one can remain true and be part of the modern world. And I suppose he tries to show that it is possible. Sometimes he shows that it is possible; sometimes he shows that it is not possible. But this is always the problem he is grappling with and, as I say, it is not so characteristic of the other Jewish writers because they have moved into the modern world and, in a sense, made peace with it. The kind of intense orthodox background, the others don't have it. And so, for him there is a problem that others don't feel actually. For others like Roth who tries to get along with his mother or father who have expectations of you that you don't want to fulfil. Not that they want you to become a rabbi. No. But they want you to get married, have a family and live normal life. But you don't because you have other ideals in life.

DV: What do you think about the different intellectual postures of Jews like Norman Podhoretz, Irving Howe, William Phillips? Would you care to comment on their views? They all feel strongly about their Jewishness. They don't play down their Jewish tradition nor are they embarrassed by it. Maybe they did once – certainly *Partisan Review* did in the old days. Only recently, they seem to be publishing articles of Jewish interest.

MS: Well, as for Neo-conservative movement, that is a very interesting development; that the fundamental position of the Jew in the last many years has been from the left. Now, they have some from the right. These are not Capitalist Jews protecting economic interests, they were considered to be anti-Semites. The most interesting thing that I see about them is that they are on the right. The other thing about them is that they are not assimilationists. I would not say that they are always such fervent Jews but they are certainly not assimilationists. They're not attracted to Christianity, they are not attracted to conversion to Christianity to their children or get Jewish education to their children or get indoctrination to their children that they are Jewish. You have a combination of people on the right which is a new stance, at the same time, rightists who are in favour of Jewish identity. Maybe they are not assimilationists – that's better way of putting it. To me, this is a novel position which you wouldn't find in Europe, you wouldn't find it in Germany. But you do find it in the United States. Perhaps, it can exist in the United States because the right, at the moment, is not inevitably anti-Semitic. If the right were the old right of Europe where there is anti-Semitism in the right, that's the reason why Jews could not be with the right because to be with the right is to ally with anti-Semitism. We know also that left is sometimes not so friendly to the Jews and had reservations about Jews. But Jews are overlooked on the left. But they didn't know that they were overlooked on the right because it was obvious and forthright and so on. So, it probably comes from the fact that there is a section of the right, which, you might say, is non-anti-Semitic. They are conservative, but they are not conservative in the sense of the French right. So, that right they can abide, that right they can live with and, in a certain sense, that right they are popular with because some of them are significant intellectuals on the right and they are playing an important role on the right. So, that's the set up that we have and it is something that one wouldn't have expected, say, in the thirties or forties when it was on the left, Jewish intellectuals were on the left and anybody who was not on the left was out of it. He did not just amount to anything. And Jews on the right in the thirties and forties – it was something unheard of. The only right you came across were the anti-New Dealers because they were protecting their economic interests, big business and so on. Even those Jews were few in number.

* * *

DV: When we met last time we talked about so many things. But we did not have time to touch up on Jewish intellectual positions. Obviously, they represent many ideologies and schools of thought – political, cultural and otherwise. Neo-conservatism, New Left, liberal – and ever so many with different shades of emphasis. Norman Podhoretz, William Phillips, Martin Peretz, Nathan Glazer, Daniel Bell and many more agree on some issues and probably disagree a great deal. *Commentary, Dissent, Nation* and these days *Tikkun* – these intellectual magazines have their own political agenda. What do you have to say about these people, and especially about Podhoretz and Irving Krystol?

MS: Let me put it this way. Perhaps the most interesting are the people on the left because, as you may well know, Jews on the left are a significant force. As Nathan Glazer made this observation long ago, that most Communists are not Jewish but most Jews are Communists, which I think is quite an accurate one. It is a little hard to estimate because the left-wing movements have changed completely in their figuration and Communist party is not a significant force. Trotskytes are – I don't know much about them now. I knew them when they were significant force thirty, forty years ago. They played a certain role. I don't think they are playing a certain role now. Trotskytes, I think, have a little magazine but it doesn't really amount to much than it used to be. So it appears to me that this tremendous activity of the Jews in the left-wing movement has disappeared. Left-wing movements are not what they were. They don't play the kind of role they once did in earlier period. It is quite a scéne to see Jews absent in left-wing movements and they do not seem to depend on Jews in America either to get power, intellectual status or whatever. The conservatism, the changes in conservatism and the Jewish input there catches everybody's eye. My eye catches almost the opposite.

DV: What are the reasons for the rise of conservative trend in America?

MS: Here you have to be an expert in History of American Communism which I am not. The Nazi-Soviet Pact did shake up the Jewish Communists and there were defections at that time. The individuals who felt that if that was the attitude of the Soviets, there wouldn't be Communists any more. The Russians have always been antagonists of Nazis, here they make a pact with the Nazis. That was one aspect of it. Then there was doctor's plot and other events in Soviet life which could be called anti-Semitic. I would call them anti-Semitic. I would not know if the Jewish Communist would call them anti-Semitic. But they were clearly anti-Semitic. The question is, what impact it would have on Jewish Communists particularly in the United States. Did they rationalize some of these things? Did the doctors merely happen to be Jews? Another theory is that the attitude of the Soviet Union towards Jews leaving the Soviet Union and the restrictions imposed on them. I don't think it would make any impact. But if you look at the situation, Jews were the only people who were let out at all in great numbers. Other Russians could not get out. Yet another theory is that the Russian attitude toward Israel which is hostile. They also get other Communist countries to be anti-Israel. And then there is blatant pro-Israel sentiment even Jewish Communists have because of their Jewish identity. Therefore, they could not look upon Israel as expendable as Russians looked upon it. Communists were anti-Israel, democrats pro-Israel.

DV: Why are Jews attracted to Marxism? Do they view it as an expression of messianic vision?

MS: That's one theory. This goes back to one hundred and fifty or two hundred years ago – almost before Marx.

DV: Some of the most important Marxists happen to be Jews. Marx himself was a rabbi's son. George Lukacs, Lucien Goldman, Leon Trotsky, Arthur Koestler and many others in this country. There must be an explanation for such a relationship.

MS: There has been a great deal of writing on that. There has been a great deal of writing on why Jews are in psychiatry and Marxism. In both these cases, the founder is Jewish. I would certainly put an emphasis on the theory that Jews are marginal to society and actually a history of pariah people. Marxism gave relief to the Jews for the first time, a status in the society, membership in the society. Even in the lands where they should be accepted or given citizenship, Jewish position is one of inferiority. That history of pariah people was there. Marxism would rip that out. In other words, Marxism would rip out the entire history of the Jew in Western society and start a new black page. All that had gone before would be destroyed or torn out. There would be a new page, a fresh page. All of these religious attitudes would be destroyed because the religion would be destroyed. All from the history of pogroms and persecution would be destroyed and medieval history also would be destroyed. A new page of civilization would start out and the Jews would be equal. In fact the Jew would be little superior because he would be the intellectual elite. If you ask any Jew, he would certainly know that Marx had Jewish background and so did Trotsky. So, I would not look up on it as much more of a result of the position of the Jew in society as the Jewish desire to change that position radically. Now the other theory is humanitarian theory that you have outlined, Jewish desire to help the other people, Jewish desire to help the proletariat, Jewish desire to help the underdog and so on. I would say the Jew is the underdog and he is helping himself.

DV: At the same time, he is helping others too.

MS: There is no question about that. There's strong humanitarian appeal here. I wouldn't deny that. But I would say that if there wasn't a self-protection or self-change in the Jewish position, it would not have assumed the proportion where capitalist Jew gave rise to Communist children. The progenitors of these left-wing children are conservatives, part of the establishment which presumably should not happen.

Normally the children should go on in their parent's ways and assume their business or whatever. My impression is that the things have changed. They have changed in the last twenty or twenty-five years on the line of the Jew being liberal particularly in racial terms. Two young Jews who were killed in Mississippi, which was celebrated incidentally with Martin Luther King's anniversary two weeks or three weeks ago, which brought back the public consciousness – apparently there's a movie now, *Mississippi Burning* (Alan Parker). You saw that movie?

DV: Yes, I did. In Chicago.

MS: Did they use the original names of the Jewish kids? What are their names in the movie?

DV: Goodman and Schwerner, I think. In fact, the KKK fanatics stop their car somewhere far away from the town at midnight and talk to these civil rights students from the north. One of them says, "You nigger-loving Jew boy," and later he kills them – all of them, a black kid included.

MS: That (the position of the Jewish youth) is typical of the West Side New York upper class Jewry of liberal variety. They are rebelling against their parents, as I understand; but they are carrying it further what their parents want them to carry. The older Communist input fifty or forty years ago seems to have in recent times become the input of liberal cause, the favourite cause being the racial cause. It's not remaking the world but resisting the racial group which has been looked upon as, to use Shakespeare's expression, "slings and arrows of outrageous fortune." So, what you do is assist them in their desire for equality. So, these people are not Marxist, they are not Trotskytes, they are liberal-left of some kind, rather vague about their politics. They want to make a better world. It's localized politics having to do with the American situation, particularly the racial situation. Now, there has been some suggestion that the people of this sort have been awakened by the Chicago convention – how many years ago was that? – twelve years ago, fourteen years ago. The blacks took over and invited the whites to get out and stressed that they have self-emancipation and let the Jews worry about their problems. They are also anti-Israel, and all of these things.

DV: Traditionally the Jews and blacks have common interests in this country. Jews generally supported the black causes. In the recent years, it appears to have broken down. The blacks on their part – one quickly remembers Louis Farrakhan, Steve Cokely, Jesse Jackson and probably many more—tend to take positions that sometimes hurt Jewish interests, indulge in a rhetoric that would be called anti-Jewish, if not anti-Semitic. But why such a change at all?

MS: I would speculate that every group confronted with problems after certain life chooses self-emancipation than the emancipation by the others. Jews did the same.

DV: But then they have strong traditions to fall back on both for inspiration and sustenance. And they are proud of their heritage. I don't think the blacks have a comparable advantage.

MS: Slavery gives them the feeling that probably it's time for them to emancipate themselves, not wait on the whites' good faith and good feeling. The only emancipation is the self-emancipation which they win for themselves. The only emancipation which is good for them is the one thing they achieve for themselves. The other emancipation is the one coming from the master to the slave, even if they are Schwerner and Goodman because they are the masters and you take over yourself the leadership of your own group. And even Martin Luther King, you know—nowhite man is allowed in the black emancipatory movement. Part of it is that Jews were more active and supportive. So, what you do is that you bite the hand that feeds you. If the group is against, in a sense, you can do business with them. If the group is your friends, they are your enemies because it is your friends who want to emancipate you. So, get rid of the people who would take over the leadership of your group. They may be supporting in good faith but your manhood is hurt by their taking over and becoming the leaders of your group. Schwerner and Goodman have the best of intentions but in their point of view the worst of intentions. You don't want assistance from the people who are not of your group.

DV: Isn't that utopian? What happened after all these movements? Not much of change in the lives of the black people. They still live in the ghettoes. Not many black kids go to colleges or universities. I don't see too many black students in American universities. The only black students I see on the campuses generally stick together and dropout rate is very high.

MS: You could say that position of the blacks is not so terrible in the U.S. If you compare the black position in America with the position of the blacks in South Africa or in any other African country, the blacks are doing comparatively well and their income is still under whites' and their education level is still under whites' but – I don't know if you have heard the sports arguments these days.

DV: Well, I have. Most of them are blacks. They get admission in academic institutions on priority basis.

MS: Well, they are the basketball players of the United States. And this new thing would diminish that really. There are protests but they seem to have won a reconsideration which would mean that that would change the marks and that one would get admission in order to play basketball.

DV: On their part, it seems to me, that the Jewish writers have reflected a sympathetic portrayal of the blacks within, of course, the aesthetic dimension. One finds this significantly in, for instance, Edward Lewis Wallant's *The Pawnbroker* and certainly in the novels of E.L. Doctorow, Bernard Malamud – to name just a few.

MS: To the black, it doesn't mean anything. Jewish writers have a sense of guilt because the situation in America is not the ideal norms we espouse. It is hard to think of a Jewish writer who has written a book of deprecating images of blacks. Certainly I don't know any one who has written all about blacks. Even in those books where the presence of blacks is incidental, that incidental portrayal is generally sympathetic. I don't think it affects black psychology particularly the blacks who are part of the current black thinking, who are active politically, certainly Mr. Jesse Jackson is not touched by it at all. As I say, I would put it obviously, the more sympathetic one is, the more one is thought of hostile to black cause. It's a crazy kind of a thing or not as in the black interests or denying the black manhood. In other words, the black would say, "get off my back, I don't want you helping me, I don't want your sympathy and I don't want anything that you do for me."

DV: I think the black priorities have also changed a great deal. In Martin Luther King's time, he was still talking about "I have a dream" which is certainly integration, being part of the American mainstream where the black and white share a common table. Now, obviously it is "the black is beautiful" story affirming, what they call the Afro-American identity. Consequently, and due to many things that had happened over the years, the black man would not or even possibly does not want to make a distinction between the white man and the Jew who happens to be white too however sympathetic or supportive he is. I think it is Jonathan Kauffman, the Pulitzer winning journalist of the *Boston*

Globe who recently has tried to reestablish the context between the blacks and the Jews in his book *The Broken Alliance*.

MS: I think it is so typical of the Jews.

DV: Coming to the young Jewish writers today, how much of Jewish sensibility do they reflect in their works? Obviously the situation has changed now. There was a time when the children of the Yiddish-speaking Jewish immigrants began to write novels, there was a protest from the gentile writers that these children with immigrant background would "spoil" the English language. Now, the young Jews consciously celebrate their Jewish heritage and certainly they are not ashamed of it as it was the case at the turn of the century or the early part of this century. With these changes in mind, how do you view the prospects of Jewish writing in America?

MS: There has been a lot of middle-brow novel and it seems to me that lot of novels of Jewish themes are being produced today. These novels are usually sympathetic, usually the grandfather comes over from Russia or the grandmother comes over from the Old Country and establishes a dynasty, dynastic novels which are middle-brow or lower middle-brow, some of them. They are generally about what happens to the first, second or third generation. The first generation is generally the good generation, the second is little crazy—this one went into drugs, this one went into sex, this one into politics, they seem to do their own thing. Their thing is not, by the way, done for the benefit of the family, is done for their own individual desires. So families begin to split apart because there is no unifying principle. One may go to Israel, by the way. Usually in these novels, the deviant goes to Israel. I don't know how important they are, whether they amount to anything at all.

DV: How important is the Jewish heritage for these writers?

MS: I am not sure whether these novels live or not. There are books that live for three years or they don't live at all. There are tens of thousands of books published in the U.S. every year. If you go into the average book store, you find two thousand books or three thousand books. The kind of books people may not read, much less popular. There are these new writers, most of them don't seem to me to be the most distinguished people. The older group has established a style of their own. Philip Roth is probably the youngest of the older group. It also gives rise to anti-Semitism or hostility because they are such leading people on the literary scene. The older group is exciting, they can go so long.

But the question is whether there is a younger group to replace it. One could see Bellow's ability when he wrote the *Dangling Man*. On the Jewish scene older writers had a Jewish perspective even though it's not primary to them, even though they frequently denied it. But they were so tied up with it, it was part of their culture. Whether or not they are conscious of it or proud of it, it was there. And the younger ones do not have such an immigrant culture. They had gone to fancy schools or universities that the older group could not even think of. My own feeling is that the younger group, unless they are conscious of it or seek to achieve Jewish identity, will not have the Jewish identity that the older group did. For the older group it was there, it was thrust upon them. Some of them were conscious of it, they even protested against it but it was there. But for the younger group it was not there, they had to seek to achieve it because they don't have that kind of intimate reaction that happens as a result of contact with immigrant life. This happened in (Alfred) Kazin's life. He doesn't come from a particularly practising Jewish family. His father did not want his *bar mitzvah* but his mother wanted. His mother seduced his father into finally accepting her view. So, he was sent to a third class Hebrew teacher for four months for his training – a very marginal character. But he was raised in Brownsville. Of course, he had a tremendous antenna, he is out all the time – very perceptive. If I were teaching the immigrant Jewish neighbourhood, I could use his book *A Walker in the City*. He had the antenna, he is getting the right signals all the time. So, he could interpret everything correctly.

DV: Do you think there is a subtle type of anti-Semitism in this country? As I come into contact with pop culture, cinema, graffiti, and talk radio, I get the feeling that it is very much there in some form or the other.

MS: It is very difficult to estimate because it is so subtle, because it is so covered over. There is so much on the other side. They say there is anti-Semitism at Columbia University. The President of Princeton is Jewish. A Jew is offered the Presidency of Yale University but he didn't even take it. He said, "I am not even interested in it." That's a *chuzpah*. You have to have the nerve. The job of the President of American University is not scholarship but money. It may well be eighty five percent of the trustees are gentiles. They may think that the Jew and money are intimately connected and the Jew may be able to raise money from the poor innocent gentiles whereas gentile cannot do it because he is just clean. The Jew is a Shylock and he can do all the manipulation. This Yale has an interesting fact because Yale has lost hundreds of millions of dollars in its endowments because it decided to go into the stock market some years ago. To speculate, most universities don't do that but Yale thought they were smart to get the right stocks. Stock market went down. They also lost millions of dollars. How are they going to replace that? This is my interpretation. They picked upon a Jew to replace the money. The Jew is smart enough to say that." So, the Jewish academic turned them down. It is hard to say there is anti-Semitism. The President of Du Pont, for number of years, was a Jew for the first time or the second member who is not a member of Du Pont family. You can find all sorts of Presidents of this corporation or that corporation. There are a lot of gentile corporations, there are Jewish owned corporations. I am talking about those which are not. So, all of these things go on. And you say anti-Semitism, where is it? There is a Jewish President at Columbia University, you say there is anti-Semitism in American academia. Yes, the President of Dartmonth is Jewish. So, what I am saying to you is that evidence on the face of it is that anti-Semitism is a dead issue. Jews have achieved this, Jews have achieved that. How can there be anti-Semitism in the institutions dominated by Jews or Jewish President? I feel there is more anti-Semitism than it appears on the surface. And the Jew feels that he has to suffer. When the things are good, he can't just go along with it. So, he would say that all of these things are bad. If he can't see it on the surface, it must be under the surface. Why can't he say if it is not on the surface, it doesn't exist? But I would claim that, say, just the academia of which I know something about, there are problems – let us put it that way. Some of these problems are individual, individuals who hate other individuals or dislike other individuals. There are persons who dislike one Jew against one gentile. I would claim that it is deeper and more pervasive than that. I would even claim that when the Jew is President of, say, Du Pont, it doesn't mean that there is no anti-Semitism in Du Pont. If you want to be more sophisticated than that, the theory I have suggested with Yale, they chose a Jew because sometimes anti-Semitic feelings push them into choosing a Jew, because they have dirty job to do, they want the Jew to do it. Just because the Jew is appointed here or appointed there, does not convince me that the picture is clean and fine. I feel there is more continuity with the past than we give credit for and that you cannot even expect that there is discontinuity with the past because people don't act discontinuously; there is some continuity in their lives. Therefore, it makes more sense to assume continuity than discontinuity. The thing here is to find continuity. It's not easy because there are federal laws against discrimination. We also have laws against the discrimination of old people. That doesn't mean there is no discrimination in the industries against people who are above fifty or more. There is a good deal of it. But how do you prove it? How do you get people to verbalize it? So, a good deal of discrimination would be under colours. They say, he doesn't know how to use this kind of computer or that – all of which is correct. Your feeling is that he doesn't bother sending him to retain him because he has twelve or more years for retirement. So, all my instincts tell me to look for discrimination, all my instincts tell me to look for anti-Semitism, all my instincts tell me that there is more anti-Semitism than it is on the surface.

DV: Now, the attitude of American intellectuals towards Israel. I think it has changed a great deal over the years, from support to criticism. You have Edward Said on the one hand and on the other hand, intellectuals of the liberal or liberal-left persuasion are vehement in their criticism against Israel, and interestingly some of the prominent critics are Jews themselves. It's not surprising to me because Marx himself wrote "World Without Jews" which is quoted conveniently by the anti-Semites living especially in Communist regimes. The Frankfurt School philosophers gave a different twist altogether to anti-Semitism in Dialectic of Enlightenment written by Adorno and Horkheimer. One also finds Israel-bashing in the newspapers . . .

MS: Number one, I don't think Said is a good example. He is an Arab. He is the president of the American-Arab federation or something. He is an intellectual, a college professor who took leadership of the Arab community in the United States. I would expect some one to do that.

DV: Gore Vidal?

MS: Gore Vidal's is a different story. He is not an Arab. First of all, I think Jews are surprised when they saw an Arab in academia and who is a loyal Arab in the sense that Arab is loyal to Arab causes. We should expect that to happen. Why shouldn't that happen? So that doesn't surprise me at all. It's part of the course – as the expression has it. Now, the most significant question is whether Jews who are disaffected by Israel are hostile to Israel. I think you are right in suggesting that in the last few years there has been more of that than ever before. And I think it is true that what has happened in Israel and the Middle East does not make the academic happy. It's not the world the academic appreciates and likes. The older approach did make the academic happy in a certain sense. The academia were not against Israel but they were indifferent to Israel. Those who were not were in love with Israel because Israel has Kibbutz. Books on the Kibbutz are being produced everyday or every other day. Articles are produced and people would go to the Kibbutz staying a day or two or months – and frequently writing about them. That was considered to be a great thing, Israel's contribution to human cooperation and to the betterment of humanity. Now in the last few years the Kibbutz scene has gone out – I mean they haven't diminished. But the emphasis is, the problems have moved away, or moved in a different direction – hostility, shooting and fighting, all things which academics are not very attracted to.

DV: They seem to judge Israel living in this country, sitting in their secure apartments and enjoying comforts . . .

MS: That's another story. Those who have left Israel and come here, that's another story. That may complicate the story. The story of Israel and its geopolitical relationship with Arab world which is manifested in the West Bank that has turned off the Jews so much. The other thing is of course the influence of the rabbinate in Israel, very conservative and orthodox, and the issues like who is a Jew and the whole approach to marriage and divorce. All of which strikes the American academics the worst kind of conservatism, the manifestation of the worst kind of clericalism. Here the Church and the State are like this. The third reason is, of course, social-political reason which in the last few years is dominated by Likud, the conservative party, which has a strong militaristic and aggressive kind of thing and not the Labour Party which the academics identify with, which is academic in its orientation. These things have worked against Israel. In other words, it isn't the kind academics are happy with. So, they are anti-Israel, they moved away from Israel in a peculiar way. They moved away from Israel for understandable reasons. Sincere identification with Israel, in majority of them, is never deep and strong, naming that Israel is right or wrong, or that Israel is so important to me that I'll continue with my pro-Israel stance despite it all. Since they don't have any despite-it-all view, I have to disagree with Israel. There is plenty to disagree with Israel in the last ten years, I would say. That's how I would look upon.

DV: One hears about Israel in American newspapers every other day, if not every day – often presenting the disturbing side of Israeli political scene or Israel's handling of the *Intifada*. Do you think that the American Press is over-sensitive to the happenings in Israel? Or are they merely publishing what sells in this country? Well, all countries have problems, India, USSR, South Africa – practically any country including the United States.

MS: India gets some place in the American Press, where there is a stealing of money, or money is skiffed off. They say that happened in India. In most cases, there wouldn't be anything. Most American newspapers are not internationally oriented.

DV: My point is, all countries have problems. Why should the American mass media be sensitive to the Israeli scene alone?

MS: I think you are right. I would say that the American mass media is fascinated with the Jews. In a way it is very surprising and sometimes even frightening. Any item that has to do with the Jew – of course Israel is quintessentially Jewish – so you say yourself, "India? Why aren't they interested in Japan? All of these are larger countries. Why Israel?" Alright it has a more strategic location than, say, Indonesia. I am not sure about that. But it does seem to be a fascination and involvement with Jewish things. It's not only hostility. For one reason or the other, the fascination with the Jew is because the country is basically Christian. Who are the anti-Christian? Well, they are the Jews. They are in dialogue with the Christian. So, you cannot pride the American newspaper without the items of Israel. There are some American newspapers who carry it further in being anti-Israel. The *Boston Globe* is a very good case in point. There is seldom a day that goes by without something that I would interpret as anti-Israel in the *Boston Globe*. I have known people who have discontinued their subscriptions to the *Boston Globe* because of that, I haven't done so. What you are going to get is that news items about Israel which are not appropriate. They should have something about India because it would have been more appropriate than Israel. Some who are involved in anti-Semitism would pick up hostile things about Israel. I feel that Jews have to take this. First of all, many Jews are not unhappy with this although I know some Jews who say that if we get less publicity, we would be better off. We are normal people. It would be appropriate if there is an article about Israel once in a month or so and articles about India every other day. Don't do us favour by giving us all the publicity. There are some Jews who feel that if we don't have this publicity, we are nobody. But I think the general feeling is that we can live without this publicity. For better or worse, the publicity is going to be there because the Christian world is not going to lose interest or fascination with the Jews. Tomorrow it's going to be war for better or worse.

DV: There are so many denominations of Judaism: Conservative, Reform and Orthodox. Where do they stand at the moment?

MS: The movement that's still alive is the Orthodox Judaism. Everybody expected the Orthodox Judaism to be dead by this time. The Orthodox Judaism is not only not dead, it has become more aggressive. It was a tremendous achievement. Orthodox Judaism was immigrant life, it would also die, some expected, when immigrant life died. But it didn't die when immigrant died. As for Reform and Conservative, nothing exciting is happening. Both of them have made extensive modifications and changes particularly the introduction of women members as the rabbis, which the Reform had introduced quite some years ago, done much more recently by the Conservative group. The Refórm group is composed of two different strata. The one is convinced Reform Jews and the other Jews who call themselves and belong to a Reform Temple because the Reform asks the least of them in terms of observance, holidays and Kosher food. So, the Reform has this peculiar set up with mainstream Reform Jews and those who belong to it because it is the least demanding. The Conservative movement thought that it would triumph over everybody because it would attract those from Orthodoxy, those who could no longer abide orthodoxy, get those from Reform who want to be part of the mainstream and who wouldn't like to assimilate. So, the Reform would be diminished to a marginal group. For a while that seemed to be the case. Conservative Judaism was growing more quickly than any other group. Orthodox Judaism thirty, forty or fifty years ago was diminishing and those people were going to Conservative Judaism.

DV: What about the Reconstructionist Movement of Mordecai Kaplan?

MS: One would talk days about it. But the Reconstructionist movement, all couldn't agree with whether it is a movement or not. It was started by an intellectual, Mordecai Kaplan. That's very bad. It never had the structure to organize it and give it solidity. It should be a school of thought. It should not have the approach of the other movements because it's an intellectual creation. People can learn from Reconstruction. After forty or fifty years, that could no longer think either, it had to become a movement or die. They established a seminary in Philadelphia, established an organization of a congregation. There is Reconstructionist rabbinical scholarship which has a fifty or seventy-five positions. But it is a small movement. It never replaced Conservative, Reform or Orthodox. Reform and Conservative don't think that it is a competitor at all. So, it has remained rather as an exotic plant. The main group is Reform, Conservative, Orthodox. They all differ in that they all have left-wing, right-wing or centre-wing. When you are talking about Reform, you are talking about an ideological cohesion. You are talking about a certain rainbow.

David Perkins

DV: What is happening to the teaching of literature now? Theory has become fashionable, acceptable to many people and some are writing dissertations in this area and others seeking tenures on these intellectual priorities. How do you view all this? What do you think about the present trends in English Departments?

DP: Well, when I entered the profession, which was about thirty years ago, I guess, there were different modes of criticism represented in university teaching of literature. For example, positivistic literary history, New Criticism, intellectual history, a sort of humanism in the vein of Lionel Trilling. But still, there was pretty much of a consensus too; that is to say there was consensus about which authors were important and which ones were not. There was something of a consensus about what was acceptable as literary criticism and what was not. And the annual convention of the Modern Language Association had far fewer different sections and sessions than now exist; and what has happened since then and really since the 1960s has been a great increase in the number of modes of criticism and, at the same time, a sort of politicization of the profession whereby add hands to a certain mode of criticism; also, form a political party, supporting each other and often quite intolerant towards other ways of talking about literature and, therefore, a decreasing ability of critics of different persuasions or schools to communicate meaningfully with each other. If you are in an order of deconstruction, you make an altogether different series of assumptions about literature than if you are a literary historian or a textual critic and the assumptions that these various modes of criticism have to make in order to practise certain amount of criticism are as mutually inconsistent. So, there is a greater diversity in most criticism and a decreasing power of communicating between them and a greater politicization of the critical scene. And my feeling is that it makes it all, makes being a scholar and critic in the field of English at the present time, more interesting than it used to be.

DV: In fact, Terry Eagleton says that New Criticism itself has a framework of politics.

DP: Yes, he thinks that. I was not very conscious of New Criticism as having a political dimension thirty years ago. It was something I taught myself in graduate school because my teachers were not themselves New Critics and it seemed to me just a right way to study poems. I never thought it was very applicable to drama or to fiction. And, I guess, that's the definition of an ideology I simply accepted it as natural and right and didn't think of it as involving political choice at all.

DV: What is the consequence of deconstruction or, if you will, post-structuralism?

DP: I think in practice in the U.S., most deconstructive criticism is in fact a very close scrutinizing of texts with an emphasis on what is problematic about them; and also, to point out the difficulty of coming to any kind of stable interpretation of a text and, therefore, it's one of many things that makes the whole problem of reading and of interpretation much more problematic than it used to seem. And I think, that is its main intellectual impact. I think that as a sort of political movement, it is waning and that we won't hear so much about it in the future.

DV: For some reason, these movements immediately catch on in American academia. I don't think that it's so popular in Europe. What do you think is the reason?

DP: I think that is a very complicated question and, in order to answer it, you'd have to take a lot things into account at the same time. If you look at the cultural history of the U.S., you will find that Americans throughout their history, at least intellectual Americans, have been very receptive to the importing of ideas and philosophies from Europe. And, of course, the particular source was Germany and, in fact, many American universities are modelled on German universities or the model of German university was engrafted on all those sorts of collegiate English structure; but also radical intellectual movements in the U.S. such as Marxism have been brought from Europe. And in a certain way deconstruction or post-structuralism is simply another example of the permeability of American intellectual life to ideas from abroad and particularly from Europe. I think that has to do with certain feelings in American national life or the psychology of Americans, on the one hand, its openness; and, on the other, it expresses also, I think, certain insecurity—and so, that's one thing.

Then I think that there's a sociological, structural reason and that is that as Ph.Ds in English are set up, you have to write something new and you have to write something new about texts about which a great deal has already been written. So, it is necessary to approach them from some new intellectual perspective and so I think the mere need of finding Ph.D. subjects creates a certain constant revolution of fashion that certain set of ideas arrives, permits a great many Ph.D. theses to be written; and once its service in that respect is exhausted it gives way to something else. Then I think that in the case specifically of deconstruction, after one has read certain number of deconstructive essays, they become a little monotonous; that is to say, the results become predictable. One is going to find that the text is, the meaning of the text is, indeterminate and, after a while, it's no longer interesting. So, I think that the sort of trendiness that you are talking about in the intellectual life of English Department is related to all those factors.

DV: What do you think about Paul de Man controversy? Some seem to believe that the theory he championed would help him to conceal his past.

DP: But I think that it's mere speculation and we can never know if that is true and I don't myself think it is proper to evaluate ideas by the biography of the person who holds the ideas. I think it's an old principle of logic that the truth of the statement has no relation to the motivation for making the statement. You judge the truth by whatever criteria you use to judge truth in your philosophy. And then there's the question whether your statement is true is entirely different and separable and the question of why a person did make that particular statement.

DV: I have seen articles about Wyndham Lewis, Ezra Pound and Eliot and their peculiar anti-Semitism. Are you saying that personal morality should be separated from their works?

DP: I don't wish to say that personal morality is not important. There are any number of writers who have led lives we might wish to condemn from the moral point of view but that still doesn't mean they weren't good writers.

DV: My question is whether the aesthetic consideration of a text has anything to do with the authorial moral situation at all?

DP: When one reads texts, one makes moral judgements as to the content of a text. But that the life of the author is separable; that is to say, when

I read "The Wasteland," Eliot's poem, I encounter a certain vision of the world and I don't think it's possible in reading to separate an aesthetic judgement from a moral judgement; from a judgement of the truth of what has been presented to me I think that one makes holistic judgements. But I think that what one is reacting to is the poem, not to the life of the creator of the poem. So when Ezra Pound might or might not be in his own person a very condemnable person, that doesn't say anything about the moral quality of the cantos. I deplore anti-Semitism and yet it would be perfectly possible for me to like the cantos if there was no anti-Semitism in the cantos. But if I encounter anti-Semitism in the cantos that would trouble me very much.

DV: What should be the province of literary criticism? I am asking this question because one finds studies like "The Image of Jew in American Literature." Such studies appear to be more sociological than literary.

DP: Well, I suppose, I might say I would call it literary scholarship if it is not literary criticism. It is at least literary scholarship; it helps you to understand how a novel came to be, what it is with reference to a particular theme; or if it points out to you something of a novel which you wouldn't have seen otherwise. It seems to be the legitimate thing to do, legitimate sort of study to be made in connection with literature. It's not interpretive but it's something which is informing you about the context in which the book is written; and, therefore, it helps you perhaps to understand certain features of it. I think the use of a lot of historical scholarship in literature is to make literature more apprehensible.

DV: Now coming to critical theories, how does a teacher come to terms with the critical theories and still practise meaningfully the profession of teaching? And what should be his priorities in the teaching of literature?

DP: Well, that's a difficult question. I think that perhaps it's possible that in different institutions, a teacher has different responsibilities, depending on what's expected to that particular institution. As Edmund Burke said in one of his speeches that the situation of a man as a preceptor is his duty. I think that in Harvard which is an—

DV: Traditionally, Harvard is quite conservative, isn't it?

DP: Somewhat though, less so now than it used to be. In any case, we have a lot of graduate students and it's a research institution and we are training people who are themselves going to be teachers and scholars.

DP: Somewhat though, less so now than it used to be. In any case, we have a lot of graduate students and it's a research institution and we are training people who are themselves going to be teachers and scholars. I think I have a responsibility to be familiar with all the different discourses about literature that are current at the present time so that I can direct students in such a way that I can help them to follow out their own interests and discover their mode of criticism they want to practise, whatever it may be. Then, of course, I also have an obligation to do research in writing myself and that couldn't necessarily be of some relatively specialized kind of theory; and then also, have an obligation to teach undergraduate students. And I think I cannot very often or very easily carry my research interests into my undergraduate teaching. So, for undergraduates, I have to teach in some way that will give them a large amount of necessary information and try to make them simply respond to and enjoy whatever it is that we are reading and think that the vehicle of undergraduate teaching is basically commentary. You just take a text and comment on it and exhibit yourself reacting to it. So, it's quite different from the way you teach graduate students as from what is going on when you are writing a paper or doing research. There is a lot of tension because what goes on in the classroom with undergraduates does not have much relation to what goes on in the library when I am being a researcher and a critic so that I think that one is somewhat divided in one's professional activities.

DV: But surely you have your own perception, priorities and assumptions of literature. How do you view them in the context of the recent theories?

DP: I have my own assumptions, my own mode of criticism which I practise. But the presence of so many other quite different modes of criticism that other people are practising makes me more subconscious about my own and make me more likely to examine my own premises. Whereas there is a great deal of controversy at the present time between different schools of criticism, the controversy is very heavy because it makes everyone more reflective about what they are doing themselves, makes them examine, makes them more likely to detest it, question it. I read literary history of modern poetry and I am now writing a book called *Is Literary History Possible*? in which I examine, write about and try to think my way through the moments in hand in the process of writing history. And I asked myself if the solutions to these dilemmas of literary historians have intellectual legitimacy. So, I'm really questioning that assumption like why have I been writing the history of modern poetry? And, of course, while writing it I was also questioning what I was doing. But I don't think that was the moment to engage in theoretical discussion of literary history. But I don't think I would be so sensitive to the fact that the assumptions are questionable while I am not living in a world in which there are many schools of literary criticism so that any one in any school feels challenged by the other school that are also present. If you write literary history, you have to assume certain things. You have to assume that there are authors, you have to assume that literature—you have to assume that authors, texts can mean, be divided into groups so that you can speak of schools, movements, periods, traditions; and in doing so, say something meaningful. If you can't speak of Romanticism or the Romantic Age or the Victorian novel or modernism and in using those terms be saying something meaningful, you really can't write literary history. Because history is by definition a record of the collective activity; and so, a literary historian is always talking about the doings of the super-personal entities such as, for modern poetry, imagism—that was a movement of modern poets—or symbolism going to have intellectual legitimacy, if they don't really refer to anything that has some kind of reality, then you can't do without history but the legitimacy of such terms can be questioned and is very much questioned within certain schools of criticism.

DV: Don't you think there is so much of intellectualization in literary discourse these days? First of all, it makes a complicated reading especially deconstruction and secondly, one wonders sometimes if it is relevant at all in the appreciation of a work of art? Or is it necessarily providing a new perspective beyond fashionable jargon?

DP: Well, I don't think reading deconstructive essays interferes at all with my enjoyment of poems of literature. I can read just as naively as I ever did when I actually have a poem in front of me. So, I don't think it's doing any harm and I think that there's a philosophical motive behind it that I respect. I think philosophy means the effort to make a true statement. And deconstruction is about the question: is it possible to make meaningful interpretations? And that is a philosophical question which is perfectly legitimate to ask. So, I say that the deconstructionists do their work and it does me no harm and it may be doing me some good. Since they normally look quite close to a text, they often see things that other people may not in them.

DV: Some critics argue that they have some kind of hidden agenda?

DP: Well, I think in many cases they do. But it's very vague what the political agenda may be. If you deconstruct an economical work, one that has been taught to generations of school children and has great authority and respect in the culture and you suddenly show by a deconstructive essay that its meaning is indeterminate, you don't know what it means, can't know what it means and is not possible to determine what it means – that's somewhat a rebellious act. It's a flow against cultural tradition. It has a political meaning. I think the deconstructionists' programme politically is simply anarchist. That is to say, one cannot as a deconstructionist enact anything but one can deconstruct monuments of cultural authority.

DV: I think it is nihilistic, even comparable to that of narcissism.

DP: Well, I wouldn't go that far. I don't think I would call it nihilistic. I think a passion for truth could underlie it though of course that it seems so naive to deconstructionist.

DV: With all the post-structuralists around especially deconstructionists, Marxist criticism suffers a theoretical backlash. What is its status now?

DP: Well, I am not a Marxist but I think that people who aren't Marxists could learn a good deal from Marxism and Marxism interests me most for its contribution to historiography, for its contribution to understanding historical happening and I think all Marxist historiography that I've seen is too simple. And that a really sophisticated historian is not a Marxist, is a more sophisticated historian than a sophisticated Marxist. But, I think that material life and economic factors and class relations certainly have a vital role in the production of an historical alibi and even have a role in the production of literature. And that Marxism illuminates. And so, I think we have a lot to learn from Marxism but I think we are naive to be a Marxist.

DV: From Arnoldian view that literature is criticism of life to various theoretical variations at the present time, we have touched many interesting literary discourses. But is there a way of synthesizing these multiple theories in the context of literary appreciation?

DP: I was saying that I read a lot of separate poetry and there isn't much criticism written about it and if I read a text or a poet whom I greatly enjoyed, whom I am therefore very interested in, I find that I very much want to read criticism; it's just in order to continue to think about the poet, to extend my own stance. So, I think that's a very important function of criticism, and of course when we are talking about Shakespeare or Milton or Wordsworth, then we are talking about writers for whom there's enormous critical tradition. If you are a Miltonist and here you have to read all the criticism that has been written and that continues to pour out on Milton because there's a law of diminishing return you have to bear with you; or that each new item of criticism brings relatively little that you haven't read.

DV: How does one profess literature at the moment? What should be the guiding forces?

DP: Well, everything I said is quite relevant.

DV: Isn't it quite problematic now? Teaching literature?

DP: No, I don't think it is because people are dying to read literature and dying to think about it. They want, they want literature very much; they want to think about it. And so, no, I don't think there's a problem at all. I think literature will continue to be read and taught because there is a demand for it..

DV: In one of your books, you talk about natural response to literature. Is it still possible?

DP: Sure.

DV: If it is possible, is it acceptable to the people who seem to exult in post-structuralism and deconstruction?

DP: I think that those people, when they just sit down and read a book and are not writing a critical essay, read it just in the same way everybody else does. Naively. I was once at a conference at which Hillis Miller gave a talk – he's a deconstructionist and the talk was a deconstruction of a little poem of Wordsworth, the one that begins with "A slumber did her spirit seal," and in his talk, he showed us a deconstructive essay a critic does that you really could not make out the meaning of the poem. It was indeterminate. But at the end of his talk, a woman in audience asked him why the poem was worth talking about in that case, why had he wanted to talk about it at all? And he gave a very naive and a very traditional answer which was that it's a very moving poem about a girl who has died. So, I think that's paradigmatic. That deconstructionists read naively just like anybody else does and it's only when they write critical essays in the deconstructive mode, that they are deconstructed.

DV: What is the role of a teacher of literature in a society?

DP: I think their role as professors of literature is basically to keep the past alive, keep the literary past alive, to be an institution through which the necessary mediation of the past with the present is carried out.

DV: Well, you have written useful books on poetry. I am interested in Jewish poetry. Now, there is a critic who says that there is no such thing called Jewish poetry; there may be poetry written by Jews. Do you think there is something called Jewish sensibility or do you go along with the critic I had mentioned?

DP: Well, no, I don't think there is a Jewish sensibility or black sensibility but I think there's a persistent attempt to invent one.

DV: Who are the important poets in America at present?

DP: I think the most important poets living are James Merryl and John Ashberry and A.R. Ammons.

DV: Does Allen Ginsberg have any reputation to speak of?

DP: Well, yes, he does. He has a very high reputation and historically was a great influence on American poetry in the 1960s. I don't regard him as such an important poet. I think he will be remembered because he did have a large historical influence on other poets but I don't think his poetry is all that good.

DV: What do you think about popular literature?

DP: I think it's not good literature; it's not, to me, important as literature but it could be very important to study it as manifestation of popular culture, what symbols are moving the people, in the country where you live. I think it is very important to understand that, understand them. So, it should be studied. But it is cultural studies. It isn't the study of literature in my opinion.

DV: In other words, it's merely a matter of sociological interest.

DP: Yes.

DV: Nothing beyond that.

DP: In my opinion.

DV: Do you think the critics like Trilling, Leavis and Eliot demand any audience now? Do you think they still have any influence?

DP: No, I don't think they are much read. Trilling, I don't think, is any more an influence. Leavis, I don't think, is any more an influence. People still read Eliot. But I think they read him, his criticism primarily in connection with his own poetry, in order to understand his own poetry. I don't think it is a force in criticism at the present time.

DV: Is this trend healthy?

DP: Well, he was a very good critic. I think Eliot is one of the best, probably the best critic of poetry to write in the twentieth century. But it's like reading Samuel Johnson or Coleridge. That's very good criticism, but it's not forming people's minds in a strong way at the present time. Eliot is not creating disciples, there's not an Eliot school of criticism, there are lot of, lot of people who are disciples of Eliot's criticism.

DV: Do you think they'll re-emerge?

DP: I don't think they'll re-emerge.

DV: Because I feel that deconstructionism has slowly fallen into disrepute, out of fashion in academia. If this is a fact, do you think the old schools of criticism and the critics will re-emerge and get accepted as major influence once again.

DP: I don't think so.

DV: Coming to Harold Bloom and his theory of misreading or misprision. Do you think it is tenable in the analysis of poetry?

DP: Well, I think that Bloom, so far he is not just a commentator. He has written lot of essays, some of them are really good, which are simply commentary on a particular poetic text. In so far as he is a theorist, I think he has particularly illuminated one question about literary history, and that is the problem of influence and he has made us think about influence in more complicated ways than we did before he wrote. And that's good, that's a gain. But I still think that it's a narrow point to focus on. There's a great deal more that one can think about in connection with poetry, in connection with literary history. So, I think he is a person who has a very limited subject or focus but that he has illuminated the problem that he focuses on.

DV: Well, obviously you co-edited a book called *Teaching Literature*. Why did you think that you should write a book like that? Do you think the context and framework of teaching has changed in recent years?

DP: Well, the idea behind that book was to ask a number of people who are very eminent in the profession of teaching English literature, eminent as scholars and critics, to talk about teaching. Most of the discussion of the teaching literature is carried on by an altogether different set of people; it's carried on by people who are coming out from schools of education. So, I thought it's valuable to have the thoughts of teaching by people who have made their enormous reputation as critics, to see what they had to say about teaching. I thought they would bring a different point of view to bear and they are asking a different set of questions and I also thought that these people who are eminent scholars and critics, also involved in teaching, doing it day in and day out and have thoughts about it.

DV: Northrop Frye is against the evaluative criticism. Do you accept such a position?

DP: No, no. I think evaluation cannot be left out of criticism. I think it's a limitation on Frye's position.

DV: But how can one know and accept that one interpretation is more authentic than the other? What are the guiding factors?

DP: The reason why evaluation cannot be left out of criticism is that it's there in all our acts of life, in all our acts of reading. When we read one thing rather than the other for some reason and, so, to ask criticism not to be evaluative is asking something it cannot do. It just has to be evaluative, no alternative. I don't mean to say only evaluative but it cannot *not* be evaluative. Now, to ask what the legitimate grounds of critical evaluation are, that's quite different question. I don't have any answer to that except that in part the evaluation is arrived at a dialogue between one self and the text and there is a personal element in it. After all, it is one's self evaluating, and the text speaks to you in some way that you have found it meaningful. And at the same time, there is the text that you are reading and a good criticism is the one which is in touch with that text in multiple aspects, just seeing a lot that is there. And I think one quality of good criticism is simply the complexity of perception. Some people would see the object as simple object, and some people would see the object as complex object. Those people who are seeing it as complex are seeing it better, I think.

DV: Do you think the context of literature as an interaction with society has a subtle political ambience whether it is willed by the author or incidental to the narrative patterns? Do you think it worth pursuing in a literary discourse?

DP: Well, I think there is a political element in all literary texts and all reading. I think that's part of life, I think that's part of all reading, part of literature and it would be artificial to exclude it. On the other hand, there is a good deal of criticism at the present time which is primarily political in its orientation. You mentioned Terry Eagleton earlier.

DV: Raymond Williams, too.

DP: Well, Raymond Williams. I am not in favour of foregrounding political allegiances, or political considerations except when the texts themselves do that. There are political poems which ask us to have a political attitude. In that case, one's response to the poem is going to include a very strong political element and any criticism of the poem would be politically motivated in part because the poem has asked for that. But otherwise, I am in sympathy with the kind of criticism, which starts from a political position that the critic is committed to and judges text from the political perspective of the critic, though it is inevitable in any reading to a certain degree.

DV: Now, you have been teaching at Harvard for many years. The general perception about this university, it may probably be true of other Ivy League Schools too, is that it is generally conservative in its institutional and curricular framework. So much so, some of the current ideas and new approaches of theory are not immediately accepted. Whether this is good or bad, do you think the situation has changed over the years?

DP: Well, over the years that I have been associated with Harvard English department, it really hasn't had any corporate position. It has simply included a number of diverse people who are all able to function in the same department because of its very loose set of rules. It basically allowed each person to teach whatever they wanted in their own way. And given that fact, it's very easy for the department to assimilate new positions as they develop because they would be the positions of a particular person, not endorsed necessarily by the other members of the department. So, I have lot of colleagues who teach and criticize literature in ways that I did not and very often the ways that I don't agree with. The dialogue, the difference, and very often the lack of communication between different modes of criticism – that's true of teaching English as a whole at the present time – exists also at Harvard and I think that's a very good thing, really. I would not go to Harvard to somehow not to incorporate all the differences that exist in our profession at the present time.

Wayne C. Booth

This interview took place at his residence in Chicago.

DV: As a teacher how do you view the recent trends in literary studies?

WB: Generally favourably. To everybody's surprise lot of my colleagues, particularly those of my age, are appalled by seeing so much happen on the literary scene – the critical scene. Wherever one looks one finds a new point of view, a new method or a new attitude and it can be disconcerting if one is brought up in a different way. On the whole, what happened in the last twenty years in the stirring up of the literary scene with the new kinds of themes has been beneficial. When I was in graduate school my teacher felt they were the only ones – people like Ronald Crane, Richard McKean and Elder Jones – who cared about relating philosophy to literature. They kept lamenting that nobody seems to want to read philosophy along with literature. What has happened in the last twenty years is that a great many people think about literature philosophically. So, the effect of deconstructionism from the people like Derrida and Foucault and the others has been to turn the profession into a more theoretical way which on the whole has been good. I think there have been some disadvantages. Some young people seem to read nothing but theory and don't read literature, novels, plays and poetry anymore. I do occasionally meet a young person who seems to be frozen in a theoretical vein and not really having a fun and profound profit of reading a novel, plays, poetry and epics. But on the whole, I think, the profession is intellectually more alive today than it was twenty or thirty years ago.

DV: Is what's happening in the name of critical theory good for literature in the long run?

WB: It is little hard to know whether it is going to be good for the actual life of the creative writers. I do know in some departments, for instance, in University of Syracuse, there is a serious battle going on between the new theorists and that part of the English Department of Creative Writing Programme. The novelists and the poets seem to be quite greatly upset by the inroads of the theorists. But that is partly because in one branch of current theory the authorial authority tends to be played down. The author is no longer viewed as the authority of the individual text. The writer produces it or the ecriture produces the text so that the author sometimes seems to be denigrated by the current theory. But I think that would pass.

DV: Is there any difference between literary criticism and literary theory?

WB: Not in my mind, there's not. I cannot conceive of doing any good literary criticism without a theoretical work. I guess in general usage criticism tries to tend to relate to dealing with the individual literary works. Theory has tended to become an autonomous separate field with doing theoretical work for its own sake, in its own right without really worrying about texts. But in my mind, they come together steadily. I never do criticism without doing theory and don't do theory without doing criticism. I think there's a slight difference.

DV: Did you change your attitude toward literature radically from the publication of *The Rhetoric of Fiction* to the recent book [*The Company We Keep; An Ethics of Fiction*, 1988]?

WB: No, not really. This recent book on the ethics of fiction, *The Company We Keep* – its roots can be found in the *Rhetoric of Fiction* particularly in the last chapter. But I become considerably more pluralistic, broad-ranging in my interests than I was twenty-five years ago.

DV: What should be the methodology of literary appreciation, now that we have seen so many theories on literary scene?

WB: I think there is no single answer to that question. That's what I mean by saying I am more pluralistic. I don't think one can even say that there is a single method. There are many different good ways dealing with literature. And consequently there must be, there should always be, in healthy condition, many different approaches, controversial rivalries. Although I think there are many bad ways, there are many good ways too. My own choice at the moment is ethical criticism. I am conducting a seminar for graduate students in ethical criticism. The methodology there is very closely related to that of *The Rhetoric of Fiction* where I assume that you start by trying to find out what the work intends and what the work is trying to do. Then you move to second level which I sometimes call *overstanding* than *understanding* which you relate the work to your own ideology, your own set of values and either criticise it or praise it according to your own understanding. I am at present deeply engaged in that kind of critical endeavour which is considerably different from what I was doing in *The Rhetoric of Fiction*. I am trying to figure out how works work out. Now I take that for granted and move on to what some people call ideological or axiological level.

DV: What do you think of Paul de Man controversy?.

WB: De Man controversy has been something I have followed but have not taken part in. I find some of his work stimulating and some of his work exasperating. And the recent revelations of his past haven't changed my feelings about his work. To me it seems useful to think of the work as independently of de Man's past. On the other hand, I do sense the obfuscation, the difficulties in his work somehow relate to his past which he somehow wants to conceal. I have not taken part in that debate.

DV: How does a teacher cope up with the everchanging and multifarious critical theories and still teach literature meaningfully?

WB: That's a good question. That's a good question at least because it troubles a lot of teachers these days. My way of dealing with it is simply to continue to teach the classics in the way I used to. But then to go and see what the new ways have to teach me. For example, many feminist movements have alerted me to ways which I was imposing in a male point of view on the classics and alert me to ways in which a given work will look different to a male reader than it does to a female reader. And that does not change fundamentally my view of what a classic is. Most of the classics I have believed in thirty years ago are still I think of them as classics today. It does somehow change one's approach in the classroom, particularly it alerts you to elicit the women's point of view also. At one time, I used to have thought there is only one way of reading. Now I am sure that some works men read differently than women do.

DV: Don't you think deconstruction is problematic to your kind of theory?

WB: Not as much as you might expect. Depends on which deconstruction you look at. There are many varieties of deconstructionism. Some of the students of deconstructionism seem to be going overboard, become monotonous in simply doing the same thing with every text. You can predict if you read the first paragraph and the last paragraph to show that the work is disorganized or fallen apart. Deconstructive analysis is as monotonous as the old style. You can read the first paragraph and the end of the essay to show, in the old style, that the work is unified as complete work. It is very different always to know what the effect will be. When the deconstruction came, I thought it will last only about five years and would fail. But now I feel it probably made a permanent contribution, loosening up of our views, of what possibilities in literary criticism. So, I don't feel personally threatened by it.

DV: How far do you go along with present critics?

WB: I have really deep disappointments with much of what they do. I don't believe that everything is language and that all texts deconstruct themselves in quite the way they do. I think some texts invite deconstruction and others you know better if you take them as creative whole – and they do hold together. They think texts are made of language and I think that the texts are made of people. So my fundamental metaphor for a poem of T.S. Eliot or whoever, is a personal relationship between implied author and implied reader. And their fundamental metaphor is the texts, or the enigma, or the linguistic object. For me the fundamental metaphor is people and for them, it is words. And that is really the fundamental difference. That is not a difference of right or wrong. I can reveal something by taking them as people and they can reveal something by taking it as a linguistic object. We do different things. But in the long run, they are not flat contradictories but parallel enquiries.

DV: Almost every critic seems to come up with his or her own theory these days. Why do you think that this has become a strong priority with critics?

WB: Well, it's hard to know where we are going. And the multiplicity of critics seems threatening. In a sense, it has been partially true in long, long time. In the thirties, there were multiplicity of points of view; in the forties there was multiplicity of points of view. In retrospect, it looks as if the New Criticism was dominating everywhere but it wasn't. The New Critics felt embattled for a long time and there were many rivals on the scene. And when I was in graduate school, the Chicago school of criticism and New Critics were combating each other tooth and nail. And other kinds of historical criticism and philological criticisms were also fighting. So I think that the controversy is endemic and permanent. It is healthy. Single view is more worrisome to me than the multiplicity of views.

DV: Is it healthy – the kind of criticisms we have to-day?

WB: Are you implying that it is not?

DV: No, I am just wondering . . .

WB: (laughs) Well, yes and no. I think there are unhealthy aspects to it. When young people think that they can embrace deconstruction and solve all the problems and they become dogmatic about it and think that's the only way to do and they lash everybody etc. who does not do it. That's unhealthy. I think there is a lot of arrogance in some of the young adherents of deconstruction. I read the pieces which make me uneasy because they seem to suggest that every body in the world is stupid except those who buy this particular way of going about things. But every movement attracts dogmatists. I am not worried about that. On the whole, the rich controversy is healthy.

DV: Has it become part of the academic power struggle?

WB: I think to some degree in our department here the debate about this subject became polarized. So far I can tell I don't see any deep personal hostilities. But we have deconstructionists, we have traditionalists, we have historicists who debate with each other but we are friendly in the department.

DV: Is it merely a literary enterprise or does it have any power struggle aspect to such discussions?

WB: Nationally it does have a power struggle aspect to it, of course. Yale English Department, when deconstruction was central then, was engaged in deep power struggle because the deconstructionists and anti-deconstructionists became really quite antipathic. Now that the most of the deconstructionists left Yale, the anti-deconstructionists have pretty well taken over. I was talking to Hillis Miller not long ago and he says there is a counter revolution at Yale. And, of course, that is a power struggle term. But we have not suffered that here. I think most departments haven't had it strongly. There is a current branch of criticism which believes that all criticism is power struggle, as you know – nothing but power struggle which, I think, is a distortion. To reduce all arguments to who has the power is to make the word meaningless to do serious criticism.

DV: Do you really trust the intellectuals in academia or do you sometimes think that literary appreciation should be left to the well-informed and educated layman or common reader?

WB: No, I think there is an expertise. If I understand your question, I think there is a real difference between those who have an experience of literature and thought hard about it, and those who haven't. There is a real training here. It is harder to point out what it consists of than physics or math. But there is a genuine training here and reasoning that counts.

DV: It also tends to be programmatic as we know in some cases of deconstruction . . .

WB: That is the danger in any period. That became true of New Critics twenty or thirty years ago. New Criticism became programmatic and, in a sense, insisted the next stage.

DV: The theories are so cerebral and complicated one wonders if spontaneous response to literature is possible at all at this point of time.

WB: Well, I worry about it. I know one young teacher who told me that she never introduces literary text without mimeographing ten or twelve interpretations first before they read the work, and then takes up the work. That seems to me destroying the spontaneity – doesn't it? – the student faces ten or twelve interpretations and then goes on to the literary text. How can you have a first hand spontaneous response to a story, a poem or whatever? There is that danger, but really good literary works have a good deal of power to defend themselves. If there is any good they don't surrender easily to the wrong kind of theory. I have a lot of confidence in literary work.

DV: What is the function of literature now that we have come far away from the liberal attitude to literature? What, in the wake of many theoretical views, is the function of literature? Does such a question make any sense at all?

WB: I want to give the same answer when I talked about the multiplicity of approaches. There are many good functions and some are bad. In the appendix of my current book [*The Company We keep*, 1988] in the last section, I have a little anthology of people's arguments of what literature is for. It is a very rich, very various collection and most of them make sense to me. For different people in different situations literature does different things. In this present moment, it seems to be that literature, if one wants to mention a single function – no, I don't – I really want to say many functions. The one function I care about is the awakening of the critical intelligence, that happens when you sit down and read a good book. I try to get my students to be the kind of people who are critically alive and who are self-starters, who continue to read on their own and are not simply uncritical absorbers of the national ethos. As they are surrounded by a great deal of destructive ideology in TV and popular literature. The function of good literature is to combat this as best as possible.

DV: Shouldn't it make us more sensitive to values?

WB: Yes, and also make us more critical of values, the values imposed by various media, especially commercial media. It seems to be appalling to me that the commercial TV is destructive of spiritual values. Just by getting the students to read good literature we are freeing them from the blind acceptance of what comes at them.

DV: Does deconstruction believe in that?

WB: Yes, you may want to look at Hillis Miller's book *Ethics of Reading*. He thinks of deconstruction as essentially a liberation from being a blind follower of what comes one's way.

DV: Would you sympathize with the view that literature also has political angle?

WB: The given society is largely controlled, if you take literature in broader sense, by the literary works, at least the art works it has available to it. The political activity of that society is very much dependent on what kind of art it has available to it.

DV: How does one canonize one work over another?

WB: One doesn't do it. The society does it. Individual or critic could say that so and so work is neglected or deserves recognition as a classic. It takes a full community of readers to canonize a work and most of the canon in a given period falls out of the canon in the next period. Only a few works go from century to century.

DV: What is your response to Allan Bloom's *Closing of the American Mind*?

WB: I think on the whole it produced a good convention. I think he is right in some of the things he says about American education – too much of its superficiality, too many people having forgotten how to read closely. I don't think his prescriptions are very helpful. He seems to be too hasty in his belief that simply by restoring the classics you are going to have the saving group or the saving remnant. I have a much stronger belief in democratic education than he does. I think his book is somewhat elitist.

DV: Some people argue that he is romanticizing the past . . .

WB: Yes, I think he does. Definitely, he is.

DV: Coming to the recent American fiction, how important is Saul Bellow?

WB: In my view, he is terribly important. He is one of the best, if not the best in American literature. He is not at the forefront of critical discussion as he was ten years ago. But it was inevitable as the man gets older. But I think his work will endure.

DV: What do you think of his recent novels?

WB: I did not like *The Dean's December* as much as his earlier novels. But *More Die of Heartbreak*, I liked again. But to me the best ones are *Herzog* and *Henderson the Rain King* – although the very early work, *Seize the Day*, is a wonderful novel. But he is still producing very good stuff.

DV: What is the contribution of the little magazines – *Partisan Review* and others?

WB: It is essential for America. It's where most good writers get their first publication. It saves them to go on and do better work, you know. Without the little magazines, I don't know where they would be.

DV: Which magazines do you prefer at this moment?

WB: Of literary magazines, *Tri Quarterly* (published by North Western University) I admire quite a lot. I usually read *Kenyon Review* and *Georgia Review*. There is rather a good little one called *Syracuse Review* that people don't know that much about.

DV: *Partisan Review,* maybe?

WB: I don't read it as much as I used to. Well, I am not talking about critical journals. I am talking about journals which publish fiction, poetry and the other creative writing. Among critical journals, I read *Critical Inquiry* published here and *New Literary History* and *Representation*, I read most regularly. Of monthlies, I read *New York Review of Books* and the *Times Literary Supplement* [that's a weekly].

DV: Who are the important novelists now?

WB: I have a little list. Lousia Edrich, American Indian novelist, is very good. Elaine Silko – she has a wonderful novel, *Ceremony*. She is an Indian too; her novel is about a half-breeder, an Indian who is half-white and half-Indian. I recommend that very strongly. It is a powerful book. Much neglected novelist who is in his seventies but sure to be permanent is a man named Wright Morris. He has done about twenty five novels. And wonderful. He would become known. Tony Morrison, the black American novelist who has just done a novel called *The Beloved* which is on the best seller list. Splendid work – really first class. And I am surprised that it is a best seller because it is so good you know. I would not have expected it to sell so well. But I like her a lot. I like the work of a lady who has done *Dinner at the Home-sick Restaurant* [Ann Tyler]. I think Philip Roth is a serious, good writer though I am less excited about him than I used to be. He is certainly a name who is very important. Robert Carver you should pay attention to. Don De Lilo – very good novelist. That's enough of a list to go on.

DV: Won't you think Bellow is repeating his themes time and again?

WB: Yes, to some degree. But as long as he engages with it, makes me laugh, makes me feel as a new insight, I don't object to it. That's true about every great author – isn't? If you look at Dickens, he covers the same themes again and again, but always coming up with a new start on them.

DV: Do you think he will survive . . .

WB: Yes, I do. Oh, yes.

DV: What difference do the intellectuals make in this country? What kind of power do they have?

WB: Less than what they do in other countries, I think; less than in the Eastern bloc. I don't know about India, but surely less than their counterparts in India. What is your impression?

DV: Very marginal . . .

WB: They have less impact here than in England, France and Germany. It depends on how you define an intellectual. If you just mean academics, then academics have quite a lot of influence. Political scientists and economists. But most of them are not what I call intellectuals. They are specialists, professionals, experts who have a given line. But they are not the people who read widely across disciplines. If you think what used to be called men of letters or people who are both in literature, philosophy and political matters – they don't have a lot of influence on public affairs. They have influence on education, I think.

DV: Coming back to criticism again, Northrop Frye seems to be against evaluative criticism.

WB: Yes, he attacks it in his book on various places. I don't understand that because he himself does evaluative criticism. He is always making clear what he thinks of great works, what he thinks are not. You cannot argue rationally about these matters; therefore, it is merely a matter of taste.

DV: In retrospect, what do you think is the lasting contribution of New Criticism?

WB: Well, I think it made a lasting contribution because people now pay attention on the way works are put together – the close reading. The deconstructionists really in one part of their works are New Critics in the sense they try to look at the work closely and deal with textual work much more closely than was common before the New Critics. At the moment, people are not discussing New Criticism. They are not high on the agenda of any critical journal. But I think their work will last.

DV: How many theories will survive initial enthusiasm, in your view?

WB: I cannot be a prophet like that. I think Northrop Frye's work will continue into the next century. I am pretty sure now that the work of Derrida will continue into the next century. I think some branches of Freudian criticism are going to endure – psychological criticism. I am sure that the Feminists have made a permanent change in people's way of thinking. Feminists will continue to be vital. What seems to be obvious is Aristotle, Plato, Samuel Johnson will be read hundred years from now – they are not going to die. I find teaching my students now Aristotle makes them excited just as anybody. And I have a student who is greatly excited by Plato. I think the classics will remain classics. There would be ups and downs but they endure.

William Phillips

DV: How liberal is America? Over the years and at the moment?

WP: Well, I have to answer that question in two ways. One, it depends on how you define the word 'liberal' and the second is I'll have to say that most of the people in America are not liberal in the most recent, current sense of the word. Liberalism in America has shifted to some extent. It's taken out a radical tinge and in that sense preponderance of opinion in America is opposed to this radical tinge that's been taken on. That's why Protestants get elected. I don't know what would happen if we had a liberalism that didn't have a radical tinge. John F. Kennedy was a liberal without a radical tinge. He was quite popular. So, I don't know what would happen if, let's say, there was a candidate of that kind. I'd suspect it'd be different. In America, most people are opposed, a majority of the people are opposed to a liberalism of a radical tinge – a radical liberalism. However, there is a division in this country. There is in the academy, and among the media that's not the case. The media are to some extent sympathetic to the radical influence and liberal opinion in this country.

DV: What is the difference between the old *Partisan Review* and the new *Partisan Review* apart from the Marxist context?

WP: Oh, there are enormous differences. There is obviously a continuity in the sense that I am there. To some extent, you can't withdraw a magazine from the people around it. And a certain mind runs it, a certain way of thinking runs it; so, there's that continuity. So, in attitude, stand and its values – these are continuous and continue. And the difference, to some extent, is in a different situation. It's a situation in which popular culture is more prevalent in this country than it was when we began. There are many more publications, competing publications, that didn't exist then. And some of the commercial publications have begun to publish the kind of writers never published before. So that we had a virtual monopoly in the field. These are some of the differences, a lot of differences in situations.

DV: Do you think it has the same kind of intellectual status it used to have when Trilling, Philip Rahv were there.

WP: I think it has a great intellectual status. I think we've got a monopoly before. We don't have a monopoly now.

DV: I met with Podhoretz some time ago. He says that *Partisan Review* has changed radically. It is not the same old intellectual force that it used to be in the old days. I think he says pretty much the same in his contribution to the fiftieth anniversary issue.

WP: That's his opinion.

DV: Nathan Glazer also felt that though the magazine was nourished by Jewish intellectuals, very few of them ever paid any attention to Jewish issues. Do you agree?

WP: We never take a count and I am not sure that it's true that most of the contributors are Jewish. I really don't know. I tend to doubt it. But many are. Well, and what was the second part of the question.

DV: The *Partisan Review* did not pay much attention to the Jewish issues.

WP: The fact that one has Jewish contributors does not mean that it is a Jewish magazine. It's more like a cultural magazine.

DV: But surely as intellectuals at least there should be some interaction with the contemporary issues like the Holocaust, Israel, the Middle East. These are important issues for Americans also.

WP: They are important but we don't feel that can be the area of our greatest concern. We are not experts on the Holocaust. Our position is clear on the Holocaust, on anti-Semitism and related questions. Our attitudes are clear on Israel. You heard about them. But that's not our main function.

DV: Does the magazine have any implicit political agenda?

WP: The implicit political agenda might be said, I think, we stand in the middle. I think there's been a polarisation of political opinion of intellectual, political polarisation of intellectual opinion in this country. Moving way over to the left and moving to the right and I think we regard ourselves as not being identified with either one, either extreme. So, we think of ourselves as independent and free to agree with certain positions that the conservatives take and agree with some of the positions that the left takes.

DV: I have a write-up here from Lionel Trilling's notebooks. He says, "I recall my non-Jewish teachers with more interest and affection than my Jewish ones of whom there are very few and it seems to me that I thought of the gentiles as having more reality than the Jews." Do you think that the Jewish contributors to the *Partisan Review* are playing down their Jewishness? And why?

WP: I am not sure they're playing it down. I think they think of themselves as people who have a certain literary and cultural role. They are writers, they are intellectuals, they are specialists in other areas. But they are also Jewish and have also a Jewish interest. The question of priorities of the centrality of one's role; it's like saying a Frenchman is a Frenchman. But he may also be a historian of the eighteenth century—that's his profession. So, his main existence is not as a Frenchman.

DV: Do you think the same thing works with Jewish intellectuals also. Because being a Jew demands certain implications, certain responsibilities and certain issues one has to come to terms with.

WP: Well, I think it does. But they are not easy and Jews are interested in these questions as you know. Many Jews are split on the question of Israeli policies. There's a split, there's a division among Jews and I consider these questions; I stand in one position and some other people stand in another position on Israeli policies. But I don't regard it as my function. I speak my mind on it and I've written on it but it's not my main function. I am a literary intellectual, that's what I am trying to emphasize.

DV: Are you trying to say that literature and politics are two different things? That's not what we see in the *Partisan Review*?

WP: They've different emphasis. They are related, they're different things. They're related but it's a question of emphasis, it's a question of priorities.

DV: What guides these priorities?

WP: It was our profession. When you are a literary critic and when your interest is in literature, that's your profession. That's your main concern. My main concern is not Jewish questions. That's not my profession. There are other people whose main concern is Israel, better at it, than I am. They specialize in it.

DV: Are you saying that personal morality and professionalism do not interact? Because the issue of Israel is both political and moral, if you view in the framework of Jewish history.

WP: I am not saying that. You've introduced another term, morality. Now, that's another question. It's a different question when you talk of politics. Now, you talk of morality. Morality is a complex question. It has to be defined. Some people take some kind of position which they call moral.

DV: Let's say politics, personal politics, and professionalism are different.

WP: They are different. Some relation, some interaction but they are different.

DV: Is this interaction, in whatever form, reflected in writing?

WP: I'll give you an example. A lot of the literature contains a lot of anti-Semitism. But you can't judge Western literature purely from a Jewish point of view. What are you going to do, dismiss Western literature?

DV: The problem in Israel at the moment is the definition of Jew. Do you have anything to say about this?

WP: I have not studied it. I tend to think that the religious groups in Israel have pushed the issue too far and have created an unnecessary question. But I say this very tentatively.

DV: What do you think of the recent Arafat issue? He is denied visa to visit the U.S. and address the U.N. Do you think that's correct?

WP: I think that was correct. I am opposed to Arafat. I think Arafat double-talks and he pretends he is one thing and he is actually another; and if you examine what he does and what he supports, he is not very helpful and honest about it. If he really supported the existence of Israel and really wanted to come to decent terms and really wanted to establish a democratic Palestinian state, I think the situation would be different.

DV: Now coming to the American academic scene. Critical theory has taken over the academia–deconstruction, post-structuralism.

WP: I am not for deconstruction. Well, I have several reasons why I'm against it. I am against some of the premises which claim that everything is relative and that you can't establish meaning and it all depends. It goes back to the reader. I don't think everything is that relative. I think there is some flexibility and relativity but Shakespeare is Shakespeare and John Donne is John Donne and John Donne is not what's his name who wrote the *Grapes of Wrath*?

DV: John Steinbeck.

WP: Yes, John Steinbeck has an identity and it's not that flexible, its meaning is not that flexible, it can't be interpreted that differently. I also think that they are really not literary critics. They are ideologists. They don't have much to do with literature. These are theories.

DV: Do you think they have vested interests, their own politics?

WP: Yes, they have vested interests in the sense that they are involved in academic enterprises. But deconstructionists of France have no school as such at all. They are non-existent in France; actually Derrida said that they have to come to America, too. Critics here are more interested in Deconstruction than the French are. And America has become, I think, an academic enterprise; it involves students, jobs, salaries – God knows what!

DV: After these theories especially deconstruction, the idea of political discourse in literature becomes problematic.

WP: Everything becomes problematic. I think there's also a hidden agenda in deconstruction, by the way, in that politics are implicit and that they never come out wholly for them. But they really support all kinds of movements of causes which I am opposed to. They want to change the curriculum, I am opposed to that and, you see, that's part of their agenda.

DV: I think its influence is waning, on the decline.

WP: I really don't know–may be waning slightly but it's quite rampant.

DV: Somehow these things become quickly fashionable in American academia. It's hard to see a literary text without its context, whether marginal or significant – although one cannot over-emphasize these to the detriment of the autonomy of art.

WP: Fashions have become important here. I get back to what I said because there are academic stakes in these fashions. If there were no academic stakes, I think, there would be no deconstruction. Most literary critics don't care about deconstruction.

DV: What is the status of Jewish-American writing now? Incidentally, Bellow is a sort of institution in my country.

WP: He has denied that he's a Jewish American writer, says he is an American writer. I prefer to think of it that the Jews are American writers who are also Jewish. They sometimes have Jewish themes, sometimes have Jewish attitudes. But most of them are primarily American writers. They've been a few but they are not major writers. One can say, for instance, there's Abraham Cahan who was a Jewish writer, to some extent. Mike Gold was a Communist, and a Jewish writer. There are some people who are more distinctly Jewish writers.

But I think that people like Bellow, Malamud and Roth – they are American writers who use Jewish themes.

DV: Are you saying that the condition of being Jewish wouldn't really effect their creative writing?

WP: No, I wouldn't say that. I think it does effect them. Well, in that sense everything effects them. You might say that they are *avant garde* American writers or they are conservative American writers or they are patriotic American writers. One component of their writing is their Jewishness. But there are other components.

DV: Maybe it's a major component?

WP: Well, let me think about that. I tend to think that it's not major. I think that people like Bellow and Malamud are steeped in the history of Western literature. They stem from Tolstoy, Dostoevsky, and Flaubert and some more minor writers like Thackery. They are part of that tradition, they're not part of that tradition of Jewish writing. They are not part of the tradition of Sholom Aleichem, I would say.

DV: What do you think about Marxism today? Do you think Marxism and Soviet Russia are synonymous?

WP: I think Marxism is dead. I think Soviet Russia has more or less given up Marxism. It realizes that it can't, well, let me say, the issue is slightly more complicated. First of all, Russia was never a Marxist country. Marx never envisioned a totalitarian society; that isn't why he wanted a revolution. So, they created it for him. It created a new form of tyranny and oppression. So in that sense, I don't think Russia was ever Marxist. But they involved the name of Marx to justify their opposition to free market, to private enterprise and so on. But they've even gone back on that.

DV: What do you think about the Neo-conservative movement in this country? Or is it a movement at all?

WP: I think the Neo-conservative movement is right in many respects and a little too extreme in some respects but it's not all in one piece. They are not going to agree with each other on every single one of their positions. Some say some things and others say other things; it's not a party line like the Communist Party. But I think they are right in many respects. That's right.

DV: At least people like Irving Howe feel that its influence is slowly declining if not vanishing altogether.

WP: There is certainly a large conservative influence in this country. That's been built up. There are more conservative intellectuals today than there used to be like with the American Heritage Foundation and like the *New Republic*, some like the *New Criterion*. I think that the core of Neo-conservatism that surrounded people like Podhoretz and Kristol has probably been dissipated. That's what I think has happened. It is very difficult to evaluate this.

DV: Who are the Jewish writers that impress you immensely among the up-and-coming writers?

WP: Well, Cynthia Ozick. It's hard to think of new arrivals.

DV: Grace Paley, Tillie Olsen?

WP: Cynthia Ozick is much better. I don't like to espouse politics either which is influencing writing. I don't want to deny Grace Paley's writing but I don't think she has the grace of Cynthia Ozick's range and power. I think Grace Paley has a certain amount of talent.

DV: Well, in the recent years people are talking about the role of the university, curriculum reforms and the things of this sort. Allan Bloom and E.D. Hirsch reflected on these issues. Do you have comments about these debates?

WP: I think that they point to a real dilemma in a real crisis. I think that their analysis is severely flawed and their solutions are meaningless. I think that they don't really understand the real problem. The real problem is not that we don't teach Plato and Aristotle now. The real problem was elsewhere. The problem was, I believe, we have mass education in this country and we can't have elitist education in mass education institutions and they haven't faced that problem. They also exaggerate the virtues of students of the past. Students weren't so bright in the past. But now, as they say, we have mass education and have many students who come to college.

DV: There are many new theories on the American academic scene. Consequently traditional view on curriculum has taken a severe rap from these critics. Gender, race, politics have thoroughly made an impact on any classroom discussion. I see this at Brandeis too. How do you view these changing responses that have overtaken American scholarship?

WP: Those who want to revise the curriculum in terms of new fads and popular works, I think that represents a political agenda. That's not for educational purposes. That's putting some kind of politics on to the university.

DV: What do you think about the foreign policy of America?

WP: I don't think America has any foreign policy. I think it is mixed up sometimes with sense, sometimes with little sense; sometimes it is illogical, sometimes it is pragmatics. I think it shifts back and forth. Maybe you watch Reagan. I think the attacks on Reagan are false. He does not represent what people say he represents. It is a big ideological war just because he wants to suppress Communism. Half the time he is negotiating, compromising, so on. Generally, I would say, we don't have a consistent and long ranging foreign policy.

DV: What do you think is the reason for that?

WP: Partly it's in the nature of the country, pragmatic country. It is in the nature of American political thinking. Another reason, it has so many conflicting interests. It has to satisfy so many different people in the country. Democracy has been carried to one extreme in this country. Probably there isn't another country, which is as democratic in the sense America is. You cannot satisfy everybody. You cannot have a foreign policy that satisfies all groups, and all interests. There is a constant shifting, rotation and adjusting and so on.

DV: Being an Indian I cannot understand the traces of strain in Indo-American relationship. At the same time, America seems to be getting on fine with Pakistan. Both India and America are democracies. Still, somehow, prospects for relationship are not encouraging.

WP: But then, media, academy, politicians, various interest groups don't have the power in this country.

DV: But sincerely don't you think that India and America should have more agreeable relationship?

WP: Yes, of course.

DV: Do you think there is a possibility of relationship between India, America, and Israel?

WP: It is possible. This country is partly cultivated by the Left, for all kinds of reasons we don't want to go into now, partly also by the anti-Semitic Right.

DV: In India?

WP: No, no; in this country. If these forces can be overcome, I think India can play a role, Americans can play a role in supporting Israel. Let me emphasize a point. I don't think one has to support every single issue of Israel to support its independence and security. Nobody is for everything a country does. I am for India, but I am not for everything it does.

DV: Who are the prominent thinkers in this country now, Jewish or non-Jewish?

WP: I don't agree with all of them. I think Irving Howe is a prominent thinker and a prominent Jew. I don't agree with everything he says but he is important. Daniel Bell, some of his policies, I don't agree. Nat Glazer, probably I agree more. Norman Podhoretz with whom I agree to a large extent but not completely. Irving Kristol I agree in segments. Very good intellectual and scholar is Irving Kristol's wife Gertrude Himmelfarb. She is more of an intellectual scholar than a political thinker.

DV: I was browsing through some of the back issues of *Commentary* where I found an article on Gore Vidal's anti-Semitism. In fact, it is a response to Vidal's article published in *Nation* called "Empire Lovers Strike Back." It is interesting that Victor Navasky, who is a Jew, had to publish such an anti-Semitic attack on certain Jews and Jewish lobby in America.

WP: Well, Navasky. Politics. *Nation* is left. Left accommodates anti-Semitic, anti-Jewish, anti-Israeli positions. I think Gore Vidal went out of bounds in this .

DV: I got the feeling that there is a general anti-Israeli stance in American media.

WP: It's all because of the left.

DV: But why?

WP: Well, partly because of the tradition. Russia is anti-Israel, Communist countries are anti-Israel. It's assumed that if you are a leftist, if you are a Communist, you are against Israel, which is supposedly a Capitalist, imperialist country. That's wrong.

DV: Also, many left-intellectuals have been Jews. George Lukacs, Lucien Goldman, Ernest Fischer and so on.

WP: I think they deny their authenticity.

DV: Is it something like a self-hating Jew?

WP: I don't think it is. I think they are adopting an ideology which is in conflict with their basic intellectual interests.

Robert Brustein

This interview took place in Prof. Brustein's office at the American Repertory Theatre in Cambridge, Mass. Presently he teaches at Harvard University.

DV: The three important American dramatists are not doing anything these days. Tennesse Williams is no more; Arthur Miller does not seem to be coming up with his best. Neither does Albee. Do you think the golden era of these playwrights is taken up by the succeeding generation of American playwrights?

RB: Yes, I think something very dramatic happened in the '60s and '70s that the older and the established playwrights didn't keep up with and that was a break in the causal nature of drama, that drama perhaps responding belatedly to the Einstein universe began in a non-causal and a non-linear way. And this was true of a number of directors and this was true of a number of playwrights. Such as Sam Sheperd, Christopher Durang and, to some extent, David Mamet and David Rabe. But they were working in a different kind of method than the realistic and sometimes naturalistic living room, bed room, kitchen environment that were common to Arthur Miller particularly and to a lesser extent Tennesse Williams. Edward Albee who had started in the absurdist view with his one-act plays had continued to explore in his first plays *Who is Afraid of Virginia Woolf*? and, I suppose, to some extent *Tiny Alice*. To my way of thinking that's too much under the influence of English metaphysical drama like T.S. Eliot, Graham Green and turning out the kind of plays that also didn't have much weight or power behind them. So, for one reason or another, also because of a whole new group of critics, this group does not appreciate the major American drama stream. Arthur Miller continued and continues to write. He comes up with a play every three or four years but they have not caught on the public or with the critics. Tennesse Williams is due for a revival; as a matter of fact, he is getting a revival of *Orpheus Descending* in London at the present time in a well-received production and will probably begin to get a number of revivals here. Albee has a new play called *The Marriage Play* coming up this year but every play he has written over the last ten or fifteen years has been manhandled by the public and the critics. So, you get to realize that we are in a belligerent and hostile theatre atmosphere here in the U.S. particularly in New York. The critics are very unfriendly to the new works themselves and there is not that atmosphere of sympathy and support that there need to be when a critic like Brooks Atkinson was writing for the *New York Times*. And this has invaded a number of theatre people particularly in New York where they can work on something for two, three or four years and in one night it is annihilated by a single review. But it's not just the review of the *New York Times* but any number of New York reviewers who have picked up on this rather savage manner of treating a new work so that you got to feel that something got to be a hit or flop and there's nothing in between; there's no room for any playwright to be supported who hasn't produced, you know, the great American play of 1989. I was just reading a report by a Rumanian director who spoke of the great supportiveness of the critics in Rumania and of the public as well. You don't feel that here at all. It's a very hostile territory for creating theatre art here.

DV: How important are playwrights like Tennesse Williams and Sam Sheperd? Some people say they repeat themselves . . .

RB: I don't think Sheperd has been repeating himself. I think his last play was repetitive and recognizable but the Sheperd who produced *Action and Suicide in B Flat*, for example, or the *Geography of a Horse Dreamer* is very different Sheperd from the Sheperd of *Buried Child, Curse of the Starving Class*. You can't really hold him to a single style; he is chameleon in that regard. So, I don't think he repeats himself. I think Williams was repeating himself toward the end of his career.

DV: In fact, I read a critic sometime ago that Sheperd is like Maxwell Anderson and he'll be forgotten after sometime. How many people remember Anderson now? He was popular in his days.

RB: Not many. There has been some talk about Maxwell Anderson recently. I think some one tried to revive one of his plays. But he was a bit of flash in the pan. There's no question about it. He gave an impression of seriousness and wrote in poetry but his plays were highly melodramatic and his themes were simple-minded. He didn't really last. But it's hard to give a final word about any American artist. We can have the case of O'Neill himself. O'Neill was praised in the early years for plays that are unproducable today, plays like *Strange Inter-*

lude, Mourning Becomes Electra, Marco Millions, Hairy Ape. I find these plays almost unreadable. They work if you translate them into another language. So you don't have to listen to O'Neill's failure as a linguist – as a verbal playwright. Then he went into decline and didn't produce anything for about thirteen years after *Ah, Wilderness*. And then he produced the great plays. No one could have anticipated that these would be as spectacular and wonderful as they were. I just certainly couldn't have. Just basing on his early plays, I was ready to write him off. I disagree with those critics who put down his later plays like *Iceman Cometh* when originally it was produced. What we had in our midst was a major, major world dramatist at that point of time. I think thirteen years of restful incubation during which he was wrestling with his own theories, about his family memories produced extraordinary work. So, I find artists unpredictable and if there's anything I can learn as a critic it's never to make a final judgement on anybody.

DV: Do you think it's difficult for an American dramatist in the unfriendly atmosphere to come up with their best?

RB: It's very difficult for them to prosper. It's not difficult for them to write and they continue to write and as a matter of fact I wrote a piece on this. I think they are probably more versatile, more changeable, more experimental and willing to risk. Precisely because they have not been picked up and lionized as the great American playwright of 1989. They have two choices to either continue and write what they believe in or give up writing altogether. But third choice that was open to people like Tennesse Williams, Arthur Miller and Albee was to try and repeat the first success and then to get back in public favour. That was not a happy choice and it caused Tennesse Williams particularly to be very repetitive; he is an oft-repeating playwright.

DV: Mamet wrote powerful plays. In his plays one sees effective use of language, dialogue and situation. But then, he is into movies now. Is this the familiar story of most American playwrights? You come up with a good play or novel which is a best seller or a box-office hit and go to Hollywood to make a fast buck. Isn't it an artistic compromise?

RB: Well, you gotta remember that there's a lot of gold out there but the theatre does not provide anybody with much money anymore. You do not have glamour anymore, or you are not provided with the status of celebrity anymore whereas the movies can. Naturally, there's a magnetic pull towards Hollywood and to establish yourself there. However, you can't generalize about American playwrights at the moment because they are not welcome anymore in Hollywood. I can't think of any American playwrights really who are working successfully in movies. John Gay wrote *The Atlantic City* and I do think he wrote another movie. The playwrights who are out in Hollywood now are secondary American playwrights people like John Patrick Shanley who wrote *Moonstruck*, Kevin Wade who wrote *Working Girl*. These are playwrights the theatre does not miss at all because they are not very powerful playwrights and they might be the kind of lighthearted stuff that the movies can pick up and make up something out of it. Mamet is an exception because Mamet is not only a playwright but a director and also an actor. And it's as a director that Mamet has established himself in Hollywood with his first two films. But one of them he co-authored and in both cases the scripts were less important than directing. They were not his most important work. But the directing that he brought to these movies reinforced and gave them a style, a power that the script itself did not contain. But I don't think Mamet is going to leave the stage; I think he will continue to write for the stage. We just produced a play on Broadway called *Speed the Plough*; he did an adaptation of *Uncle Vanya* for us last year which was very beautifully written and very successful. And he is working on a play right now.

DV: Do you think the present attitude towards Communism and liberalism is possibly the major reason why the drama of the thirties is viewed unfavourably? Or do you think the theatre of the thirties deserves any attention at all?

RB: I think that there are plays in the '30s that do deserve attention; certainly. I do think that critics and audiences today tend to believe that the ringing affirmation of these plays is rather naive and unsophisticated and especially in the light of what happened to the Communist Party, and what happened to the Soviet Union during the period of Stalin. But the energy that came out of that attitude of revolt and protest was real electric energy that possessed Clifford Odets. That energy is still vital today even when the characters and plots seem a little old-fashioned. But I guess I will be agreeing with you that the attitude towards Communism certainly and to a lesser extent liberalism does affect the way we view these plays today. They seem a little simple-minded in their affirmation and a little melodramatic too in Lillian Hellman who was a very good friend of mine up until her death. She still wrote melodramas. There were the good guys vs bad guys and bad guys were the Fascists and the good guys were the liberals and Communists and you can't decide the world that way in art, the way they wanted to do in politics.

DV: Do you think playwrights shouldn't have any political agenda of their own reflected in their works – either explicitly or implicitly?

RB: I think the playwrights can have any political agenda they want. Personally, I think if they are going to write political plays, these plays are going to be very complicated. They can't simply be agit-prop or political activeness or cries or appeals to workers to get up and strike; and those things are exciting at the time but they quickly fade and become old-fashioned.

DV: At the same time, I see political implications in Arthur Miller's plays too.

RB: Yes, I think you can clearly extrapolate political implications in his plays. Sometimes they are quite voluble and straight-forward like in *Death of a Salesman.* When you hear comments like "attention should be paid to such a man" or "You can't throw away man like a piece of fruit", this has political implication although they are never spelled out. There is a certain tendentiousness in Miller's plays, to be sure. I think Mamet is a deeply political playwright, for example. But he never really spells out his political intentions. The society he paints in each of his plays is a very banal and savage society in which people go out at each other for their own advancement and it's dog-eat-dog in the jungle. The Marxists can draw very strong conclusions from a play like that but Mamet doesn't draw any conclusions; he just paints the reality and critic or the political thinker draws the conclusions.

DV: What's the justification of theatre in a society?

RB: As far as I see it – any society? – I wouldn't want to generalize about any society because each society needs a different kind of theatre depending on its state in any given time. For example, in South Africa, I would think an activist theatre would be very necessary. In a state of crisis, you don't look for complication and people get really upset with those who don't want to see things in terms of black and white. I remember a play by Robert Sherwood called *The Petrified Forest* in which the leading character was on the fence regarding whether he was going to be against the Fascists or not and at the end he gives his life against the Fascists and what the play was saying is: You can't be on the fence; you can't weigh too many complications in your life; you really have to act and you are the sum of your actions; and, therefore, you must act morally, you must act politically. But that play hasn't lasted either and the plays that have lasted are the ones that are full, ripe picture of the human kind in all its complexity, in all its darkness and multiplicity and those are the plays that excite me because they fight through the everyday cant with which we live our own lives and remind us the need for toleration, the need for responding to our fellow human beings with some kindness and some depth.

DV: What's the contribution of the avant-garde in American theatre? Living theatre, for instance. Shocking audience has been their consistent concern, it seems to me, and also theatre has become a kind of elitist activity with this kind of intellectualization. Would you comment on this?

RB: I think you got two different ideas. I don't think Living Theatre was elitist, I think Living Theatre would shoot you if you call them elitist. Avant-garde? Some avant-garde is elitist and some of the members, populist. You really can't generalize in that way. The true avant garde is always elitist because the meaning of the word is to be in the vanguard and therefore not a collective majority. Now, if they were not elitists, there wouldn't have been a Stravinsky, a Joyce, a Picasso or there wouldn't have been any major artist in the 19th or 20th century because by definition they wanted to be popular, they wanted to appeal to a large number of people and therefore they wouldn't go with the tribe and troop. You wouldn't even experiment, you wouldn't even try anything new. Stravinsky would be no Stravinsky, though. No Bartok. Right now they are populist because the people have caught up with them. Mere phrases "populist" or "elitist" I find to be useless. The word "elitist" used to have honorific meaning, it was an honorific thing to be in the vanguard and try to bring the people with them and not to ignore them but to introduce them to new methods, new terminologies, new essence. But if you are willing to take risks and be alone for a while society is going to stand still and after sometime it is going to become a museum. There's a great play by Ibsen called *An Enemy of the People* and there's a line in that: "He is strongest who stands alone." And what he means by that is that he has to collect the majority slowly, doesn't collect around a new idea very quickly.

DV: Who are the enduring playwrights in America at the moment; the ones you are most interested in?

RB: The playwrights I am most interested in? David Mamet, pre-eminently . . . I think he is certainly going to be considered a major artist of our time. David Rabe has written a play that I have a great respect for called *Hurly Burly* and it encouraged me to believe that he is going to do a lot more very interesting plays as well. Sam Sheperd – if he'll ever get out of Hollywood and stop being a movie actor. He is not writing in Hollywood; he wrote a movie but he is not writing; he is acting and as far as I'm concerned it's a waste of his time and his talents. Some day he's going to wake up and start writing plays again. I like Christopher Durang's satires very much. I like Don De Lilo (who is essentially a novelist); he wrote his first play which is, I think, as good a first play as ever written called *The Day Room*. I think Arthur Kopit occasionally has a good play in him; whom we are leaving out. Lots of people. Alfred Uhry, who wrote *Driving Miss Daisy*, I would like to see his next play . . . I think that was a poignant work. Craig Lucas who wrote *Reckless*. On the basis of that play I'd say he has a great future ahead of him. It's very unusual play which is to theatre what the movie *Blue Velvet* was to the movies. It has that same off-centre view of the American optimistic illusion. Howard Quarter is very exciting young playwright. He wrote *Boy's Life*. We are about to do two plays of his here in the spring called *Fun* and *Nobody*. Those seem to be the chief playwrights to me.

DV: What do you think about Saul Bellow's *The Last Analysis*?

RB: I think it's a very interesting novelist's play and I don't think it's a great play and I don't think it shows any particular difference in the theatre.

DV: What is the distinction between Broadway and Off-Broadway or even Off-Off-Broadway, for that matter? Is it a matter of economics or do they have different philosophies of theatre altogether?

RB: Well, at present there doesn't seem to be much of a distinction whatsoever. Off-Broadway is seen just as breeding ground for Broadway now. Places like Manhattan Theatre Club, the Second Stage, Circle Rep etc., – they are just try-out homes for Broadway plays. So that if something clicks, they transfer it to Broadway. I don't see too much of a difference. There's an Off-Off Broadway movement that remains relatively chaste. Richard Foreman's Ontological-hysterical Theatre, naturally anything Robert Wilson does. There's a real distinction between those kinds of works than the works you find on Off-Broadway and on Broadway.

DV: Is there any sort of negative attitude towards realistic drama at the moment?

RB: Yes, there is. There is always a negative attitude towards realistic drama on the part of the alternative theatre. There was a time when realism was the alternative theatre and it opposed realism and naturalism, to the existing artificialities of the well-made play, i.e., Ibsen, Strindberg, Chekhov – people like that. But then that entered the mainstream and imitation of their work became the mainstream theatre and therefore alternative theatre became more of a dream-theatre, more of a non-causal, non-linear kind of theatre that called itself up as the option.

DV: How much of patronage does it receive?

RB: Depends. Varies from time to time. Only we consider ourselves a resourceful theatre. Some years we are 100% sold out; some years 65% sold out. It depends on how the public responds in a given time. Somebody like Philip Glass or Robert Wilson can become icons for short periods in New York and works like *Einstein Beach* did not look the same as before. But it becomes after ten years a great success one can't get tickets any more. But these are the fashions and the critics create the fashions. Their fashions come and go. What is important is they continue to write.

DV: But some say that you are a demanding critic yourself.

RB: I try to be . . .

DV: Musicals made a permanent impact on Broadway. It is hard to think of a season where a musical is not present. Why do you think this is the case? Although one surely recognizes that producing a musical is an expensive project. Also, when I see the *Best Plays* of the American Theatre series, I quite often find musicals included in these selections.

RB: When someone is trying to choose the *Best Plays* of the so-called American theatre, they are only talking about New York. They fail to see the fact that American theatre they talk about does not exist in New York anymore. There is theatre activity in the fifty states of America. Each state is a member of very important theatres. Many of them are doing new plays. Some of them are very good in New York. Given the slim picking of New York and the fact that nothing can survive on Broadway if it is not essentially a musical or a comedy, naturally they tend to choose the same as the so-called American theatre. But they are not the American theatre and they are not good plays. So, that's my feeling about musicals.

DV: Well, theatre reviews are generally disliked by dramatists. For instance, Albee is quite critical of theatre-critics. Some people feel that they make or break the plays. For instance, any review for or against a play in *New York Times* makes a tremendous impact. Do you think critics should have that much of power?

RB: Well, of course not. I think if the critic has any power, it is the function of the critic to otherwise elucidate a text or analyse and elucidate a theatrical evening. Naturally a judgement of values is necessary that the judgement of values in the sense that it is good or bad. It is the least interesting part of the critic's equipment. The trouble is that he is never accountable for this opinion. Clearly we don't have the final judgement on a work of art, the final judgement belongs to posterity. I think we should be judged as harshly as we judge the work of art and judge if we are thoroughly intimate in our judgement. And it is a very dangerous situation for a critic to have the power that some critics do have today. And I have been fighting all my life to try to weaken that power.

DV: Theatre-goer does need some kind of guidance – doesn't he? – or some kind of information.

RB: I prefer that the theatre-goer choose on his own or on her own. I don't think he needs to be told where to go. I think that's one of the problems with the American theatre and New York audience. Again we are talking about New York and not the rest of the country. New York audience is like a bunch of sheep and they have to be guided away to the next hit. That has created a market-place mentality in which only the minimum number of plays can survive because they have been identified as the next hit and everything passes by the wayside because the sheep won't follow that particular path. I think the New York theatre-goer should develop a mind of his own, choose a play on his own and recognize on his own but the price of the New York theatre tickets does not allow that to happen. Until that happens, you are not going to have a healthy theatre in New York. In other countries, theatre-goer does not follow any critics. In this city, for instance, Kevin Kelly (*The Boston Globe*) is the leading critic. He batters us (*The*

American Repertory Theatre, Cambridge) time after time but our audiences continue to come to our plays. They got their own minds. They are not following his opinion. They are familiar with the theatre and its aims and they know that if they come here, they are certainly going to have something which they haven't seen before. It is not going to be a conventional experience. Whether they like it or not, there is going to be something exciting for them. And also they don't listen to the critic telling them where they can safely go.

DV: Because Brustein is a big man . . .

RB: It is nothing to do with me. It's nice of you to say that, but . . .

DV: People respect you. And you have written about theatre extensively. People care about your writing and what you had to say in them. You have written, after all, great stuff.

RB: Yes, I wrote. But it is not the question of respecting me in order to come every year to every show. In contrast to New York, they certainly make up their own mind. So, they think it is because of the theatre itself and not because of me. The theatre has provided them in sufficient ways and certainly some satisfaction.

Nathan Glazer

The interview took place in his office at Harvard University.

DV: How is it that "liberal" is a dirty word to-day?

NG: First of all, I don't think it is a dirty word in Cambridge or Boston or on editorial page, of the Op-Ed page of the *New York Times* or the editorial page of the *Boston Globe*. The only place it is dirty is if one has to make a mass appeal and get a majority of voters, then it turns out that it is not so useful. But among intellectuals there's no question that majority of them still see themselves as liberals. They are very positive about liberals – liberalism. If you want to know why it is a dirty word among the non-educated Americans or the less educated Americans or the working class Americans – that's entirely the result of the position of liberals on certain social issues, not on economic issues. Their position on crime or the rights of the accused criminal, pornography, free speech, on abortion, on school and so on – and all these issues which the ordinary American, lower-class working-class American tends to support. These are the issues a liberal opposes. So, if you want to get the ordinary lower-class or working-class support, don't call yourself a liberal.

DV: But I believe in Presidential Campaign George Bush talks about ACLU liberalism. And I thought he was using it as a pejorative or derogatory expression – and indeed he uses it to score a point against his rival, Michael Dukakis.

NG: Yes, but the position of ACLU liberalism is that the ACLU liberalism doesn't take any position on economic issues; it takes position on just those social issues. And that's one way of tarring your opponent. The problem of any campaign in this country, whether Democratic or Republican, is that the Democrats on economic level have an appeal to low-income voters. So, the Republicans have to find an alternative appeal. And their alternative appeal is to social issues. Where working class or lower class is conservative, liberals have opposed them.

DV: Is this an international trend? In Europe, Margaret Thatcher also . . .

NG: Well, I don't think in Europe it is the same because when we say liberalism is a dirty word here, at least in my view the issue is a social issue, not the economic issue. I don't think there is such an automatic thing in free market positions in this country. It's true, on the economic issues there's been certain swing as in Europe. But I don't think the social issues play a large role in Europe. Those issues I referred: crime, pornography, abortion. I don't think they have any weight in Europe as they have in this country.

DV: Do you associate yourself with neo-conservatism in any way?

NG: Well, I think the problem of the term neo-conservatism is that initially neo-conservatism referred to a number of positions. They weren't complete philosophy. On some of these issues, I could be called a neo-conservative. But recent neo-conservatism almost identified totally with foreign policy positions. And foreign policy of Norman Podhoretz and my friend and collaborator Kristol, I don't agree with. I don't agree with their position on Israel. I don't agree with their position on Russia. I don't agree with their view that there's a need for strength internationally—defence-strength and so on, on the suspicion of changes in Russia. So, since that has become a definition of neo-conservatism, I shy away from that term. If the definition of the neo-conservatism has remained or included, specifically identified with other positions I have taken like critical of certain elaborate social positions, critical of affirmative action, then I would call myself a neo-conservative. If it tends to mean the things I don't agree with, then I don't.

DV: In the article you have written for the *Partisan Review*, you have mentioned that it hasn't paid that much of attention to Jewish issues?

NG: That's right.

DV: But why? It has mostly Jewish contributors, I thought.

NG: It was probably mostly Jewish contributors. By the way, if you looked at the editorial group it was only half-Jewish probably. Maybe. It has two non-Jewish people. The initial editorial group. Dwight McDonald and the artist George L.K. Morris. How big a role they played I don't know.

DV: But most influential are William Phillips and Philip Rahv.

NG: Yes, Phillips. Philip Rahv. Then, Trilling in so far as he involved and (Sidney) Hook. Delmore Schwartz. William Barrett is not Jewish.

Why weren't the Jewish issues prominent? I think it's because they are very much under the spell of Marxism. If you are under the spell of Marxism, you think in terms of class. And you think race, ethnicity, and religion as survivals, as things that simply left over from the past or the things that don't play any important role. In fact, they could never really come to terms with most of the artists they admired. I mean they couldn't – for instance, they did not know what to make of T.S. Eliot they admired. But they didn't know what to make of his Anglicanism. Meant nothing to them. So, they were simply not responsive to religious issues or ethnic, national issues because they were so much under the spell of Marxism. And so Jewish issues were not relevant to them.

DV: What about the present position of the other groups? For instance, *Dissent* of Irving Howe and I believe *Tikkun* also?

N.V.:Well, I would say that all Jewish groups to-day, all left-wing Jewish groups or left-wing groups of Jewish intellectuals are much more Jewish than they were in the forties or even the fifties. As the Marxist ideology declined, it was clear that the religious or nationalist issues have not disappeared. In fact, they are more and more important. And may be if you are a fossil like Chomsky, who is literally a fossil, whose ideas have moved, I suppose not a millimeter since he was a young Marxist in the late forties and the early fifties, then you can still ignore these issues. Then you can still think in terms of class, that Zionism represents imperialism and Jewish middle classes. And you can have such idiotic illusions as he sometimes does. A working Arab and Jewish working classes combining against the upper classes. These nonsensical issues. But Jewish intellectuals see the significance of religion-national identities. You can't explain Jewish-Arab conflict in class terms. These are national or religion-national conflicts and issues. So, I suppose my view would be Jewish intellectuals learned. And they realized that the Marxist-framework was meaningless and explained nothing. And so they have changed. So, whether it is *Dissent* or *Tikkun* or even, for that matter, some of the old Jewish Communists, even they have become more Jewish. Someone like Maurice Shafiz. They may still hang on to something but very little.

DV: But, at the same time, there is a subtle anti-Semitism in this country, I feel – in academia and elsewhere.

NG: Well, that's a question, I would say, compared to what. Compared to the twenties and the thirties there's much less anti-Semitism. Compared to the forties, there's much less anti-Semitism now. In view of the provocation, there's much less anti-Semitism. Jews are very prominent in academia. But I don't see much by way of anti-Semitism. I don't feel I do, at any rate.

DV: Not so much in outrageous terms, may be. I remember Gore Vidal wrote an article long ago called "The Empire Lovers Strike Back." And it was published in the *Nation* edited by Victor Navasky who was Jewish.

NG: Yes, Gore Vidal is in Venice after all. And he is not very much in academia. He is very much a writer. He is a successful writer. But there's a distinctive slant. There's always been something of a conflict between two wings of American intellectual life. One is young Southern conservative homosexual and the other is North-eastern Jewish. And many years ago Leslie Fiedler wrote an essay describing the tension between these two elements who would meet in New York. Now, by the way, not that all the Southerns are homosexuals but lot of them were. But tension even exists with regard to Southern writers. There is peculiar meeting ground. Southern writers who have come up from Southern region and emphasizing tradition and the virtue of Southern culture. And there's that kind of tension. And Gore Vidal is not particularly a Southerner I think but he represents that kind of point of view. And others, of course, specific issues one could disagree. But his views on Norman Podhoretz are obvious because Podhoretz is one of these intellectuals who took stand that homosexuality is wrong. It is not just a sexual preference. Well, you can realize that Gore Vidal is not going to like that. I don't think Gore Vidal represents anything in particular.

DV: How do Jewish intellectuals view the Middle East situation and Israel?

NG: I think they are divided. There is clearly a division, let us say, between Norman Podhoretz and Martin Peretz and Irving Howe or, for that matter, Michael Lerner of *Tikkun*. All of them support Israel in some way unless you get to some one far left like Chomsky. There is a kind of anti-Israel tendency among a few far left Jewish intellectuals. All of them want Israel to survive but there's a difference in perception between dovish and hawkish wing. Dovish wing which thinks that there is chance of place in Israel with Arabs and they want to explore trading of territory for peace and the hawkish wing which says that this is futile and doesn't want to explore it. So, that's the division and that division is sharp. It's become sharper. I would say that it didn't exist much in the sixties when everyone was on Israel side. It didn't exist in '73 when every one was on Israel side. I think in post-'73 years and particularly after Begin became the Prime Minister of Israel in '76-'77, it became clear that the assumption of American Jewish intellectuals that Israel would be willing to trade land for peace was not true. It was not true for the dominant political forces, and so that led to certain disillusionment. And Lebanese war in '82 similarly—the first war Israel did not fight in self-defence. So, I think there's that division.

DV: What do you think of the recent Paul de Man controversy?

NG: I don't think much about it at all. Lot of his students and supporters are Jewish, aren't they? Because they are in literary world, literary criticism. They want to pursue anything new, and he is new. Structuralism, deconstructionism—whatever it is. And I don't think it's going to have an effect one way or the other. There are different number of controversies these days. There is one around T.S. Eliot and the notion whether Jews should support the creating of scholarship in his name. There is a debate going on that. *Times Literary Supplement* and elsewhere. And there's Heidegger who is such a prominent figure in the field of philosophy. And how to interpret his pro-Nazism and so on. I suppose there's a recent biography of Pound, has been reviewed in *TLS.* I suspect what's been happening in these controversies about Pound, Heidegger, Eliot and de Man is the relationship between modernism and pro-Semitism or anti-Semitism. Jews always seem to be modernists—people of the new. They are kind of suppressed in the forties, *Partisan Review* days. The contradiction between modernism as represented in people like Eliot, Lawrence and Milton Hindus's great idol Celine, is the contradiction between modernism and liberalism. And these contradictions lead Jewish intellectuals to think more about it whether there is any organic relationship between modernism and anti-Semitism that surface in some of these figures.

DV: There was a time when there was a great relationship between the blacks and Jews. Somehow it appears to have strained to a certain extent now.

NG: Well, I think the primary reason for the split – I think there are two reasons. Jews would not go along with blacks on the affirmative action, affirmative action being preference for blacks. When there was anti-Jewish and anti-black discrimination, Jews and blacks would agree on a race-blind planned policy, because it is good for Jews and good for blacks compared with a race-conscious policy that was discriminating. But when the race-blind policy did not do much, then they went on to demand race-conscious policies that favoured blacks. Well, if they are going to favour blacks, they are going to disfavour Jews. The decision also went against the grain of Jewish liberalism. So, that was one issue. The second issue was the issue of Israel. If the black intellectuals are going to identify themselves with the third world and the third world would see Israel as Western imperialist intrusion and be critical of it, that would be a problem. Let me ask you one thing. During your stay at Brandeis, did they ask you about Indian position on Israel? . . . Well, it's part of non-alignment policy, the problem of interpreting Zionism as a force of imperialism, not to mention the occupation of Arab lands and so on. I don't think Indians are anti-Semitic. Do you see *India Abroad*? Recently some Jewish delegates met Indian officials. For the first time, a group of Indian journalists is going to visit Israel. So, the relationships are improving.

DV: Most of the academic left is obviously anti-Israel. Maybe they equate Zionism with racism of some sort. Considering the fact that most articulate and vocal theoreticians are Jewish like Lukacs, Trotsky or, for that matter, Marx himself, their anti-Israel stance is puzzling to say the least.

NG: Yes, Marxism is opposed – well, it is a complicated story – to make nationality, religion prior to class interests. So, that's the explanation for that. True Marxist is not going to be a friend of Israel.

DV: As the time goes on the Jewish intellectuals in this country seem to have found sustenance in Judaism and Jewish heritage. I see Harold Bloom trying to link up Kabbalah with his brand of critical approach. Geoffrey Hartman recently put out a book called *Midrash and Literature*. Derrida himself has been considered in terms of Rabbinic Judaism in *Slayers of Moses* (Handelman). Why such a sudden need for extensive Jewish scholarship with parallel critical trends?

NG: I would say this was not with the Jewish intellectuals of the forties and the fifties. I say in general about the Jewish intellectuals that Marxism opens up the other alternatives, religion, nationality and so on. Whether this would apply to literary criticism, I just would not know. This is one subject I wouldn't like to hazard anything on.

DV: How influential are American intellectuals?

NG: They are influential – they are influential in academia. How influential they are in general in terms of effecting American policy on economics, I think not very. Certainly influential in shaping academics in such a book as Allan Bloom's *The Closing of the American Mind*.

DV: Do you go along with Bloom's assessments and prescriptions in the book?

NG: I think he is extreme. Here again, my non-conservatism. I simply do not see how one can justify the primacy of single canon, you know, of authoritarian works anymore. One can always justify because they are influential and they are important. But the notion that they imply wisdom. If you don't know Aristotle or Plato, you are in some sense defective in wisdom. This is something which I do not simply accept. So, I think Allan Bloom is simply extreme. And as a matter of fact, even I think depending how it's done, one can find wisdom from studying contemporary works too. Basically I don't go along with him – his critique of curricular change and so on. I would agree if he were making the point that curriculum is weak and flabby but it is strengthened necessarily by the classic study of political philosophy. May strengthen mathematics or sciences, or general knowledge of literature, or history of thought.

DV: Now, about American foreign policy. America supports Pakistan at the same time it supports Israel too. Do you see any problem here?

NG: Sure there's a problem. America supports Saudi Arabia too. Kuwait against Iran. There is this complexity – an enemy of your enemy becomes your friend, if not on some other grounds. So, Pakistan is not a Communist country. On the other hand, it is anti-Communist strongly because of their position or because of their ideology. So, if they are anti-Communist in some sense they are a friend of the U.S. So, we basically support them from the viewpoint of a big bi-polar controversy. Now, in that bi-polar controversy, India – again the enemy is your friend – India has tensions with China now for thirty years and so is Russia. So, they become allies for complicated reasons. I hope now that relations with Russia are improving, America will find less to support Pakistan.

DV: What do you think about Gorbachev's reforms in Russia?

NG: Whether he survives or not is a different question. People have doubts on that. But that he certainly wants to reduce Russia's confrontation with the West; he wants to reduce Russia's investments in arms and increase investments in civilian production – that is clear. He wants to loosen up Russian controls. That's also very clear. There is no doubt that he intends change. That's also for the best certainly.

DV: Do you foresee any possibility of improvement in Indo-American relationships? We both are democratic nations.

NG: Well, that always has been my position. International tensions have overruled democratic community. I think a lot depends on Russian American development. I think if the things continue to move in the direction, if those relations improve. There's another reason why America supports Israel, there are five and a half million Jews. I am sure if there are five and a half million American Indians, our relations will improve. They have already improved with half a million Indians. Million Indians, it would be even better. Because that's the way American foreign policy works; it works through democratic political influences.

DV: You just came back from India. How do you view Indian political scene?

NG: Let us not get into that. That's so complicated. Well, you know it's very discouraging. India needs two-party system. It's very hard to create it. It needs an opposition. I think the Congress needs a strong party to oppose it because of what happened, so much of corruption, so much of ineffectiveness. But, as you know, opposition consists of regional parties, it is so difficult to make them a coherent group just as it was difficult to make Janta a coherent group. So, it's very difficult. I don't know. That's internal politics.

DV: There's so much illiteracy in India. Does it disturb you as a social scientist?

NG: Sure, illiteracy disturbs me, even more, the fact that, whatever it is, 200,000 villages, only 80,000 don't have the drinking water. What disturbs me is that India's economic progress has been so modest even compared to China according to recent figures – very modest compared to Korea or Thailand. Nevertheless, I think that it's stuck with a system of governmental control of recovery that is very inefficient,

inefficient that cannot be shaken. I mean the relationship between bureaucrats and the protected companies is so close that there's no way of opening up the economy. I was seeing some figures that there are ten or twelve times foreign investment in China than that is in India. Now, if China can afford foreign investment, why can't India? There are ten or twelve times foreign investment in Thailand than in India. So, it's very discouraging that the liberalization of economy hasn't moved fast.

DV: Do you see any hope in future?

NG: Well, it's hard to see any hope. It's hard to see any forces that bring about any change. I may be wrong.

Conversations with Bellow: A Personal View

Very few contemporary novelists seem to have attracted as much critical attention as Saul Bellow over a long period of time. It speaks of enduring interest his works have evinced in the readers. His novels have certainly created a wider readership in my country, India, where research students often consider him as a prospective target for term papers or dissertation. In a comic way, Bellow has foreseen this as one would expect from such an ingenious writer. So, then, it is not surprising that Charles Citrine, buttonholed by a student-interviewer who wanted to know details of his poet-friend's personal life, says this: "Young people, what do you aim to do with the facts about Humboldt, publish articles and further your careers? This is pure capitalism."[1] But then, why am I talking about this? Because I too was one of those enthusiasts, only this time it was Bellow. I met with him at his apartment in South Chicago (December 24, 1988) on a winter day. I too have questions but I discretely avoided personal queries. Mark Harris's[2] book, written in frustration, did not induce me to pursue my curiosity in this direction although I do not find it objectionable that the reader wants to know about the writer he/she admires – notwithstanding the disapproval of such an act at the moment by some theorists. So, we moved on to that subgenre, if you will, called American Jewish literature which also gave currency to the term "Jewish-American Writer."

The term "Jewish-American Writer" has always been problematic to many writers of Jewish origin over a long period of time. So much so, the *Contemporary Jewish Record*, the forerunner of *Commentary*, asked some of the emerging Jewish writers in 1944 to express their views on how their Jewishness determines their work, especially against the background of the all-pervasive anti-Semitism at that time. Among them were Lionel Trilling, Muriel Rukeyser, Delmore Schwartz, Alfred Kazin and Isaac Rosenfeld. Many of them treated this idea with indifference and even with a sense of disdain while Schwartz and Rosenfeld either affirmed their Jewishness or found a useful paradigm in Jewish context for the modern *angst*. Trilling, for instance, stated that modern Jewish religion did not produce a single voice "of religious authority."[3] Further, he knows "no Jewish writer in

English who has added a micromillimetre to his stature by 'realizing his Jewishness', although I know of some who have curtailed their promise by trying to heighten their Jewish consciousness."[4] In mid-fifties *Congress Weekly* and in 1961 *Commentary* again provided a forum on this subject. But now the views of Jewish writers dramatically changed for the better in the sense that they accepted it and, in some cases, even celebrated it. Much later in his career, Trilling himself outlived his views and found rabbinical overtones in Wordsworth's poetry.[5] I thought Bellow, certainly the foremost of the Jewish-American writers, would have his thoughts about it. His reflection on it came as a surprise to me. The people, he says, who use this term are not always friendly people. Most of these WASP critics consider the first generation writers as "foreigners" contaminating the pure English idiom. Therefore, these writers of immigrant background and, at least, initially of bilingual context, can never be part of the mainstream literary ambience, for, somehow, they 'fail' to reflect archetypal America. On the other hand Jewish community considers the predominance of Jewish writers good public relations. Public relations, Bellow explains, in America means advertisement. It is an advertisement for Jewish community because traditionally Jews have been viewed as Shylock-types. Jewish contribution to science, literature and art possibly subverts this myth. Also, the WASPs "didn't always like it that the foreigners or ethnics of various kinds came to America and wrote in English."[6] Bellow does not think that it is his role as a writer to improve the reputation of Jews though he sympathizes greatly with them. He is not interested in public relations either – theirs or anybody else's. He does not like to be put down for being a Jewish writer nor does he think that he should be apologetic about it.

Can a Jewish writer be an American writer also? This question is never addressed with such earnestness in the case of other ethnic writers. It is as if one is introducing the age-old dual-role of the Jew in Western Civilization. Traditionally, the Jew is rarely, if ever, viewed as a part of the mainstream culture. They are 'aliens' with loyalties elsewhere – the state within state. Much damage has been done with these notions. When one introduces these arguments in literary terms, its implicit menace should be properly recognized. Bellow's reluctance, in a way, is justified. But when he goes further and states that the American Jewish committee views it as a publicity (i.e., advertisement), I think it is slightly overstated. When I sought clarification on this issue, he said he was merely explaining their positions.

I said that one could be both a Jew and American writer. Thus, the context of the Jewish writer in America continues to be a debatable issue.

Then we moved on to his novels. His characters think about their past all the time. They talk about their parents, cousins and uncles – the family structure, in other words, figures prominently in his work. And also, they crave for Old Country culture and values in their search for security, sustenance, and spiritual fulfilment in gentile America. To this observation, Bellow says that there are two kinds of Jews in the Western world: assimilationists (viewed derogatively as *maskilim* in the nineteenth century) and those who believe in their Jewish identity. Obviously, Bellow has no sympathy for the assimilationists because one should not forget one's history. Bellow says, "what does one assimilate to? America does not hold steady." When these changes provide enough room for authentic self, it is a different matter. Uncertainties, need for communal identity as well as personal order call for uncompromising values. The failure, if it could be called that, and personal discord of Bellow's people eloquently testifies to the fact that the contemporary world proclaims little hope to man's soul. But they don't give in; instead, they put up a battle in order to restore full dignity to man's estate by reconstituting the usable past. In this regard, the function of memory, *zakhor*, is significant since it gathers up subdued, forgotten or lost elements of dignity. It works as an antidote to intellectualization of our perceptions. Thus, Bellow's people are family-bound. He further states that in "America it is rather exotic to have an attachment with family because the family is in the process of disappearing. For many Americans family does no longer matter very much. So, that's almost exotic, strange in a writer who doesn't do that. I explain to you my nephew is dead and I go to see my sister. Well, not all Americans do that kind of thing."[7] Herzog, Citrine, Henderson, Elya Gruner love their family. For Elya, Sammler in *Mr. Sammler's Planet* represents spiritual and intellectual nourishment; indeed, the very sense of the Old Country. And also America changes every five years. For these family-oriented, order-craving people, memory of the old days is sacred, though their attachment to these memories is seldom viewed with favour by other people. In *Humboldt's Gift*, for instance, Naomi's father Doc calls Citrine a foreigner, "a green horn," simply because he reads poetry to his daughter. Citrine's own brother tries hard to subdue his brotherly affection and rejects past as useless mental baggage. It is not American to exhibit family feelings openly. Nevertheless, Bellow seems to sacralize such moments in life. But why do they stumble on in life, people like Herzog? Partly because they have such un-American orientation towards life; partly also because their partners often do not share such passions any more. Herzog's problem, as Bellow puts it, is the problem of intellectual climate in Western world and the situation of an intellectual in its context. The much revered and canonical writers like Marx, Nietzsche, Freud, seem to privilege the kind of the heavy weight theories which dominate the climate of opinion in academia. Bellow goes on: "If you are a Marxist, they tell you that your family doesn't exist any more, it's gone. Capitalism has destroyed it. Revolution would further destroy the family life. If you have in mind Nietzsche, he tells you that God is dead, you are in a condition of nihilism . . . I could have gone to Freud as the third. . . . Freedom for them is throwing off all the tradition of your fathers and starting a new page for yourself. And you become successful by doing this. You become an intellectual and you are rewarded for demonstrating these characteristics. But in your private life, in your inner life, you feel disoriented by this."[8]

And yet, significantly, by writing a foreword to Allan Bloom's celebrated book *The Closing of the American Mind*, he affirms his belief in the Great Books philosophy. This Great Books course was initially introduced at Columbia University as an introduction to the classics of Western Civilization. Later, it has inspired a series of scholars like Mortimer Adler and Robert Hutchins at Chicago University also. Even so, Herzog mocks at the failure of academic training in the universities. Modern Western thought to which one is exposed inevitably in schools does not help very much in a crisis. Herzog, by writing a series of letters to these thinkers, dead or alive, makes fun of the futility of these theories, intellectual life; much valued for professional or careeristic purposes, the life of the mind becomes a burden to an already disorderly life.

After tea and cookies, we deliberated on Israel which incidentally led us to *Mr. Sammler's Planet*. Sammler's response to Israel, I thought, was not adequately clarified in the novel. I wanted him to probe into this aspect although it was not the central focus in the novel. Commenting on it, I said that it is not convincing to me that Sammler, having gone to Israel, the Holy Land, during 1967 as a journalist, goes only to the Christian sites. For a survivor, Israel should have a greater importance, now a haven for the persecuted and damned of the Western society for centuries, helplessly savoring humility and simultaneously yearning for Zion. Sammler is a thinker, now divested himself of the burdensome notions of the West. Israel, for the post-Holocaust generation, and to the people who have survived the second World War, is certainly more than a nation-state. It is probably the only novel of Bellow which at least touches on the Holocaust theme, though it never faces it squarely. Bellow says that Sammler feels 'so Jewish' and therefore goes to Israel. He is also an assimilating Jew. Further, Bellow wants merely the survivor's view of America. Besides, at his age Sammler wants to read his Christian mystics and live alone. Interestingly, Bellow writes a personal account of his visit to Israel. He, like Sammler, was a journalist during the 1967 war. Although in the novel he appears to be mute on many theoretical issues of the Holocaust and Israel's peculiar situation in the Middle East facing a threat of extermination any moment, this book on Israel takes these issues head on. His profound views are evident, for instance, when he analyses certain themes like the refugee problem, PLO, the West Bank occupation and so on. Israel-bashing has become a journalistic game these days especially with the liberal-left. They forget the fact that with such harmful criticism, they are not only destroying the prospect of the only democracy in the Middle East, but also the home for the oppressed Jews all over the world. The problems of Israel are not uncommon in this turbulent century which has already seen two world wars. Refugee problem, for instance, is in India, Africa, Europe. Would there be peace in Israel and a solution to the Middle East crisis? Bellow says this: "A person with a trained logical mind says to a problem, there's a solution. That may be true for mathematics, that may be true for physics. But that's not true for human affairs." Also, "we suffered a great deal from people who thought they knew what the solutions were"[9] – people like Hitler and Stalin who, in the name of providing solutions, killed millions of innocent people.

The situation of the Jewish intellectual, to say the least, is essentially eclectic. Most of them have come-of-age in the thirties, almost always in the *Partisan Review* environment. Some moved away from traditional Left positions to its numerous variations. Thus we have Irving Howe and his *Dissent* making a case for democratic socialism. Norman Podhoretz's *Commentary* presents neo-conservatism as an alternative. It appears that some very influential thinkers like Irving Kristol and Nathan Glazer seem to share their views with Podhoretz. Their critique of literature is greatly influenced by their socio-political positions. Bellow would not have anything to do with these people, because "the people who do not have poetry in them are politically dangerous". *Partisan Review*, which published *Seize the Day* when he was seeking literary reputation, does not interest him any more. Their perceptions of literature are ideological. "Well, as a writer, I think they are guilty of a very poor taste . . . That means a lot to me. Literature is something like my religion. So, if I say they have a poor taste, they somehow crippled themselves in a very important aspect of life. They disqualified themselves in making intelligent judgements about a lot of things."[10] They have a political agenda and literature is viewed in that perspective.

Podhoretz-Bellow connection is yet another matter. *Commentary* did not take notice of Bellow's recent novels. In fact, Bellow told me that Trilling advised the then young Podhoretz to write an unfavourable review of the just published *Adventures of Augie March* to make a literary reputation. Podhoretz recounts his version of the matter in *Making It*. He says that it was Bellow's fantasy. But Bellow has his way. Podhoretz believes that he also persuaded many of his friends that it was so. Three years later, "one of America's eminent poets," Podhoretz does not name him, told him in a drunken state at a party that "We'll get you for that review if it takes ten years."[11] When I met Podhoretz at his New York office, he appeared to be a genial and well-meaning person. In fact, he did not betray any malice towards Bellow. On the contrary, he asked me to read his book on Israel for its perceptions. About his rift with Trilling, it was merely the critics' invention. He always had a cordial relationship with Trilling.

These are some of the thoughts inspired by my conversation with Bellow. At 74, Bellow is still publishing masterful works although he is not at the forefront of critical discussion now as he used to be, say, ten years ago. In fact, how many writers can boast of producing outstanding works over a span of three decades. Richard Stern, his friend, says only three writers come to his mind: Henry James, William Faulkner and, now, Saul Bellow. Bellow offered to drive me to my apartment on the North Sheridan Road which is quite far away. On way, he told me interesting anecdotes. Finally, time to say farewell. In retrospect, I know this for sure. Whatever may be the vicissitudes and eccentricities of literary reputations, contemporary literary world would be poorer without Bellow's enigmatic presence.

NOTES

1. Saul Bellow, *Humboldt's Gift* (New York: The Viking Press, 1975).
2. Mark Harris, *Saul Bellow: Drumlin Woodchuck* (Athens: The University of Georgia Press, 1980).

3. Lionel Trilling, "Under Forty," *The Literature of the American Jews*, ed. Theodore Gross (New York: The Free Press, 1973), p. 360.
4. *Ibid.*
5. Lionel Trilling, "Wordsworth and the Rabbis," *The Opposing Self* (New York: The Viking Press, 1955).
6. Saul Bellow, in a Personal Interview with the Author.
7. *Ibid.*
8. *Ibid.*
9. *Ibid.*
10. *Ibid.*
11. Norman Podhoretz, *Making it* (London: Jonathan Cope, 1967), p. 160.

Ideology in Saul Bellow's *Mr. Sammler's Planet*

> Of course, assuming that we do not live one of these ideologies (religious, legal, political, ethical) as truth . . . we admit that the ideology we are discussing from a critical point of view, examining it as the ethnologist examines the myths of a 'primitive society', that these 'world outlooks' are largely imaginary, i.e., do not 'correspond to reality'.[1]
>
> Louis Althusser

Ideology, in Marxist context, is generally viewed as false consciousness that is imposed by a dominant class on others, the proletariat, for example, in order to perpetuate their interests. Georg Lukacs calls it 'reification'[2] which signifies that though one may perceive particular social reality as truth, it is often merely an illusion and thus the perception reinforced by the process of 'reification' can only lead to false conclusions. In fact, there is a greater element of truth in Adorno's comments that, "To-day ideology means society as appearance."[3] Although, for certain German thinkers like Max Weber[4] and Karl Mannheim,[5] ideology does not have the same connotations, it is in the Marxist sense, the term is used here. Thus, in the present view, ideology is "a system of interested deceit"[6] in order to subjugate or exploit the disadvantaged in a society or their cultural manifestations.

How does a writer grapple with such imaginary relations to perceive the truth in a social reality? Or should he accept Karl Mannheim's view in *Ideology and Utopia* that all our knowledge of truth is relational since we achieve such knowledge through the prism of ideology and, therefore, should give up hope of ever finding the truth? It poses infinite problems for a creative writer, Saul Bellow in our case, who pretends to reflect or comment upon a particular social ambience. This is also not to deny that the writer may choose to spread ideological positions for his advantage in case he belongs to the same class or supports it as part of his political agenda. If creative writing embodies such complexities of imaginary relations since they are very much part of the ideological syndrome, the implied reader of any book should be extremely cautious in his/her response to these works. One has to necessarily wade through the hypnotic human dimensions of a work of art to encounter the invidious network of 'false consciousness'; otherwise, he/she too would be an unwitting partner in propagating the author's ideology. Consequently, the critic/reader slips into a position of an adversary; but probably that is an essential price one has to pay in interpreting any literary product or, for that matter, any work.

It is in this background, Saul Bellow's *Mr. Sammler's Planet*[7] is discussed in this paper with a special reference to his portrayal of the New Left and other related matters. As I go on with this paper, I am constantly, and certainly profitably, reminded of Walter Benjamin's view that the author is a producer – and, therefore, a different structure of associations have a suitable place in any analysis of a work. Bellow's political positions, his angles of vision of contemporary American reality inevitably guide his perceptions of a given cultural domain. How these political or social ramifications are refracted through the ideological creative process on to the final product of a work, need a specific emphasis to deconstruct the superstructure of explanation and, if possible, meaningfully posit the creative impulse in its proper atmosphere.

In order to get at the genesis of Bellow's critique of the generation of the sixties, one has to restructure some of his possible perceptions out of which such meditations, as in *Mr. Sammler's Planet*, take root. Even a cursory reading of the novel would give the impression that Bellow clearly has no sympathy with the radical politics, the New Left, avant-garde in art and theatre and other protest movements. The general history of the decade of the sixties has to underline the Civil Rights movement in the South especially the outrageous acts of the KKK against the blacks, the Vietnam War, the racist segregation. The counter-culture made an imprint on its life. Joan Boaz refused to pay taxes because the money would be used in subjugating the defenseless people of Vietnam. Bob Dylan fervently thought that the "times they are a changing." He asked passionately: "How many years can people exist before they are allowed to be free?" The youth rebelled against the establishment because, they felt, it had no right to dignity when it did not recognize dignity of other people. The sixties is the decade of the youth, the New Left, the Yippies, the Woodstock. If this is the case, what better way to subvert the sixties than introducing a rhetoric which apparently suggests that the youngsters are not only irrationally rebellious but they are also ignorant, lack in etiquette, and are inadequately informed. Bellow obviously believes that the youth indulged in over-confidence, intolerance, ruthlessness and cruelty. Anarchistic imagination ruled art. The Living Theatre productions were hysterical. In other words,

America became Sodom and Gomorrah, thanks to the New Left politics. To make matters worse, the New Left was also anti-Israel. Not for a moment, Bellow was willing to consider if these student movements had any positive element at all. He would never grant, for instance, that to live with the knowledge that their country was molesting another poor country, Vietnam, did not enthuse sensitive, value-oriented youngsters. What was more problematic was the fact that the philosophy of liberal education and humanities at the universities ill-equipped a generation, which, if any thing, needed authenticity, moral strength and integrity. Since these were not forth-coming, they had to take to streets, make protest marches, to tell America that it "stinks." Even so, it would be naive and intellectually irresponsible to absolve their excesses but their concern for justice and a need for change in domestic and foreign policies cannot be underwritten.

Although, Sammler is genuinely astonished at his encounters with the American scene, there appears to be an expectation on the part of the writer that Sammler personifies certain European sobriety which is strangely not available in the New World. But to equate Europe of the Great War and especially Germany and the America of the sixties is not only absurd but also ideological. In fact, the failure to see any genuine substraction in the New Left movement forces Bellow—probably it is self-willed—to view America with extreme skepticism and cynicism. It is precisely this ideology that spells doom for the novel. The novel itself may appear to be a survivor's view of America. But why only the America of the sixties distorted through intemperate ideology? For instance, look at Sammler's personal history. He was an Anglo-phile, working as a journalist in England for a Polish newspaper. His entire family perished in the Holocaust. He was shot himself, though he somehow survived it. Presently, he lives in New York City with his nephew's help. His nephew, Elya, wants him because Sammler provides certain spiritual order in his life. America with shopping-mall culture and now, as Bellow would have it, the student lawlessness is not the place where one can establish personal order. Sammler's meditations on the America of that time are frequently connotative of the tragedy of the Holocaust. One is, Sammler feels, for ever presented with themes and explanations but "being right is a matter of interpretation."[9] Sammler evokes Bellow's sense of reality as he perceives it. After all, it is the arrogant cerebration and solution-seeking arguments of the New Left that one needs to suspect. They believe that they have issues and, therefore, lcok for solutions. Predictably, the youngsters never make an impression on him.

Thus, Lionel Feffer, who used to read for him, is a hustler, go-getter, philanderer, public relations personality, always looking for some kind of finder's fee; full of new ideas, he comically plans to make it in materialist America. He also seduces a young lady, confuses old Sammler into accepting to give a talk at problem-ridden Columbia University – supposedly for the benefit of children. He is to talk about the British scene of the thirties. By introducing the context of the thirties, Bellow cleverly attempts to debunk the New Left – as opposed to the Old Left of the thirties. In the forties and the fifties, most of these fervent communists of the Old Left became subdued apologetics or ex-Communists famously proclaiming the God-that-failed message. In fact, strange as it may sound, the New Left disavowed itself from the Old Left. If we have to accept the deliberate misreadings of the New Left especially by people like Melvyn Lasky,[10] most people of the radical movement are either poorly informed of Marxism or they simply did not think it important enough to make any theoretical change in their programme – if they have any. Sure enough, in his talk on the British Thirties, Sammler introduces George Orwell, who systematically subverts totalitarian – Communist? – regimes in his two important books *Animal Farm*[11] and *1984*.[12] He also quotes Orwell to say that the British radicals were partronized by the Royal families. This is a clever argument on Bellow's part aimed merely to scandalize the New Left. It also disregards whatever role the Old Left had played since most of them "disappeared" into various political positions. Of course, Sammler is not allowed to complete his talk. A bearded fellow interrupts him, insults him and, in a way, drives him out. Interestingly, in Mark Harris's book on Bellow – supposedly a biographical venture which came to almost nothing except sparing personal anecdotes – a similar incident is narrated which seems to have taken place in Bellow's personal life.[13] If this is true, Sammler is evidently Bellow's persona and by bringing the Old Left in the New Left context, Bellow seems to equate one with the other, at least in their ultimate consequences. On his way home, Sammler encounters the black pick-pocket, this time to be harassed and forced to a corner where the blackman exposes himself. An orchestration of threat? Certainly. But is there a single youngster in this novel who has a word of approval from the author? Elya's daughter, Angel, is absolutely with the time. Independent, she indulges in luxury with a huge stipend her father allots to her. For her, sex is a matter of routine, pure entertainment. The relationship with her boyfriend, Horricker, does not go very far. Also, she does not seem to mind group sex.

Having learnt of this matter, Elya is disturbed. At a time when Angel should have shown a gesture of repentance to her dying father, she startles Sammler by coming to the hospital in a tantalizing apparel. Her brother, Wallace, is not much of an encouragement to the concerned father of theirs. He is full of plans too. Always a beginner, he never succeeds in anything. He senses somehow that his father stashed away large sums of money he received as a favour from his mafia connections – which, after all, turns out to be true. This, too, shows the decadence of the times. Wallace wants to find the treasure so that he can use it for his innumerable projects.

The narrative, thus, becomes problematic, thoroughly confusing various themes, when the perceptions of the New Left are piled together with other insanities of the sixties, mostly the inherited horror and the legacy of the Holocaust. Contemporary America itself has problems of various kinds especially the unaccommodating contexts of the black man. There is an incident in the novel where the black gangsters do not seem to follow the boy's appeals for life. They do not share the same language any more. Bellow also introduces Walter Baruch, a survivor of the Holocaust, who has a fetish for large female hands. Rumkowski, the so-called Jewish Prince, who helped Nazis in his fashion, is an unwilling participant in carrying out "the final solution." The scenario is very grim indeed.

What happens when the New Left views of Bellow are contextualized along with these commonly agreed responses to the American scene and the recent human massacre in the gas chambers? The equation is clearly fallacious. It debunks whatever good there is in the New Left and their contribution to the American society. Bellow's understanding of the New Left is, without doubt, a deliberate exercise in ideology. He is known for his strong opinions. Once he is convinced that the radial youth is dangerous for whatever reasons, he quickly introduced his theory in the narrative. It gets submerged in the over-all critique of the Western decadence. Since other arguments are already well-accepted, the New Left disorder, if that, also is taken for granted. Thus, Bellow very cleverly generalizes – and surely benefits from such an act – and imposes his view with a subtle artistic sense in this novel. Noam Chomsky, commenting on the period in a personal interview, has this to say: "In the nineteen sixties . . . there were lot of popular organizations, lot of development among general population, began very much among the young people and spread to the various sections of the people. New questions were asked, there was lot of dissidence, there was skepticism, activism, refugee political organizations and so on. All of that terrified elites; elites want the population to be passive, apathetic and weaning—they are expressive about it."[14] Elites, academicians and intellectuals single-mindedly supported the Vietnam war. It is the masses and the youth that protested against the war. In almost all these protest marches, intellectuals conveniently stayed aloof. It is in this context such works as the one under discussion should be analysed. America to-day, Chomsky believes, is more civilized than it used to be. Bellow's views on the novel changed as the time wore on: "it's my first thoroughly non-apologetic venture into ideas . . . here I am baring myself nakedly."[15] Five years later, he says that, "I think of *Mr. Sammler's Planet* as a sort of polemical theory."[16] Afterwards, he would go to the extent of saying that it was a novel with no artistic control. Also, if one sees any point in Chomsky's argument, how is one to respond to Bellow's book? More significantly, what is the status of an artistic product when it takes up themes such as these? A part of the answer to these questions is also the problematic of the holistic discourses, the interpretive approaches which diligently take up various insights of a work of art and put them together in order to reach a general conclusion. While the general tenor of the novel may be suggestive of this aspect, such categories sometimes can also underwrite the structure of ideology. These categories naively and, therefore, dangerously function as arbitrary justifications for lapses, misreadings, authoritative superimpositions in terms of social biases. Without doubt, such attempts would continue, gain patronage from both the establishment and academia; more so now, since the liberal-left or other variations of left struggle to put their agenda honourably in American context. Novels like this perpetuate and legitimate these misconceptions in the guise of predictable generalized artistic arguments. Time and social situation are never more fertile to provide the breeding ground for such acts. There are attempts already to write off an entire generation of the sixties, no matter what its ambition was, by the people whose credentials are as circumstantial as they are suspect. But that would be yet another story.

NOTES

1. Louis Althusser, *Lenin and Philosophy*, trans. Ben Brewster (New York: Monthly Review Press, 1971), p. 162.
2. Georg Lukacs, *History and Class Consciousness*, trans. Rodney Livingstone (Cambridge, Mass.: MIT Press, 1971).

3. Theodor Adorno, *Prisms*, trans. Samuel and Sherry Weber (Cambridge, Mass: MIT Press, 1982), p. 31.
4. Max Weber, *The Protestant Ethic and the Rise of Capitalism,* trans. Talcott Parsons (Ithaca, New York: Cornell University Press, 1981).
5. Karl Manneheim, *Ideology and Utopia: An Introduction to the Sociology of Knowledge*, trans. Louis Wirth and Edward Shils (New York: Harcourt Brace, 1936).
6. Myra Jehlen, "Introduction: Beyond Transcendence," *Ideology and Classic American Literature*, ed. Sacvan Bercovitz and Myra Jehlen (Cambridge: Cambridge University Press, 1986), p. 5.
7. Saul Bellow, *Mr Sammler's Planet* (New York: Viking Press, 1970).
8. Walter Eenjamin, *Understanding Brecht*, trans. A. Bostock (London: New Left Books, 1973).
9. Saul Bellow, *Mr. Sammler's Planet*, p. 3.
10. Melvin J. Lasky, "The Ideas of '68: Revolt After 20 years," *Encounter* (November 1988).
11. George Orwell, *Animal Farm* (New York: Harcourt Brace, 1946).
12. George Orwell, *1984* (New York: Harcourt Brace, 1949).
13. Mark Harris, *Saul Bellow: Drumlin Woodchuck* (Athens: The University of Georgia Press, 1980), see especially pp. 118-44.
14. Noam Chomsky. In a Personal Interview with the Author.
15. Jane Howard, "Mr. Bellow Considers His Planet," *Life*, 68 (3 April 1970), p. 59.
16. Robert Boyers, "Literature and Culture: An Interview with Saul Bellow," *Salmagundi*, 30 (Summer 1975), p. 22.

(Con)Texts of the Secondary: Twentieth Century Literary Criticism and Theory

> Theory is what is generated when some aspect of literature, its nature, its history, its place in society, its conditions of production and reception, its meaning in general, or the meanings of particular works, ceases to be given and becomes a question to be argued in a general way. Theory is what inevitably arises when literary conventions and critical definitions once taken for granted have become objects of generalized discussion and dispute.
>
> Gerald Graff

> No intellectual change is ever universal.
>
> Perry Anderson

Rene Wellek in a book which he co-authored with Austin Warren called *Theory of Literature* (1949) makes a useful distinction between literary theory and literary criticism, the former as "the study of principles of literature, its categories, criteria, and the like" (38) and the latter as studies of concrete works of art. He also suggests two approaches for the study of literature: extrinsic approach and intrinsic approach. Before we move on to the twentieth century literary criticism and theory, it would be instructive to note that M.H. Abrams himself posits four different theories:

1. Mimetic theories;
2. Pragmatic theories;
3. Expressive theories; and
4. Objective theories.

He bases this paradigm on four essential elements, namely, artist, work, audience and universe.

The artist produces a work of art to be consumed by the audience and the work may also reflect the universe – depending on the subject matter. "Although," Abrams adds, "any reasonably adequate theory takes some account of all four elements, almost all theories exhibit a discernible orientation towards one only." (*The Mirror and the Lamp*, 4) Thus, mimetic orientation believes art as principally an imitation of aspects of reality;

pragmatic theories reflect on art's effect on the audience; expressive theories view art as merely an expression of poet's mind; and, finally, objective theories focus on the text itself, text as "a self-sufficient entity." (21) This construct provides a neat framework for theoretical activity. It would be even more interesting, however, to take some examples of the twentieth century criticism and theory to formulate certain arguments and points of view. To begin with, the view that literary criticism and literary theory are different, deserves some comment. No literary criticism is possible without theory. The very fact that one chooses to ponder over a particular text from one vantage point and the comments and judgements one makes on it pre-suppose a theoretical structure. But, increasingly, in recent years, theory began to occupy a separate status with its self-chosen and, if you will, self-legitimated intellectual priorities—and no longer a subsidiary to literature. Graff rightly points that "literary theory is a discourse concerned with the legitimating principles, assumptions, and premises of literature and literary criticism." (*Professing Literature*, 252) Here literary criticism is subsumed under literary theory.

With these few remarks, we now turn to various schools of literary criticism. Biographical criticism, sociological criticism, moral criticism, and psychological criticism always have their own antagonists. For instance, in 1910, Joel Elias Spingarn declared that, "we have done with all the Old Rules . . . We have done with the genres or literary kinds . . . We have done with technique as separate from art . . . We have done with moral judgments of literature . . . We have done with the race, the time, the environment of a poet's work as an element of criticism." (quoted in *Modern American Literary Criticism*, 1) The lecture in which he made these comments was called "The New Criticism." Spingarn, clearly, shows tremendous impatience with extrinsic factors of criticism. And he visualizes a time when a work of art would be discussed for whatever it seeks to communicate—in other words, intrinsic analysis. His daring prophecy did not materialize immediately, and it had to wait some three decades for the new movement to emerge although the New Criticism he talked about should not be confused with the Ransomite dogma. In the meantime, psychological criticism flourished especially in America, thanks to the availability of Freud's writings in translation. Ludwig Lewisohn's *Expression in America* (1932), which was later reissued as the *Story of American Literature*, reflects a tremendous influence of Freudian thinking. One also finds Freudian overtones in his novels such as *The Case of Mr. Grump* and his play *Adam*.

Similarly, Van Wyck Brooks and Joseph Wood Krutch were also greatly influenced by Freud. The New Humanism, on the other hand, looked for inspiration and sustenance from pre-nineteenth century past; and they took up the role of defending the older order with their emphasis on dualism of man and nature, "inner check," reason and judgment, and the idea of cultural and social elite. These conservative thinkers, masterfully represented by Irving Babbitt and Paul Elmer More at Harvard, felt that it was the express purpose of the American College to give training to the elite who would eventually provide the leadership to the people. It was further surmised that the term "humanity" was rather misapplied, often confusing it with humanitarianism. Even as the scholars were advancing these theories which were evidently undemocratic and right-wing, American social scene was undergoing an enormous change with massive immigration from especially Eastern Europe at the turn of the century and in the early decades of this century. In the twenties and the thirties, the second generation immigrants were interacting with the mainstream America. With magazines like *The Masses*, and later the *New Masses*, and *Partisan Review* with a new editorial policy, offered a forum for their cultural and political criticism. More often than not, these contributions came from non-Protestant background, influenced by the knowledge of daily struggle their parents had undergone and were undergoing in the New York sweatshops and elsewhere. The Great Depression of the thirties made these immigrant children, who already had the benefit of socialist background at home, realize that capitalist America was indeed on the decline. Granville Hicks, Mike Gold, Max Eastman, Philip Rahv, William Phillips, Kenneth Burke, Edmund Wilson, and many more strongly believed that literature has a social function – and they truly belong to the Marxist tradition. *Partisan Review*, at least for sometime, could be called probably the most influential intellectual magazine. Ultimately, it was in this background, the ideology and the context of the New Criticism, which became influential in the forties and the fifties, should be understood, apart from the useful service it rendered in bringing us back to the text instead of overly argued impressionism. With the decline of the left-wing scenario, the New Criticism rose to prominence bringing a revolution in teaching and appreciation of literature. It too has made certain terms popular – terms like ambiguity, structure, texture, irony, paradox, the verbal icon, well-wrought urn, affective fallacy, intentional fallacy and so on. They used both *Kenyon Review* and *Sewanee Review* for propagating their ideology. In one stroke, they strove to delegitimize biographical, sociological and Marxist orienta tion to literature. Instead, it was the text-as-such which was privileged. John Crowe Ransom, who was the high-priest of this movement, in his book *The New Criticism* (1941) appealed for the need for an ontological critic. Allen Tate, R.P. Blackmur, Cleanth Brooks gathered around Ransom at Vanderbilt University. Ransom also ran a journal called *The Fugitive* (1922-25) for a brief period. Although Ransom did not seem to have appreciated Eliot's *Wasteland*, he was generally agreed to be an early influence. These critics quickly produced text books which later served at least two generations of students. As it happened, in the post-war situation, their approach had been co-opted in the academia. Any number of students who flooded the schools under GI Bill found "close reading" interesting and convenient. But it does not necessarily mean that there were no critics of other theoretical persuasion. Obviously there were. Probably this is the principal lesson one could draw from any major trend at any time. It just happens that one theoretical system gets privileged. In any case, the success of the New Criticism, at least in some ways, was due to certain excesses done in the practice of biographical and Marxist criticism. Even so, the belief that it is only "close reading" with no hidden agenda is debatable. David Lodge, who edited a book on literary criticism, writes in a note that they "also shared religious, political, and cultural convictions of a traditional, conservative character, coloured by a special allegiance to the American South." (*20th Century Literary Criticism*, 227) In 1930, the Fugitives, as they were also known, published *I will Take My Stand: The South and the Agrarian Tradition* (1930). They were trying to recover the old values of the South and were clearly protesting against the industrialized North. And the North, especially New York, also was the centre of ever-increasing immigrant presence who seemed to be finding their entry into cultural America. So, the "close reading" also had a social gospel, after all. The text-as-such also dominates the focus of much of theory from structuralism to post-structuralism, although the centrality of a single valid interpretation is not in favour. For the New Critics, text was still stable and "close reading" attempts to analyse an authentic structure and texture. The invasion of the French theories on the Anglo-American institutional structure brought on a radical skepticism or, to use Eugene Goodheart's expression, skeptic disposition among critics. Suddenly, Arnoldian humanism, Eliot's 'tradition' and the 'unification of sensibility,' Leavisite faith that criticism of literature as criticism of life and his genuine belief that literary culture has humanizing impact on society, have been put under rigorous critique – eventually only to bypass them. Although structuralism still posits meaning, it is not the authorial intention that can be decoded from the text but the meaning that is possible due to the exigencies of the linguistic system. In other words, meaning is generated through linguistic structure. Structuralists analyse the sources of meaning (how communication is possible in the first place?). Structuralists built their theory from the works of Ferdinand de Saussure, a Swiss linguist, and Levi-Strauss, a renowned anthropologist. In order to reflect on the object of linguistic investigation and the relationship between words and things, Saussure introduced two key terms: *Langue*, which is language system that pre-exists its actual usage; and *parole*, which is individual utterance. One is necessarily born into a linguistic community and when one begins to utter something, he or she is already actualizing the sources of the system which is already available. Meaning is achieved through a linguistic relationship, and not otherwise. Therefore, relationship between words and reality is arbitrary. Language communicates because of difference. In this view, words do not correspond to things, rather they are called signs with two sides – signifier and signified. In this connection, Peter Brooks' observation is succinct: "Structuralism is clearly designed precisely to make the movement from the world of words to the world of reality a difficult one, and to explore the ramifications and the structures, the complications of the world of words, before one engages in the question of reference."[1]

Of course, structuralists immediately proclaimed the death of the author and they also made a distinction between writerly text and readerly text. They also problematized the significance of referentiality of the traditional humanist view which was brought under attack. Although the New Critics also declared the autonomy of the text, they still had humanist pretensions since they believed in unified structure. The moment the structuralists put "referentiality" of the text on trial, the critical scenario had changed radically. While talking about the traditional view, Abrams says: "The writer is conceived in Wordsworth's terms, as 'a man speaking to men.' Literature, in other words, is a transaction between a human author and his human reader. By his command of linguistic and literary possibilities, the author actualizes and records in words what he undertakes to signify of human beings and actions and about the matters of human concern, addressing himself to those readers who are competent to understand what he has written."[2] For structuralists, such a point of view, may not be acceptable because authorial intention does not get any emphasis in their practice. However, their contribution to narratology and especially Roman Jacobson's distinction between metaphor and metonymy drew particular attention. Structuralism enjoyed vogue for sometime and with Derrida's emergence as a major thinker in Parisian circles and, more significantly, in America, one could perceive a dramatic change in the seventies. Derrida's presentation of a paper called, "Structure, Sign, and Play in the Discourse of the Human Sciences" at Johns Hopkins University created some kind of a stir but his ultimate contribution in giving a new turn to critical theory came when it was finally anthologised by Donato and Macksey in the *Structuralist Controversy* (1972). Whereas structuralists could still visualize a possibility of centre and, therefore, stable meaning as such, the deconstructionists would not accept this at all. The idea of determinate meaning is structured on the premise that there is the ultimate *presence* or transcendent signified or ultimate referrent that it can refer to. The belief in metaphysics of presence or a foundation beyond the langauge system is forever present in traditional view as an "ultimate, terminal, self-certifying, and thus adequate to centre the structure of the linguistic system and to guarantee the determinate meaning of an utterance within the system."[3] Positing presence is the essential desire of Western metaphysics to establish certainty and foundation. The omnipresence of the Logos, gifted and guaranteed by the divine erects a regular foundation for much of the philosophical enquiry. Derrida questions this logocentrism/foundation in a series of books. Once the presence is questioned, the determinate meaning itself becomes suspect. His strategy of deconstruction, therefore, causes only an endless "freeplay" of undecidables, aporias, and indeterminacies. Although there is no absolute foundation for language (this is to continue Derrida's argument), it stiil works through our speech acts or oral communication. The text, for instance, is lisible, "legible." And it appears to have determinate meaning. But, Derrida says, this is wrong because what you have are the "effects" of "ideality," of signification, effects caused by the differences within the language itself. And then he sets out to deconstruct these effects to show that since they lack presence, it is merely a simulation. In order to deal with the predicament of *presence*-less situation of language, he invents, game-like, a series of neologisms, pseudo-terms, sometimes he uses the word and crosses it (under erasure) to deconstruct the logocentric view. The institutional impact of deconstructionism is another matter again. Paul de Man was the chief exponent of this school and it flourished magnificently in the Ivy-League atmosphere of Yale University where Professors including Harold Bloom, Geoffrey Hartman and J. Hillis Miller with continual presence of Derrida showed enthusiasm although the first two were marginal. Gone were the days when Harvard used to be the leader of the English Departments in America. Now, Yale established itself for such a central role. Suddenly, the enthusiasts of deconstructionism were in demand and theory-courses had an attraction for student enlistment. Certain academic journals like *Diacritics*, *Glyph*, and *Critical Enquiry* evidenced their exclusive commitment to theory whereas older journals like *Georgia Review*, restructured their editorial policy to be conducive to theory. They also flourished in their own way by establishing a forum for the like-minded theorists. Professionally speaking at least, there was so much at stake. Also, for the sixties generation of the New Left and Marxists, the seventies was a decade of a lot of soul-searching. At least some Marxists perceived a positive note in this thinking. They felt that since the presence was devalued, much of bourgeois rationale that brought them together, could also be delegitimized, thanks to deconstructionism. Michael Ryan's book *Deconstruction and Marxism* (1982) belongs to this category. This did not last long. Deconstructionists observed an apolitical stand – they supported neither conservative thinking nor radicalism. Deconstructionism, imported from Parisian intellectual circles, reflected our ever-vanishing Marxified culture. The other post-structuralists like Michel Foucault and Roland Barthes, Lacan, Levinas and others had surely outlived their Marxist phase. Lukacsian terms like "totality" and "Integrated Civilizations" did not mean very much to them. If anything they attempted to subvert such notions. Obviously, Marxist flirtation with these theories should have rationalization because most deconstructionists did not respond to the charge that they were political. So much so, although Michael Ryan had theorized a context for deconstruction and Marxism on the premise that the former destabilizes the bourgeois conceptions that deter revolutionary praxis, in the recent years there emerged a serious critique of deconstruction from Marxist critics. Marshall Berman's comments on Foucault situate a general state of the French intellectual scene of which Derrida is a significant part: Foucault "offers a generation of refugees from the 1960s a world-historical alibi for the sense of passivity and helplessness that gripped so many of us in the 1970s. There is no point in trying to resist the oppressions and injustices of modern life, since even our dreams of freedom only add more links to our chain; however, once we grasp the total futility of it all, at least we can relax."(4) Even as deconstruction is holding a sway in the universities, several other critics have advanced their own theories. Their theories have been roughly categorized as reader-response theory, New Historicism, Hermeneutics, Dialogic theory, and Feminist theory.

Addressing a Lionel Trilling seminar at Columbia University, Meyer Abrams remarked that the Age of Criticism of the mid-century had been replaced by the Age of Reading. He calls them New readers. Since the author is dead anyhow, the reader has become a favourite subject for discourse. Now, it is the reader who creates the text and each reader may create his own variety of text depending on what he brings with him by way of influences and background. This has something to do with the phenomenological view of man as the meaning-giving subject. The text is often discussed so far in terms of its autonomy, as the product of authorial actualization of his/her intention, or a reflection of particular societal context with its ideology and contradictions. But very rarely till now, did critics bother to theorize systematically the reader component in literary appreciation. Is the reader male or female, underprivileged or bourgeois, the oppressed or the oppressor? These priorities surfaced in critical enquiry. The terms like "implied reader," "competent reader," "ideal reader" found legitimacy in literary parlance. And the reader's actualization of the text is greatly influenced by his or her ideology, self-interest and, among other things, politicization of all of these. However, is it possible that the writerly text also determines, at least to a certain extent, the reader's actualization of the text? Among the prominent critics in this category are Wolfgang Iser, Stanley Fish, Norman Holland and David Bleich. The subjective aspect here is very significant; for them, the individual mind is the origin of all meaning. This view, which suffered a setback in post-Romanticism, has come back into reckoning with reader-response theory. Indeed, it is upto the reader to fill up the blanks and gaps every text purports to have. Gerald Prince also differentiates between a narrator and narratee, narratee being the person the narrator addresses his tale to although all types of readers tend to read the text including possibly the narratee. The other related expressions which came into vogue are "implied reader," "literary competence," "affective stylistics" and so on.

Among the other theories that crowd literature programmes at the moment, Feminist approach definitely has the potential to go on for quite sometime, partly because of the societal prescriptions and institutional coercion that have been subsumed under the theories of knowledge; and partly also because its presence or non-presence is inextricably linked with ideology and power through knowledge. Feminists seek to deconstruct the politics of body and reexamine the discourses that have, for centuries, manipulated the institutions to subdue and subjugate the status of women.

Literature, they have reason to believe, is one such institution where patriarchal despotism has subverted the authentic being of woman. It is ironical that literature, at least English Literature and particularly novel, which has mostly female readership is dominated by male writers. This itself would cause a major debate in the Feminist circles. Institutionally, literary appreciation is largely left to the male teachers. How many female teachers hold influential positions at the universities that matter? Some of the female writers have to take a male name to get accepted in literary establishment. Here too one finds relevance in Foucaldian power and knowledge paradigm. However, the modern Feminists received tremendous support during the New Left years. It was at this time, they fought against sexual segregation. One of the recent books on Feminism enthusiastically discusses the ideas of Herbert Marcuse, that grandfather of the New Left movement. In any case, the Feminist theory at least has three major phases:

1. the images of women in the works of male writers;
2. the critique of female authors; and
3. prescriptive criticism.

Like any other system of thought and practice, it also has shifting points of view and evolution. The foundational generation of Simone de Beauvoir and others like Kate Millet, Germaine Greer, and Betty Friedan, it appears, have their antagonists. Others like Mary Ellmann, Elaine Showalter and Toril Moi have brought in a more vigorous critique to the *body* of knowledge. Although it is naive and self-serving to doubt its legitimacy and importance in socio-political context, it raises certain questions, as some have already pointed out, about its objectivity in literary analysis. But then, they would quickly problematize the notion of objectivity as a patriarchal weapon to eliminate any oppositional discourse.

Finally, I would suggest three critics, among others, who deserve consistent attention: Harold Bloom, Mikhail Bakhtin and E.D. Hirsch, Jr. Of course, Marxist critics like Raymond Williams, Terry Eagleton, Perry Anderson, E.P. Thomson, Fredric Jameson and the Frankfurt school variety and many more have already left an impressive body of theory, moving, in some cases, beyond historical materialsim. Their contribution is bound to create useful framework in post-post-structuralist ambience. But of the three critics I mentioned earlier, Harold Bloom is more prolific and eclectic. His theory of "misreading," "misprision" and the anxiety of influence may not sound unfamiliar; but he systematized his theory in a series of books. He believes that every poet struggles with the tradition of their counterparts. The originality and creative success of a poet depends on how successfully he overpowers his predecessor in this parricidal agon. *The Map of Misreading* (1975), *The Anxiety of Influence* (1973) and *Agon* (1982) reflect on the dynamics of this view. He also tried to apply his knowledge of Jewish mysticism, Kabbala, to secular literature. Mikhail Bakhtin, on the other hand, resurfaced to prominence only posthumously. He was associated with Russian Formalism in his early days; and his contribution to the recent theory debate was his concept of dialogic criticism, enunciated in his book on Dostoevsky's poetics. This is also happily suggestive of Martin Buber's I and thou relationship. "Dialogic critics believe that individual voices take shape and character in response to and in anticipation of other voices."[5] Thus, polyphony, heteroglossia, carnivalesque shaped much of his theory.

E.D. Hirsch, Jr. has introduced dualisms, such as understanding vs. significance, interpretation vs. criticism. For instance, meaning is something one willed to convey and significance seeks a relationship between text and external structure; understanding is authorial construction of meaning and interpretation is its explanation to others. Incidentally, he is heavily interested in cultural literacy these days.

After an overview of literary criticism and theory, it would be interesting to reestablish and review the status of critical practice or, as George Steiner would have it, the culture of the 'secondary cities.' There was a time when criticism was aspiring to have a separate status, not merely the subsidiary role it was perceived to perform. It was also the time when critical practice was not a victim of unabashed skepticism. Criticism, in some way, had something to contribute to society as such. Now, most critical practice is confined to academia, and almost written for the specialists. In other words, critical practice has become strongly hermetical. This is rather ironical the moment we situate the function of English Departments with a large section of the faculty who are paid and well provided for by a particular system. Terry Eagleton, while writing about the function of criticism, has this to say: "criticism today lacks all substantive social function. It is either part of the public relations branch of the literary industry, or a matter wholly internal to the academies." (*The Function of Criticism*, 7) He was referring to the time when criticism had a "substantive social function," the days of Dr. Johnson, Matthew Arnold, F.R. Leavis and so on – even if he has disagreements with them on some accounts. Structuralism and post-structuralism, in retrospect, seemed to have ushered in an age of skepticism and disbelief.

With the absence of presence, nothing appears to hold steady. George Steiner, in his most recent book, *Real Presences: Is There Anything in What We Say*? (1989), attempts to address some of these problems to rearticulate the *presence*, not least the God's presence, without which order, meaningful discourse, and humane culture is an impossible dream. He argues that "any coherent understanding of the capacity of human speech to communicate meaning and feeling is, in the final analysis, underwritten by the assumption of God's presence."(3) And then, he moves on to the business of criticism. The book is written with indignation and anger. Coming from a humanist like Steiner, it should not be surprising. He says that criticism belongs to the realm of the secondary. Even so, the most enduring contribution to it is made, not by the literary journalists or academic critics, but by the creative writers themselves – only by re-reading and, therefore, re-visualizing the comparable classics of the past. Thus, Dante's (*The Divine Comedy*) reading of Virgil's *Aeneid* is a superb job. Joyce's *Ulysses* is a re-experience of Homer's *Odyssey*. Henry James's *The Portrait of a Lady* is a creative and profound reading of George Eliot's *Middlemarch*. Tolstoy's *Anna Karenina* is a re-vision of Flaubert's *Madam Bovary*. If this is the situation, what is the status of sundry critics who crowd the academic institutions? Steiner asks: "To what, save pride of intellect or professional peerage, is the reviewer, the critic, the academic expert accountable?" (8) And in this age of hermeticism, the theorists are probably accountable to their own respective coteries and certainly to the by-now-all-too-familiar-professionalism/ tenurism. Accountability and answerability understood in the societal context is something that gets minimal attention in these discourses. If Allan Bloom wrote that book, namely *The Closing of the American Mind* (1987) at a time when theory was a paying fad in America, it was also to reformulate the situation of the university in a society and its humanizing culture. The fact that such an academic book was a regular best-seller speaks volumes of the shared anxiety of many people. Steiner, too, performs the thankless job of putting the clock back, as John Bayly, an Oxford Professor, rightly commends.

It is safe to conjecture that after the clap-trap of the fashionable fads of literary enquiry, the long-cherished view of literature, in whatever way it is understood, would eventually gain academic fervour; and it is good also for the survival of English Literature as an academic discipline. However, it is not to underwrite the healthy climate of discussion that it had created in the past decade or so, although there were some acrimonious debates at MLA meetings between traditionalists and the theory enthusiasts as if the traditionalists themselves were not defenders (for instance, the New Criticism?) of some school, at some point. One such painful discussion took place between J. Hillis Miller, who travelled from Geneva school—its practitioners are also known as critics of consciousness—to the present deconstructionism and the renowned scholar of Romanticism, M.H. Abrams. This too, for a student of the history of literary criticism, is not entirely astonishing, for the newly converted surely acts with lot of conviction. Walter Jackson Bate, a Harvard Professor, was saddened to see so much of scholarly attention given to such topics like aporias or indeterminacies in literature. Paul de Man, in the meantime, suffered a slump in his reputation posthumously. His collaboration with the Nazi newspaper *Le Soir* was discovered in the later part of the eighties; and some began to surmise that de Man's gospel of deconstructionism is merely an attempt to absolve or, better still, rationalize his past associations with Nazism. Norman Podhoretz, for one, suggested that in so far as deconstructionism is an apotheosis of skepticism and nihilism, it has something in common with the Nazi philosophy. That it has changed the institutional structure is to be admitted even if one does not go along with it. The after-effects or side-effects of it both in teaching or literature and the institutional status of English Departments is yet to be assessed thoroughly.

So, the status and scenario of English Departments in *fin de siecle* America as well as in other countries, it seems to me, is to reconstruct literature at least in essential sense of traditional view and combine it with the beneficial side of recent trends in theory to bring back and re-cognize, as it were, the Holy Grail of meaning, value, intention and other humane contexts to resituate the battered soul of the modern man in this unwholesome century.

NOTES

1. Peter Brooks, "The State of Criticism," *Partisan Review* (3, 1980), p. 422.
2. Meyer Abrams, "How to Do Things With the Texts," *Partisan Review* (4, 1979), p. 566.
3. *Ibid*, p. 569.
4. Marshall Berman, *All that is Solid Melts into Air: The Experience of Modernity* (New York, 1982); quoted in Martin Jay, *Marxism and Totality: The Adventures of a Concept from Lukacs to Habermas* (Berkeley: The University of California Press, 1984), p. 517.

5. Don Bialostovsky, "Dialogic Criticism," G. Douglas Atkins and Laura Morrow, ed., *Contemporary Literary Theory* (Amherst: The University of Massachussetts Press, 1989), p. 214.

WORKS CITED

1. Abrams, M.H. *The Mirror and the Lamp: Romantic Theory and Critical Tradition*. New York: Oxford, 1953.
2. Anderson, Perry. *In the Tracks of Historical Materialism*. Chicago, IL: University of Chicago Press, 1984.
3. Bloom, Allan. *The Closing of the American Mind*. New York: Simon and Shuster, 1987.
4. Bloom, Harold. *The Anxiety of Incuence: A Theory of Poetry*. New York: Oxford, 1973.
5. -----. *The Map of Misreading*. New York: Oxford, 1975.
6. -----. *Agon: Towards a Theory of Revisionism*. New York: Oxford, 1982.
7. Eagleton, Terry. *The Function of Criticism*. London: Verso, 1984.
8. Goodheart, Eugene. *Skeptic Disposition in Contemporary Criticism*. New Jersey: Princeton, 1984.
9. Graff, Gerald. *Professing Literature: An Institutional History*. Chicago, IL: University of Chicago Press, 1987.
10. *I'll Take My Stand: The South and the Agrarian Tradition*. New York: Harper, 1930, 1962.
11. Lodge, David. *20th Century Literary Criticism*. London: Longman, 1972.
12. Macksey, Richard and Donato, Eugenio, ed. *The Structuralist Controversity: The Language of Criticism and the Sciences of Man*. Baltimore: The Johns Hopkins, 1972.
13. Ransom, John Crowe. *The New Criticism*. Norfolk, Conn.: New Directions, 1941.
14. Ryan, Michael. *Deconstruction and Marxism*. Baltimore: The Johns Hopkins, 1982.
15. Steiner, George. *Real Presences: Is There Anything in What We Say?* Boston: Faber & Faber, 1989.
16. Sutton, Walter. *Modern American Literary Criticism*. Engiewood Cliff, New Jersey: Prentice-Hall, 1963.
17. Wellek, Rene and Warren, Austin. *Theory of Literature*. Middlesex, England: Penguin, 1949, 1973.

Autobiography as History: Alfred Kazin's Autobiographies

No autobiography can boast of being predominantly personal and devoid of any social reference. Social turbulences and its patterns, the agony of confrontation between personal choices and institutional prescriptions become part of man's life, more so in the lives of minority people like Blacks, Jews, Puerto Ricans and Hispanics. The minority man in America has the burden of confronting two levels of experience: one, his life as part of the minority culture; and two, his response, either voluntary or circumstantial, to the mainstream culture. This becomes a source of perpetual agony particularly in the generation which is in the throes of assimilation. And Jews are no exception to this situation although assimilationist theories pompously give the consolation that Jews can be part of the American system and thus, avoid the crises that are otherwise inevitable. But Jewish experience over the years belies such possibilities. Consequently, Jewish autobiography reflects the Jewish response to the American experience and its attendant miseries and triumphs. Thus, personal story becomes a source of social history since reactions to the social patterns are reflected in these conflicts. Reading Jewish autobiography, in a way, is an act of participation in the history of Jewish life in America. That autobiography implies a social measure can be understood from the theoretical propositions of critics. James Olney in *Metaphors of Self* states clearly the merits of this:

> Historians impose, and quite properly, their own metaphors on the human past. History, as almost everyone acknowledges, is an objective collection of facts but one historian's point of view on the fact: a point of view that, taken as a sum of what he has experienced and understands, reveals to us the historian. As readers we go to history, as to philosophy, to autobiography and poetry, to learn more not about the people and the past but about ourselves and the present.[1]

For a student of Jewish studies, Jewish autobiography offers an understanding of events at a given time and period that are part of the writer.

Thus, any "autobiography asks to be judged skeptically as a version of history. . . . As the articulation of past and present motives, impulses, and ideals, autobiography becomes a kind of case history."[2]

There have been enthusiastic attempts on the part of Jews to put their lives into words ever since the great flood of immigration in America at the turn of the century. Mary Antin's *The Promised Land* and Abraham Cahan's fictionalized autobiography entitled *The Rise of David Levinsky* can be considered as the first major attempts. Strangely enough, these two autobiographies touch upon two major themes of Jewish-American literature. While Mary Antin's autobiography implies excessive enthusiasm to be part of the American mainstream, Cahan's *David Levinsky* bemoans the loss of Jewish identity after assimilation. Together, these autobiographies underline the theme of confrontation between assimilation and alienation. The Yiddish poetry of the time bears sufficient testimony to this fact.

Functioning in such a tradition of Jewish autobiography, Kazin touches some of the most eventful circumstances of Jewish life in America. His three autobiographies—*A Walker in the City* (1951), *Starting Out in the Thirties* (1962) and *New York Jew* (1978)—can be considered as sources of Jewish history narrated from a personal viewpoint. This argument is further strengthened when he says that "history exists, that it is still meaningful, and that we can read our fate in the book of history. That gives the courage to write (autobiography). To write is in some way to cut the seemingly automatic pattern of violence, destructiveness, and death-wish. To write is to put the seeming insignificance of human existence into a different perspective."[3] Further, he states that even the masterful autobiographies are case-histories in one sense or another. While affirming the significance of this sub-genre, Robert F. Sayre says that since it is written at all times and by a variety of people, it reflects the nation's sensibility, "it is the true song of My Self. And Ourselves."[4]

Written with much conviction of the self as history, his autobiographies can be read as social document which focus on the three most important aspects of American Jewish history: immigrant experience in *A Walker in the City*, Jewish radicalism and other social patterns of Jewish life in *Starting Out in the Thirties* and the post-Holocaust angst in *New York Jew*. Although there are other aspects in these books, the aforementioned themes will be the major part of my discussion.

A close analysis of *A Walker in the City* would articulate the story of immigrant Jews and their impoverished state of life. In the succeeding years, the sentimental description of Alfred Kazin is to become an archetype in Jewish American literature. The separate sections of the book become the necessary paradigms of Jewish life. The kitchen, the synagogue and the block and beyond take on metaphorical realism with multiplicity of meanings which subsume the Jewish consciousness. These layers of responses can be perceived with ingenious stresses in art, literature and politics. The immigrant loneliness, family, gentile presence, dreams of becoming part of the mainstream America – all of these suggest themselves in the narration of Kazin's autobiography. Since we do not have enough of space, I would like to concentrate on *Starting Out in the Thirties*, to illustrate more significantly the basic argument of this paper. It tries to tell the story of the thirties seen from the Jewish point of view. In both the autobiographies Kazin is obviously writing about his experience. But his life is so interwoven with the social events of the time, at least as it mattered to the Jews, it becomes difficult to ignore them, for doing so is in a way rejecting a significant part of his life. Consequently, his autobiographies become sources for the social document of the Jews. In the second autobiography, which is not exactly a sequel and hence avoids a possibility of repetition, he tries to systematize the thirties. It was the time when art and social history went hand in hand. Artists participated with zeal and enthusiasm in the turbulent ideologies of the time. Writing about the thirties is to write about Clifford Odets, Communism, the Spanish Civil War, Hitler-Stalin Pact, Moscow Trials and the disenchantment of the intellectuals in the late thirties. Kazin like any other intellectual of the day, was a socialist, for not being a socialist or a Communist brought one to the other extreme situation where you belonged to the inhuman and exploiting capitalist class – in the thirties one happily made the class distinction in principle – which was responsible for the Wall Street Crash of 1929 and ushered in the dread of disenchantment – the Great Depression. Even Edmund Wilson, who wrote the most original book on modernist poetry, *Axel's Castle*, said in his chapter on Marcel Proust that he was "the last great historian of the loves, the society, the intelligence, the diplomacy, the literature and the art of *Heartbreak House of Capitalist Culture*"[5] (italics mine). Listening to Norman Thomas, Earl Browder, Mike Gold and reading protest literature of James T. Farrell, John Steinbeck, Robert Cantwell, Josephine Hearbst and watching the plays of Clifford Odets one was convinced that Communism alone could save America from the present disaster of the Depression. While talking about these social facts, Kazin concentrates on some people like John

Chamberlain, Otis Ferguson, Malcolm Cowley, Sophia, I.F. Calverton and, most important of all, Clifford Odets.

Although *Waiting for Lefty* was the angry voice of the thirties, it was *Awake and Sing* that impressed Kazin most. Set against the background of the times, the play presents the crisis of a Jewish family in the throes of assimilation. The old man, Jacob, with his faith in moral values and the contention that in America life is printed on the "dollar bills," the almost absent Jewish father and painfully intervening Jewish mother (one recalls Philip Roth's *Portnoy's Complaint*) forever concerned with the future of her children sometimes to the point of irritating them, and the dreamy children who always want to escape the suffocating atmosphere of the Jewish home – these are the aspects Odets discusses in the play. Agony and glory are part of the immigrant Jewish life. And watching the play, Kazin feels even a sense of remorse and acceptance.[6]

Even *Waiting for Lefty* was symbolic of the decline of capitalism. Being a Communist was like being a good "guy" and it gave the moral courage that they were on the right side. Marxism promised many things, talked about the common man as the centre of the historical process and capitalists were the victimisers. In Depression America every one was a common man and Jewish intellectuals could only see Hebraic humanism in Karl Marx, the Rabbi's son. Listening to Andre Malraux, Earl Browder, Norman Thomas and reading Cowley in the *New Republic*'s back page, these intellectuals felt a deep sense of belonging. It took a long time to realize the political evil behind the Moscow Trials and the expulsion of Leon Trotsky. But in the later part of the thirties, the growing menace of Hitler, Mussolini and Franco made many writers sympathetic towards Communism. Later they knew what had happened and was happening and guiltily cursed themselves for being indifferent and ignorant of the killings. They realized how a fanatic submissiveness to a particular ideology could make them oblivious of the grotesque inhumanity of political evil. The Moscow Trials were a mockery of humanity and the ideology that gave power to a few people to exercise their authority arbitrarily, they felt, was a curse on man. Even the procedure of the trials were farcical, because the victims

> confessed that they had landed at airfield that had never existed, and they had plotted with "Hitler agents" in Norwegian hotels that had burned down years before the alleged meeting – they had done this in order to dismember the Union of Soviet Socialist Republics, to

> provoke attack on [it]. . . . They had done all this in order to restore capitalism, and to put a little money into their pockets.[7]

What happened to these intellectuals was part of the story depicted in Richard Crossman's *The God That Failed*. Even people like Ignazio Silone and Arthur Koestler, now ex-Communists, spoke against the system with ignominous repentance. Not surprisingly, the political turmoils became part of Kazin's autobiography. The book concludes with his relationship with Nora and Naomi. Intermittently, Kazin also writes about anti-Semitism in Hitler's Germany, Gentile indifference to the Jews especially in the particular incident at home when Ferguson, his gentile friend, is invited. The book ends with an anecdote in 1945 about the gruesome experience of watching dead bodies of the World War II in a newsreel which becomes a major discussion in the recent *New York Jew*. In the last sections of *Starting Out in the Thirties,* Kazin writes about literature and ideology which is a constant topic in the *New Masses* and *Partisan Review*. Mike Gold, Philip Rahv and many leftist intellectuals theorized endlessly on this point. For them "a piece of writing was not real unless it appeared in the immediate social response in convention, rebuttal, polemic. Literature for him came out of social tension, and to social tension it had to contribute; literature was the product of social debate – and Rahv's ideal aim was to add to it."[8] Many of them reconsidered their ideas in the post-Depression years and some stuck to their ideas. The social history of the Depression with its turmoils is implicit in Kazin's memoirs.

In *New York Jew* (1978), he ponders over the theme of the Holocaust, the climate of the Jewish intellectuals in the forties, fifties and sixties, and his personal life as related to these experiences.

George Steiner in *Language and Silence*[9] extends the discussion of the world's "inactivity." Even the allied forces are, Steiner feels, more interested in bombing Berlin when they should have destroyed railroads which might have saved thousands of Jews. These inherent contradictions are to haunt them forever. Hannah Arendt's *Eichmann in Jerusalem* blamed every one for their meek acceptance and indifference. She criticised Jews in Germany and Poland for accepting their fate meekly without resistance. She even stated that some Jewish leaders cooperated in the extermination of their fellow-Jews. It was a book written in rage and in an accusatory tone. There were violent reactions to this book. Many Jewish intellectuals – Lucy S. Davidowicz, among them – felt it was objectionable. Written in the heat of times, even this, many felt, could be understandable. Years later, after the formation of Israel, these Jewish intellectuals fervently visited Israel, wrote supporting articles and funded generously. Kazin himself visited Israel, met concentration-camp mission, and listened to their reflections. After the Six Day War of 1967, there occurred a permanent bond between American Jews and Israel. It is as if, the fate of American Jews cannot be dissociated from that of the Israelis. His visit to Russia and his short teaching stint at Cologne University where German students applauded him in the post-War enthusiasm to make up for the crimes against Jews evoked a sense of Jewishness. The heart-rending experience he had in England at the time of the war would never leave him. It was there he knew the full story of Hitler's "final solution." Kazin, in his usual inimitable style, says:

> Late one Friday afternoon near the end of the war, I was waiting out the rain in the entrance to a music store. A radio was playing into the street and standing there, I heard the first Sabbath service from Belsen. . . . Belsen was the first Nazi Camp to be exposed to the world, and the London Times correspondent began his dispatch: "It is my duty to describe something beyond the imagination of mankind." Now I heard the liberated Jewish prisoners in Belsen say the *Shema* – "Hear O Israel the Lord our God the Lord is One." Weeping in the rain, I said it with them. For a moment I was home.[10]

The aspects of the American scene and the Holocaust are narrated with involvement. Equally important and fascinating are his accounts of his family – the death of his father, ever lonely Sophie, the all-sacrificing Jewish mother and recurrent evocations of his Jewish consciousness. Time and again, the experience narrated in *A Walker in the City* and *Starting Out in the Thirties* are retold, sometimes by way of reconsideration and often in moods of reiteration. Written in the agonising pressure of the post-Holocaust era, the book is abundant with his thoughts on the Jewish question which haunted even those Jews for whom death camps were a matter of news learnt from rumours and news papers. After such a blow, even the American assimilationists suddenly took Jewish causes and firmly affirmed their Jewish identity. Kazin himself has done this. In his masterpiece, *On Native Grounds*, he does not talk about the flourishing Jewish writers like Meyer Levin, Henry Roth, Daniel Fuchs, Mike Gold and Abraham Cahan in the thirties even when he has a chapter on the literature of the thirties. Whatever may be the reasons for this, he clings to his religion so fervently after the war. His tribute to his Socialist father and especially his concluding remarks to the books is a testimony in itself to such an affirmation:

> Standing by the grave, I shakenly say *Kaddish*. My proudest memory of my father is that when I was a boy and stood with him on Sunday mornings as he waited in the crowd of house painters on Pilkins Avenue to be tapped for a new job, he would shyly but with unmistakable delight introduce me around as his Kaddish. "*Meet my Kaddish*." Meet the son and heir who will see me to the grave and say the last prayer over me.

Remembering the past is a way of catharsis. For once, a sense of remorse, agony and pathos overpower the mind of Kazin. Everything, even the impoverished life of immigrant fathers of the thirties and the Jewish radicalism of their children, death-camps, American purges of the fifties seemed to have a connection. Even the image of the failed-father in Jewish literature has some connection. And Kazin can figure everything and, at last, accept it with pride and humility.

The aforementioned presentations of self in sociological context eloquently point out an essential association between autobiography and history—in this case Jewish autobiography. Thus, Jewish history starting from the turn of the century immigration to America to the post-war ambience has been viewed from a personal vantage point. What makes these autobiographies more authentic is the fact that it is necessarily concerned with Kazin's life under an inevitable context of societal turbulences. Therefore, it takes on historical dimension though they are refracted through the prism of personal observation. Unfortunately, neither the professor-critics nor academic historians showed genuine interest in this genre. In any case, their relevance to historians, apart from its literary quality, should be a matter of acceptance and an irrefutable fact.

NOTES

1. James Olney, *Metaphors of Self* (Princeton, N.J.: Princeton University Press, 1982), pp. 36-37.
2. Albert E. Stone, *Autobiographical Occasions and Original Acts* (Philadelphia: University of Pennsylvania Press, 1982), p. 5.
3. Alfred Kazin, "Self as History," *Telling Lives*, Marc Pachter, ed. (Washington, D.C.: New Republic Books, 1979), pp. 87-88.

4. Robert F. Sayre, "The Proper Study: Autobiographies in American Studies" in *The American Autobiography*, Albert E. Stone, ed. (Englewood Cliffs, N.J.: Prentice-Hall, 1981), p. 11.
5. Alfred Kazin, *Starting Out in the Thirties* (Boston: Little, 1965), p. 5.
6. *Ibid.*, p. 81.
7. *Ibid.*, pp. 96-97.
8. *Ibid.*, p. 160.
9. George Steiner, *Language and Silence* (New York: The Viking, 1967).
10. Alfred Kazin, *New York Jew* (New York: Alfred Knopf, 1978), pp. 140-41.

Changing World and Jewish Experience in Soviet Yiddish Fiction

> "The Revolution we will say 'Yes' to it, but are we to say 'no' to the Sabbath?" began Gedali winding about me the straps of his smoke-hidden eyes. "Yes, I cry to the Revolution. Yes, I cry to it, but it hides its face from Gedali and sends out on front nought but shooting."[1]

The ambiguous response of Jews to the Revolution is aptly expressed in Isaac Babel's story wherein the devout Jew, Gedali, is perplexed to see the winds of change at the turn of the century in Soviet Russia. While many Jews felt that the Revolution was a blessing, since, it might liberate them from Czarist Pogroms and official anti-Semitism, some, especially the orthodox sections, felt uncomfortable because the Bolsheviks rejected religious practices. Gedali, in Isaac Babel's story, becomes an archetype for the Jewish response to the changing world. As Leon Trotsky says in his book *Literature and Revolution*, "Russian workers are not religious at all" (40) and goes on to state the purpose of literature:

> The art of this epoch will be entirely under the influence of Revolution. This art needs a new self-consciousness. It is, above all, incompatible with mysticism, whether it be frank, or whether it masquerades as romanticism, because the Revolution starts from the central idea that collective man must become sole master, and that the limits of his power are determined by his knowledge of natural forces and by his capacity to use them. This new art is incompatible with pessimism, with skepticism, and with all the other forms of spiritual collapse. It is realistic, active, vitally collectivist, filled with a limitless creative faith in the Future.[2]

The responsibility of the writer is to promote Socialist Realism which, in due course of time, ushers in the Socialist Culture. The Socialist Culture is possible when the Revolution achieves its perfection. By focussing on the proletariat as the centre of creative writing and by depicting his hold on the history of events and his final victory over the bourgeois, the writer creatively participates in the struggle against the subversive forces. Trotsky's prescriptive theories do not permit creative writing as an independent act of an individual. He denies autonomy to the work of art, it cannot be dissociated from the social fabric where one necessarily sees a conflict between the bourgeois and the proletariat. The importance and the merit of the writer lies in how convincingly he brings out this conflict in his work of art with a final conclusion that the proletariat is the only benevolent force. What Trotsky, like other prescriptive theorists, ignores is that no writer can ever work with a thesis or to a certain set of patterns, for, such a concious attempt may disrupt the artistic excellence or aesthetic integrity. What happened to Leon Trotsky himself and Socialist Realism is a matter of much literary speculation. Whatever may be the significance of Trotsky's theories, the strange but poignant problems of Yiddish writers in Soviet Russia have been avoided in his book. Therefore, it is worthwhile to bring in Isaac Babel's* Gedali again and compare his predicament against Trotsky's theory of Socialist Culture. Gedali does not really understand the "benevolence" of the Revolution, because, although it grants freedom to Jews it also takes his phonograph – "Hand your phonograph over to the State, Gedali" (71) – which is symbolic of the fact that the state owns every thing. Gedali even touches another issue which bothers him: "But the Poles, kind sir, shot because they are the Counter Revolution. You shoot because you are the Revolution. But surely the Revolution means joy. And joy does not like Orphans in the house. Good men do good deeds. The Revolution is the good deed of good men. But good men do not kill. So it is bad people that are making Revolution. But the Poles are bad people too. Then how is Gedali to tell which is Revolution and which is Counter Revolution?"[3]

Isaac Babel, thus, presents the Jewish crisis during and after the Revolution. If one has to read Leon Trotsky and then read Isaac Babel immediately after, he cannot but feel the ambiguity of response to the Revolution. Trotsky represents the Jew as a Bolshevik who took active part in the Revolution, whereas Babel floods his short stories with its ominous irony and unexplained violence, suggesting the paradox of the Revolution. This mixed reaction to the Revolution becomes an archetypal theme in Soviet Yiddish literature. Isaac Babel was eventually forced to live in concentration camps along with five hundred other Yiddish writers who were subsequently killed as part of the Moscow Trials which became widely known as Stalin Purges.

---

* Isaac Babel basically writes in Russian, exploring the crisis of the Jew and his response to the October Revolution.

In this essay an attempt has been made to discuss the Jewish experience to the changing world, taking a few important Yiddish writers like David Bergelson, Moshe Kulbak and Der Nister. Apart from the ambivalent response to the Revolution, there appears to be some kind of wonderment at *Haskalah* (The Enlightenment era) which gave them the necessary freedom to finally move out of ghettoes and shtetles. The immediate result was the secularization of Jewish life. This inevitable change in Jewish life has also been created in the Tevye stories of Sholem Aleichem which were dramatized and staged as *Fiddler on the Roof* on Broadway. Even in such an entertaining play like *Fiddler on the Roof* one can see that something disastrous is happening to Tevye's family and they are forced to move out from their home town. A sense of homelessness and the metaphor of the Wandering Jew are classic themes in Jewish literature. David Bergelson is a major Yiddish novelist who consistently projected the Jewish sensibility in his fiction. In *Joseph Schur* (1913), he presents two facets of Jewish life namely, the conventional life of Joseph Schur and the almost secular and political life of the Rappaport family. Together, they underline the social patterns of Jewish life with its attendant conflicts.

The novel begins with Jacob Nathan, the Talmud teacher of Joseph Schur, who takes up the traditional role of *shaddoch*, the matchmaker to negotiate a marriage between his student and Moishele Levine's daughter. Both Moishele Levine's daughter and Jacob Nathan themselves have discordant lives. Jacob Nathan left his wife and never bothered to support her. Levine's daughter had to face a grave problem, for, when her father died, her mother married "*this Lag b'Omer* * to that fellow from Riga" which created displeasure among the Rappaports since she married within the year of her husband's death, flaunting the traditional practice. After this disturbing experience, Levine's daughter came to Abraham Rappaport, her uncle, to stay with him leaving her mother and stepfather.

When Jacob Nathan begins to perform his role of a *shaddoch*, he has some interesting experiences especially when he waits for the train from Kiev. When the train came at last, Jacob Nathan found a place in a spacious white washed car filled with secular, clean-shaven Jews of various ages – the sort one sees travelling from one large town to another. Jacob Nathan felt himself

> a stranger among them. For the most part they sat in separate shirt-sleeved groups, their teapots and their food spread out around them,

---

* Lag b'Omer – a holiday between Passover and the festival of Shavuoth.

> and in cheerful conversation with a member of females who gave every indication that they were camp followers travelling constantly from market fair to market fair . . . . In this crowd of secular Jews eating forbidden food stuffs in mid-Passover he, Jacob Nathan, was the only one dressed in pious black and wearing a silk hat.[4]

This is the generation of *Haskalah*. It desperately struggled to become part of the mainstream life. Their response to the freedom and opportunities of the Enlightenment era is overwhelming, for they seemed to wrestle out of the restraining ghetto-life, forever hoping that the good is yet to come and Jews are safe at last and no Pogroms and official anti-Semitism can ever stifle the Jewish consciousness. Jacob Nathan feels repulsive of this change and the experience of the secular Jews can sum up the irony of such a hope which drove them to the other extreme far from the Jewish identity. Their attempt at assimilation did not come about when Jews were massacred in Moscow Trials. Jacob Nathan's isolation and rejection of secular Jews is as much part of the Jewish life at that time as the formidable curiosity about and the participation in the gentile culture. But there are some Jews who are essentially traditional despite their participation in secular activities. Abraham Rappaport is a wealthy Zionist, has business concerns and, yet, he keeps a Kosher kitchen, maintains the family charities and wears "a prayer shawl and phylacteries during morning prayers." (39) This shows the resistance to those forces of Enlightenment which demand the sacrifice of national identity. But strangely enough, his niece, Levine's daughter has a very secular life. Thus, we see that there is a conflict between the tradition and change. Although there is a change in Abraham Rappaport lately for he has skipped morning prayers altogether, it does not mean he has become secular completely. The Zionists generally paid more attention to the political side of the regeneration of Israel than the ardent religious practices. He became a free thinker and even had a gentile tenant, but there is a basic contradiction in his life. Despite his ways of a free thinker, he remained a superstitious man in his own fashion.

As for Joseph Schur, he was born of "spite-marriage" for his father married again in old age and is a fanatic Hasidic father who never allowed his sisters to stay with him. Before his death he repented for all his lapses and wept "because he was living an ugly life." (49) Joseph Schur had both a religious and a secular education. He is a traditional Jew untouched by secular life. The writer also focuses on the lives of the Rabbi of Great Setternitz and his son and old Moreiness and his daughter, to recreate the

Jewish life of the times. These two facets of Jewish life sufficiently sum up the variations of conventional Jewish life. The Court of the great Rabbi is a symbol of the vanishing Jewish culture. Known for his scholarship and learning, the great Rabbi has no patience or strength to conduct a congregation in his old age. His son falls in love with a girl – "a woman in white" – and does not like to take up the rabbinical heritage from his father. Again, old Moreiness and his daughter travel in great style with "imported suitcases." This accounts for the fact that after the *Haskalah* many Jews used to go to Germany and other countries for education. Even the Rappaport and Schur families had a liking for an "imported" son-in-law. Here Bergelson is critical about the Jewish life, for his ironic mode in the novel is not so much an attempt to denigrate as to warn against these practices.

Finally, when Joseph Schur goes to the Rappaports to ask for the hand of Moishele Levine's daughter, he feels extremely isolated in their family because he learns that these Jews have deep political convictions and are fervent Zionists. Sarahle, Levine's daughter, did not bother to recognise his presence since the cultural gap between Joseph Schur and Sarahle is simply overwhelming. She is enlightened and had reaped the "fruits" of the *Haskalah*. She travels extensively and participates in secular life whereas Joseph Schur is quiet and subdued, unpretentious and not aware of the changes in Jewish life. He is more or less a Community man of the Jewish Ghetto. Abraham Rappaport feels sorry for him and even wonders, "What sort of features does a rich young bachelor have to have these days that would make a marriageable woman unwilling even to be seen by him?"[5] The intended marriage does not take place. Joseph Schur is left alone only to have a sympathetic conversation with Nesse but he is aware of his alienation from the otherwise knowledgeable Jews who seem to have liberated themselves by choosing their part in secular life. Joseph Schur is too committed to his life and Sarahle is too blinded by her enlightened life to choose personal relationship with Joseph Schur.

Abraham Rappaport's home becomes a metaphor of Jewish culture. David Bergelson, using the ironic mode, suggests that the Jewish culture is at the cross-roads of modern history. He carries the same approach to other novels also, such as *The Hole Through Which Life Slips* and *Civil War*. The former is about a writer who faces an impasse in his career. He bears the brunt of several blows during the violence of the Revolution. His wife leaves him only to become a Bolshevik. Eventually his servant also leaves him. The writer does not trace "the hole through which his life has slipped." The violence he sees around him and its presence in language – "Eve rattled like a machine gun" – paints the picture of the Revolution in all its reality. As a Jew, David Bergelson was aware of crimes perpetrated against Jews during the Czarist regime and he cannot see any justification in the mass killings during the days of the Revolution. It is worth remembering that Kiev and some Jewish villages in Ukraine are the worst-hit areas of this destruction. Caught in the trap of this atrocious environment, Yana finds himself at a loss for words. Bergelson brings out the waste land atmosphere and spiritual vacuum Yana faces in his life through the suggestiveness of the language probably for the reason that explicitness might involve him in complications with the authorities who were desperately executing the "campaigns of corrections."

Yana, at last, faces the reality of his crippled creative self when his friend reveals why he has stopped writing: "What pinched you all these years? Society. Capitalism pushed you to invective. The devil take you! Since you're a man of delicacy and vulgarity is foreign to you, your feelings channelled themselves into a stream of perceptive articles. Now that the Bolsheviks are here, it's clear: perceptiveness is irrelevant."[6] The gulf between his dream and the ugly reality forces him to face the peculiar predicament of the Jewish intellectual in Russia.

In *Civil War* (1928) he touches on the enormity of violence as a result of the war between Germany and Russia, in a bid to own a part of Ukraine. It is about the experience of Botchko and Zeek, two gentiles, who have had to live miserable lives because of the war. However, it is also significant in terms of the Jewish experience since it also deals with Jewish Bolsheviks. The novelist also touches on anti-Semitism prevalent among gentiles. The malice of the gentile servant to the Jewish landlord is relevant for two reasons: one, the acceptance of gentiles in Jewish homes which is rather unconventional; and two, the gentiles' anti-Semitism. The maid servant does not like Jews and here is the poignant expression of her dislike expressed by the author: "Filled with spite, she wanted the Jewish bastard whom she suckled to ache with stomach cramps. She purposely ate gassy foods – may the devil take him – for reluctantly, from day to day, she was falling more and more in love with him, the alien bastard. Wasn't she right? After all, her employers were only 'filthy Jews'."[7]

Both German and Russian soldiers took their anger out on the Jews by killing and physically humiliating many of them. One such incident occurs when the Jews are immersed in penitential prayers on the Sabbath. They run away to their families to save their lives. The civil war in Kiev and other parts of Ukraine where the Jews lived, created an atmosphere of insecurity since they were the victims of the soldiers' caprice. The reluctance to accept the Jew as Bolshevik becomes obvious in an interesting conversation among peasants who talk about Germans. Germany, after a long war with Russia, at last prepared herself to leave but not before doing enough damage to the Jews of Kiev. When a peasant says that Jews are not on the Czar's side the other peasants ask him to shut his mouth. As if to disprove the prejudice of the gentiles, the writer introduces "a Jew Comrade." Leyzerke is a Bolshevik and fights against Germans in Alexandrouka. It was an era of uncertainty and elderly Jews are concerned about the Jewish community, since their participation in the Bolshevik cause may become the cause of their own extermination. However, it does not stop Leyzerke from becoming a comrade. By projecting the Jew as Bolshevik, Bergelson touches yet another aspect of Jewish life during the Revolution. In the three novels, Bergelson attempts to sketch Jewish life at the turn of the century and during the war. The old pattern of the ghetto life seems to be slowly giving way to secular life and the aftermath of such a liberation generally created a gap between religious and secular cravings of Jews.

Moshe Kulbak's *Zelmenyaner* (1931) explores the transition from the old and devout Jewish life to the secular life in Russia with its Bolshevik convictions. Zelmenyaner family is a microcosm of Jewish experience. Grandma Boshe belongs to the old ghetto life with its strong roots in orthodox life. And her children – Zishe, Itche, Yude, Folye, Haye, Moshe – are caught in the winds of change. And the third generation – their children – seem to accept the Revolution and other changes, rejecting conventional Jewish life. This transition is convincingly brought out through a series of events in their lives although the thesis of writer's vision is a matter of speculation especially when he makes the third generation utter sarcastic comments on religious practices. However, his approach throws light on the mixed reaction to the Revolution.

The court of Reb Zelmele is a world in itself. His children and grandchildren form the typical ghetto-like life. As the writer himself says, Grandma Boshe does not realize that world has changed. She becomes a symbol of the world of old values and traditions which are slowly vanishing. Uncle Itche's son Berre Chvust becomes the hero of the new world which is in direct contrast to the world of Grandma Boshe. He questions religious practices and traditions much to the consternation of his father and his uncles who are not willing, at least initially, to accept the change since they are also deeply rooted in Jewish life. Their conflicts are narrated through folksy Yiddish humour. The writer, unlike Isaac Babel and David Bergelson, seems to have a positive attitude towards the Revolution. He even talks about *Com-Youth* (the Communist Youth Organisation) which takes up the task of educating people. Aunt Malkele benefits from this possibility, thanks to the efforts of Berre. He also takes Hayele as his wife without any of the usual ceremonies, though the ritual is arranged later. Berre even brings electricity to the courtyard and then radio. The elderly Jews react violently to all these changes but, with the passage of time, they begin to accept them. This marks the beginning of the deterioration of the old world of the Jews. Later, Sonia, Uncle Zishe's daughter falls in love with a gentile who is willing to become a Jew and marries him. The old generation cannot get used to these changes. Uncle Yude goes back to reading the Talmud as an escape from the impending "chaos" from the new world. Uncle Zishe makes ironic comments: "Nice children." Uncle Itche is perhaps flexible but upto a certain point only. Later Uncle Folye destroys the electricity installed by Berre which results in a tussle with Berre.

In due course of time, the old generation accepts the changes. Uncle Itche joins the procession of Bolsheviks and boasts that his son is a Bolshevik too. His son gets an order from the Red Flag. The celebration of the Revolution becomes a major theme in the novel. Consequently his attitude to the change in the life-pattern of the Jews is positive and he affirms this change. The Jews ultimately become part of the Bolshevik Revolution, losing their particular Jewish identity—at least their religious identity. Their participation in the Revolution is the basic reason as to why the old generation willingly accepts the change, despite its uncompromising blow to the traditional life-style. Berre, due to his progressive spirit, does not name his son after his grandfather, Reb Zelmele. Instead, he names him after Marat, a revolutionary in the French Revolution. The death of Grandma Boshe is the symbolic death of the old world. The rituals are not performed properly and the young generation comments overtly on their practice. They seem to be responding to the Bolshevik ideology with Berre's influence. Uncle Zishe also dies in grief after his daughter's marriage to a 'goy'. This is a vanishing world and the writer seems to suggest that these conflicts are inevitable in the transition period. At the close of the novel, Uncle Yude wants to be associated with farming—"Red Acre"—or Jewish collective. Uncle Itche shaves off his Jewish beard. A sense of ending of the old world is explicit: "The pillars of the family are missing. Gone uncles, the two able leaders who, for many years, had turned the wheel of Zelmenyaner history."[8] The glorification of the Revolution and Jewish Bolshevik can be explained in many ways. Many Jews became Bolsheviks and supported the Revolution because they had hard times under the Czars who had blamed the Jews for every political and social crisis and institutionalised pogroms which took a toll of Jewish life. The Revolution appeared to suggest a glimmer of hope from such a perdition and it took no exceptions on religious grounds. Jews could participate in the political movement which was possible for the first time. Deprived of opportunities for many centuries, Jews took the opportunity with over-enthusiasm although some Jews were still skeptical about its benevolence as the writings of David Bergelson and Isaac Babel sufficiently testify. Moshe Kulbak took a favourable stand and hence the affirmation of changes in Jewish life even if they are at the expense of Jewish identity. Assessing the novel with this perspective in view, it appears as though the writer over-did his presentation of Jewish life. The scenes wherein the "new generation" makes fun of the Grandma Boshe's death and Itche's comments that he does not mind shaving his beard if only he is given sometime to settle down to the idea may appear little exaggerated to bring in the effect of the writer's positive stance towards the Revolution. Once he took the positive stance, he had to present the traditions in a disapproving way. Although there are some serious gaps in the thematic technique, the author does not fail to impress the reader. For a literary historian, this novel is useful because it is the testimony of over-enthusiasm on the part of Jews who, nevertheless, had to face the doom of Moscow Trials. Their over-enthusiasm is an effort to impress other Bolsheviks too. A word about the language and Yiddish humour as fictional technique will elaborate the aesthetic excellence of the Yiddish fiction. In *Zalmenyaner*, the narrator is extremely involved and he affirms change and the Revolution. Humour becomes the major fictional technique but beneath the layer of the Yiddish humour, there is a sense of pathos, sadness and serious purpose. An illustration will help to elucidate this point. While describing the peculiar traits of Zelmenyaner the writer comments:

> Besides all habits common to our family, Uncle Itche has worked up a habit of his own. He sneezed with a loud cry.
>
> Once, when she heard him sneeze, a neighbour fainted. In the tense times of the Civil War the people in the countyard were upset by his sneezing. Uncle Zishe even found it necessary to visit Uncle Itche in

> order to discuss this subject.
>
> Itche, do you know that because of your sneezing we stand in mortal peril?[9]

Here, humour is interspersed with the Jewish predicament during Civil War which suggests that Jewish towns are vulnerable to pogroms. Yiddish literature is generally rich in humour and no genre of it is exempt from it. In fact, many Jewish writers in England and America used this technique extensively. While discussing Jewish humour in American Jewish literature, Sarah Blacher Cohen says:

> Jewish humour was also the salvation of the powerless against the powerful. The Jews of Eastern Europe from whom the majority of twentieth-century Jewish-American comic performers and writers descended were victims of a ludicrous irony: they were divinely designated to be Chosen People, yet they were treated like rejects. To fill the gap between glorious expectation and miserable reality, they wryly deprecated their persecutors and bittersweetly mocked themselves. In jests, their adversaries were dimwitted and besotted; in turn, they themselves were *schlemiels*, *schnorrers* and *luftmenschen*: bunglers, beggars, and failed speculators. When they immigrated to America, their marginal status again prompted them to make comedy out of constraint. But this time their Jewish jokes were limited to *shtetls*; they told them before the delighted audiences of burlesque and vaudville halls and later devised elaborate comic routines for radio, TV, and movies. Yet they still employed the staples of ghetto humor. Their English, like Yiddish, was earthy and verbose. They mimicked the same losses and magnified their plights. They needled the audience and jabbed at their own vulnerabilities. These comics made America receptive to Jewish wit and acted in part as models for Jewish-American writers, even for the most cerebral of them, Saul Bellow.[10]

Consequently, in the fiction of Bernard Malamud, Stanley Elkin, Cynthia Ozick, Tillie Olsen – to name a few – and even in the writings of popular novelists like Cynthia Freeman, Harry Kemelman and Bel Kaufman, a streak of inherited Yiddish humour finds expression perhaps in a different circumstance. Black humour of Bruce Jay Friedman and Joseph Heller owes much to Yiddish humour.

Both Bergelson and Kulbak explore the Jewish response to the changing times and the Revolution, though they have different viewpoints on some issues. Bergelson seems to be critical about the violence and the human loss and depicts the Jew as Bolshevik rejecting the gentile prejudice that Jews are anti-Bolshevik. Kulbak affirms the Bolshevik Revolution and tries to look back from this perspective to evaluate Jewish sensibility. Consequently, his assessment appears to be more theatrical and stylised, at least in some ways, than realistic. Surely, the Jews never accepted the winds of change without the maximum of resistance. It is possible that Kulbak is confining his aesthetic vision to the "Campaign of Correction" though this may not be proved for certain. The refreshing Yiddish humour and the love-hate relationship among the people, make it extremely sustaining as a narrative discourse. Together these novelists project the sociological pattern of Jewish life and the reluctant but inevitable adaptation to the changing circumstances.

Der Nister, pen name of Pinhas Kahanovitch, in his novel *Under a Fense: A Revue* (1929) focuses on yet another perspective of Jewish life. He attempts successfully to present the crisis of the Jewish intellectual who is forced to accept the party line and betray his creative spirit only to appease others. When it appeared in 1929, the editor had to confess that it has "a ring of allegorical and symbolic tales, mutually intertwined, expressed in rich rhythmic language. . . . It is a kind of confession, an enunciation of the idealistic view of the world." (193)[11] The editor was extremely conscious that it might create an uproar; and his penitential editorial note is an attempt to avert this crisis. Unfortunately, he did not succeed in convincing others. The story is extremely suggestive and no one in the early thirties can miss its message. It is a commentary on what happens to a writer who makes a pact with the official party line and suppresses his inner creative urge. The writer in this story is torn between his loyalty to the official party line and his inner urge which somehow tells him that he is practising intellectual hypocrisy. He feels the burden of guilt and the story is an attempt to externalise the psyche of the guilt-ridden artist.

Although it appears in story form with realistic characters, at least some characters are symbolic personifications. Thus, the symbol of false literary urge is suggestive of the party line and the artist's daughter is his authentic creative spirit. Dustman becomes the source of the writer's guilt. Once this is recognised, the theme of the story falls in perspective. The Circus is the world of the reader or the audience of literature. The Circus performer is the writer himself often performing to the tune of others. The harassing intensity of the writer's guilt for his self-betrayal and the betrayal of his calling is presented through dream sequence where he is put on trial by his pupils—or literary disciples?—and his own teacher (Medardus) is the judge whom he had criticized exposing him to the perils of party officials. The charge is that the writer's daughter (his creative urge) is injured in the circus where the writer lured by Lili's beauty, the party ideology, takes his daughter to perform in the circus. Lili hates his daughter and deliberately lets go of her during the performance. Thus, his daughter is injured for which the writer is ridiculed and humiliated. A group of people come to his house to stone the artist. He becomes delirious and then the dream sequence begins. Suddenly the court, the writer and his students appear and he is the accused and they are the accusers. His defence, which is a confession, is the testimony to his guilt and the genesis of his downfall:

> And when we are cold we hug anything that can keep us warm, any garbage or filth, as long as it covers us. And we wear anything, even rags or flesh-coloured rights, as long as it's clothing. And when we are hungry and have no work, being a clown is a work, after all. And when we have no home the circus can be home. And the circus is as it is. Your life is cheap. You are there only to gratify others. Your soul hangs by a thread, and your life is unimportant, so is it wonder that your child is unimportant too, and that you can sell her to the tight rope for a trifle, for your breakfast?[12]

In the meantime, the dustman arrives and says that the writer's "father," "mother," "children"—his forced literary endeavour—are full of straw, meaning that they are artificial creations and are not convincing aesthetic figures. Then follows another scene where his teacher is attacked for his free spirit of creativity and the teacher turns into a bird, flies off which suggests the immortal nature of his literary efforts. Later the dustman burns the straw figures and takes the writer to the public and reads out the writer's demeaning blunders. Finally, the writer is sentenced to death by fire (catharsis?). All these sequences occur in his dream which throws light on his guilt-conscience.

Der Nister's interior landscape of the guilt-conscience of the writer is an archetype of the Jewish writer and the necessary conflict that arises when the writer is forced to conform to official caprices. In fact, Der Nister foretells what is to happen to writers like Osip Mandelstam, Boris Pasternak, Isaac Babel and many Yiddish writers who became the victims of the Stalin Purges. To be sure, the novels discussed so far must have created an uproar among the party officials. Bergelson's essentially Jewish cautiousness to any supposed "liberal policy," Kulbak's unconditional acceptance of the Revolution and Der Nister's crisis of the Jewish intellectual when he is asked to perform to an official tune, portray the mixed reaction to the changing scene of Jewish life. Taken together, these writers cover major aspects of Jewish life in Russia. An explanation is necessary as to why they choose indirect fictional modes to communicate their thematic concerns. Allegory, symbolism, unspecified irony, violence, anthropomorphized description become the fictional devices, for they help the writer to convey the unpalatable truth indirectly. And being Jewish made these writers peculiarly eclectic in their response:

> The mere fact of being Jewish made a good many of the writers feel uneasy. They might compose agit-prop verse or stuff their novels with uplifting Bolshevik sentiments, but memories of what Jews had suffered in Old Russia and fears of what they might yet suffer in the New Russia could never be shaken off. The mere fact, too, of writing in Yiddish, a language notoriously entangled with national and religious traditions was cause for nervousness. . . . Into their poems, novels, stories and plays, the Yiddish writers packed, or hid, all the intellectual pressures, moral quandaries, nerve-shattering anxieties and inescapable betrayals of time. No literature could easily bear this, and an unfree literature least of all. Yiddish writers had to keep looking over their shoulders not only with the fear every other writer in the Soviet Union as sooner or later felt, they also found themselves responding to the cultural authorities with the deep rooted habits of an oppressed people. Yiddish critics had to be sure that not only did they hew the party line but that as Jews they shared a little extra zeal, proof of caring more about "Socialist Realism" than about the writer who had been their friend for decades. It was an atmosphere that made for distrust, paranoia and sometimes betrayal.[13]

Moshe Kulbak, David Bergelson, Der Nister, along with many other Yiddish writers, were forced into concentration camps in the wake of the Moscow Trials. Their works were vulnerable and the officials read more violence and national spirit in them than the anguish of a Jewish intellectual and his response to the changing world. Perhaps, it may be difficult to find logic for their fate, for, so much is undisclosed and unavoidable for scholarly discussion. Joseph Brodsky and Chaim Grade could never forget the traumatic experience in Russia even after their secure settlement in America. They are torn between their love for Russia and the official anti-Semitism. No one can express their tragedy more succinctly than Chaim Grade who knew many of the poets and, better still, knew their fate was beyond the intensity that words could find expression :

> Murdered poets: no vengeance for your blood.
> Turned into a crowd of ghosts. What stood
> watch over you – gates, guards, bars – gone;
> till it seems you are skimming my window under the moon.
> Sometimes you are the wind and the fog from the sea,
> sometimes a shadow.[14]

The death of the Yiddish writers is a severe blow to the Jewish life. It reinforced official anti-Semitism which disillusioned many Jews who glorified the Revolution. Reading Yiddish literature with the perspective of Leon Trotsky may be ironical in many ways. Hard pressed by the enormity of reality, the Yiddish writers wrote about their agonies and the Jewish life which they knew from close quarters. In a changing world, Yiddish writers wrote about the Jews they knew and the predicament they shared for being Jews. In fact, Trotsky is an extreme example of the Jewish intellectual who showed commitment and enthusiasm to the Revolution. He was to suffer a miserable death himself, thus becoming the prototype of the Jewish intellectual in Russia. The journey from the life pattern of Jewish people in Kiev and other Jewish towns to the Jewish Bolshevik marks a new, but sad, chapter in the Jewish history of Soviet Union which finds expression in the Yiddish literature that is known for its idiosyncracy and humanism.

NOTES

1. Isaac Babel, *Collected Stories* (New York: Criterion Books, 1955), p. 70.
2. Leon Trotsky, *Literature and Revolution* (Ann Arbor: University of Michigan Press, 1960), p. 15.
3. Isaac Babel, *Collected Stories*, p. 71.
4. David Bergelson, *Joseph Schur*, in Irving Howe and Eliezer Greenberg, *Ashes Out of Hope*; major discussion is on the novels from this anthology (New York: Schocken, 1977), p. 38.

5. David Bergelson, *Joseph Schur*, *Ashes Out of Hope,* p. 66.
6. David Bergelson, *The Hole Through Which Life Slips*, *Ashes Out of Hope,* p. 82.
7. David Bergelson, *Civil War*, *Ashes Out of Hope*, p. 94.
8. Moshe Kulbak, *Zelmenyaner*, *Ashes Out of Hope*, p. 191.
9. Ibid., p. 128.
10. Sarah Blacher Cohen, *Comic Relief* (Urbana: Univ. of Illinois Press, 1978), p. 8.
11. *Ashes Out of Hope*, p. 193.
12. Der Nister, *Under a Fense: A Revue*, *Ashes Out of Hope*, p. 201.
13. *Ashes Out of Hope*, pp. 14-15.
14. Irving Howe and Eliezer Greenberg, ed., *A Treasury of Yiddish Poetry* (New York: Schocken Books, 1969), p. 342.

Narrative and Ideology in E.L. Doctorow's *The Book of Daniel*

> To restructure the problematic of ideology, of the unconscious and of desire of representation, of history, and of cultural production, around the all-informing process of narrative, which I take to be . . . the central function of or *instance* of the human mind.
>
> Fredric Jameson[1]

To be able to believe that narrative is merely a technique in the art of fiction is to invite a series of problematic assumptions in a critical discussion. Narrative assumes certain projection of authorial presence and thus becomes a means of communicating its possibilities. In other words, it is an actualization of authorial viewpoint, one cannot be isolated from the other. Authors who choose especially political themes or an event of history run into pluralistic perceptions and bias and it would be often times difficult to fully participate in the narrative discourse without decoding the conditions of its place in the total form and meaning. If, to make matters even more complicated and confusing, the available historical situation of the writer's product is heavily influenced by everchanging views and/or conditioned by the political institutions, it would further complicate the writer's attempt at handling such an ambience without pushing oneself to one position or the other. Such ideological postures are not uncommon in the modern world. Therefore, political novel/art has not only survived the critical judgment of the classical and still very much active canon-makers who believe strongly and sometimes naively that it is not the province of art to make political judgment—for isn't a point of view a form of perception, position or judgment?—much less take a position on political issues; but has also outlived almost pejorative aspect that is customarily associated with it. That Solzhenitsyn, Koestler, Malraux and the generation of American writers in the thirties have made a contribution to an emergence of political aesthetics speaks for a legitimacy of their view. To say that literature is a non-referential dialectic of aesthetics not only appears to be elitist but also intellectually irresponsible.

This brings us to an inevitable aspect of literature, and particularly of political art[2]: the structure of ideology. Ideology, at least in Marxian terms, is assigned to superstructure in the dialectics of materialism. Superstructure also includes, as Jameson[3] rightly observes, culture, political structures and the State. Together, they create a false consciousness through a process of reification.[4] Lennard Davis, while discussing the need to "resist" novels, enumerates the structure of ideology a la Raymond Williams[5]:

1. The belief system of a particular group or class;
2. A system of illusory beliefs – false ideas or false consciousness – as contrasted with true or scientific knowledge.
3. A semiological system or system of signs which produces meaning and ideas in society.[6]

It is in this context that E.L. Doctorow's *The Book of Daniel* (1971) can be interpreted. Doctorow is to respond to the two extremes in the recent American history. The well-publicized Rosenbergs trial is viewed both as an American tragedy or a vindication of justice – depending on whether you are a liberal or conservative. Some would argue that the electrocution of the Rosenbergs was the last-ditch attempt of the establishment to destroy the legacy and hope of Communist Party of America; others view that they were suitably punished for the heinous crime of supplying the secrets of the bomb to the Russians. Doctorow handles the problems by introducing two types of narrative. The first-person narrative is that of Daniel, the son of the now deceased 'traitors,' who does not know whether his parents deserved such a historic judgment. If his parents were innocent, would it be possible for him to seek justice in an emotionally charged mass media or public outrage both of which largely influence the establishment? He tells the story of their parents legacy which destabilizes any facile understanding of America or coming to terms with it. His sister, always extremely sensitive, first abortively attempts to commit suicide and taken to an asylum instead of a hospital by the police, eventually dies. She protests against the Vietnam War and sadly realizes that her parents are nothing to the so-called New Left. "The Isaacsons are nothing to the New Left. And if they can't make it to them who else is there?"[7] The story of Susan is the anguish of the left-tradition in America. In Daniel's narrative one recognizes the tremors of an age, viewed not with cool objectivity but with concern, sympathy and acceptance of a sad chapter in the nation's part. The novel ends with his ironical submission of doctoral dissertation: "A Life Submitted in Partial Fulfilment of the Requirements for . . ."[8] It suggests that how academic the subject has become leaving the perils of personal confrontation to the children of the deceased who cannot even confess to their identity. The fact that Doctorow has to change the names of the dramatic personae itself needs some explanation. I will come to that later.

The second technique is that of third-person narrative which is arguably disinterested, objective and dispassionate – showing instead of telling, to borrow Wayne C. Booth's term[9] – as if there is one all-seeing and all-knowing person somewhere, trying to 'tell it like it is' – as Americans say. Possibly Doctorow felt that by positing the two angles of vision he is situating historical context and individual presence, both notably interact, clash, conflict, mutually supplement or subtract – finally providing the reader an essence of truth of human affairs in a polity. However, this too can be debatable. Even this "showing" instead of "telling" implies selection, organization or shifting through of massive material which means one has to have some perspective of guidelines which can be either ideological in so far as it supports the establishment's version or demythologise it for the sake of history. By structuring the novel with different narratives, the author provides a background for a necessary conclusion. After all, the novel, as our never-yielding gray beards say, has to have a beginning, middle and an end. The point, however, is whether such a conclusion is political or aesthetic. Or to put it in a different way: does the writer have to sacrifice one for the other? Such a dilemma is as disturbing as it is unsolvable to the satisfaction of all. Probably these complexities drove critics to avoid the political novel whenever they could. In aesthetic terms, the conclusion of the novel could be explained in terms of Daniel's personal exorcism with his own fate. The death of his sister, the travails after the ignominous execution of his parents and its aftermath lead to a catharsis. The verbal violence and the imagery point to the violence of the period that somehow intruded into personal terrain, making some people victims or vanquished and others the purveyors of justice or victors.

But what to make of its political context? The ideology demonstrates dissent, terrorizes its supporters. The ubiquitous mass media not only breaks news but presupposes the outcome of a trial: "Long before the trial the Issacsons were tried and found guilty in the newspapers."[10] Anti-Communist hysteria, McCarthyism, the oppression of the blacks, the Vietnam War, the Cold War, the New Left comprise the genesis of the times. History, the author seems to suggest, is yet to pass a judgement on these people who became the arbiters of justice, carelessly deciding the fates of the people.

The eclectic narrative touches all of these and establishes a postscript for an understanding of the Rosenbergs trial. Though the name as such is never mentioned – they are called the Isaacsons – the suggestiveness and the parallels are unmistakable.

Changing the figures of actual history also contributes to the writer's narrative strategies. It brings a human factor to those people who suffered death and whose legacy is death-in-life for their children. For once they are noι political cliches, predictable stereotypes, 'bad guys' in good America. They achieve humanity. Even Selig Mendish whose confession becomes a major argument for the government to indict the Isaacsons/the Rosenbergs, is presented as a suffering old man, probably used by both the government and the friends.

Daniel, for whom life is a series of confrontations, has to restore a perspective and conclude, this inconclusive, politically-charged milieu. Even the book's title is profoundly suggestive, the analogy with the biblical story being that the Jews in an alien situation are at the mercy of the Greeks and Daniel having to somehow bear the responsibility of leading his people to survival. At that particular time, Nebuchadnezzer's rule demands that all the Jews, who never believed in idolatry and have nothing but monotheism, are forced, one and all, to bow before the golden calf and worship it. Or all of them would perish under the fury of the omnipotent ruler. The narrative of *The Book of Daniel* in the Hebrew Bible itself has many shifts. Starting with Hebrew, as Biblical scholars tell us, it smoothly moves on to Aramaic. Again, Daniel's dreams and visions also shift from third person to first person, the first unit of dream being in the third person, while others are in the first person. Historically establishing himself as a riddle-solver – isn't a dream a riddle after all? – he climbs to a position of a ruler, a triumph for his God and his people. Instead of going extensively into the various interpretations that supplement a general reading of the book in Rabbinic Judaism and Jewish mysticism, suffice it to say that in the context of the novel our Daniel also attempts to solve a political 'riddle' to make peace with himself and confront the times meaningfully for a prospective history. Strangely enough, *The Book of Daniel* also suffered certain identity problems since there was no agreement on Daniel's prophetic stature among Jewish and Christian scholars. These parallels proclaim the complexity of the novel. Daniel's role here is not only to exonerate his parents but also to save 'his people' – the liberal-left, progressive, socialist sections of Americans! The apocalyptic strain in biblical story somehow gets secularized in Doctorow's novel. More to the point in the context of the narrative, this analogy points to those people who named names, though they knew they were lying outright, to save their skin. It is political and social hysteria that demanded human sacrifice. If there were no victims, they had to be created. Otherwise, Doctorow seems to suggest, how else one can justify frequent lapses in judicial procedures of the trial. The people have to 'fry' in order to illustrate a point that any one who dares the establishment would meet the same fate. The chill of Cold War paralyzed the thinking people into complacency of complicity.

To achieve such a political vision, Doctorow does not take the actual names. Because it puts a limitation on the author's perception of reality, which does not necessarily have any documentation or, if it has any at all, there are many contradictions in it. Also, he may have to restrict the narrative to the details that may or may not give any opportunity to integrate the disaster of the trial with the political climate of the sixties and the seventies. By elevating art to the study of political hysteria, the creative art performs a ferocious feat of imagination that also touches the heart of the matter in terms of history and human fallibility. The issue, then as always, is not merely a few people supposedly committing a treason, but the need for any establishment – liberal-democratic or totalitarian – to use people as a ruse to orchestrate its political agenda. Probably by bringing the politics into the domain of art, Doctorow seems to absolve that section of suffering humanity whose history would be as problematic as it is painful. And yet to ignore its existence is to throw the realms of art to the ivory-tower myth which, to say the least, is ideology. Doctorow debunks this ideology on two levels: the novel as an art-form free from politics and the Rosenbergs case as an exigency of oppressive ideology.

The narrative only adds to this authorial position. In the first page itself, the narrative jumps from the third person to the first person and back again. The present clashes with the past, confusing or fusing, and sparkles a little in that clash to throw a momentary light on history. Even the first person is not always Daniel, it could be his grandmother or his father. The novel has three conclusions, once again questioning one-dimensional view of history or that kind of history which usurps personal life. First, Daniel visits his parents' home now inhabited by a black family. Second, the tuneral of his sister and also, symbolically, of his parents. Third, ostensibly, his dissertation submitted in partial fulfilment of his life. The book, the dissertation, if you will, is about his father as well – a life refracted through the prism of subverted and subverting political institutions. Having survived the purgatory, Daniel, at last, believes that "I think I am going to be able to cry."[11] Such a catharsis in his life is achieved through a magisterial technique of narrative that struggles to break free from the ideology.

NOTES

1. Fredric Jameson, *The Political Unconscious* (Ithaca, New York: Cornell, 1981), p. 13.
2. A reasonable case could be made to the view that all literature is a game of politics to some degree. Literature always has a political dimension to it either to perpetuate the ideology of a particular society or to subvert it. Similarly, there is certain section in critical theory which strongly believes that all criticism is politics, a matter of power.
3. Fredric Jameson, *The Political Unconscious*, p. 32.
4. George Lukacs, *History and Class Consciousness*, trans. Rodney Livingstone (Cambridge, Mass: MIT Press, 1971).
5. Raymond Williams, *Marxism and Literature* (Oxford: Oxford University Press, 1977).
6. Lennard J. Davis, *Resisting Novels* (London: Methuen, 1987), p. 15.
7. E.L. Doctorow, *The Book of Daniel* (London: Picador, 1971, 1982), p. 159.
8. *Ibid*., p. 309.
9. Wayne C. Booth, *The Rhetoric of Fiction* (Chicago: University of Chicago Press, 1961).
10. E.L. Doctorow, *The Book of Daniel*, p. 227.
11. *Ibid*., p. 309.

Index